PURITY AND PROVOCATION

DOGMA 95

Edited by Mette Hjort and Scott MacKenzie

 Publishing

First published in 2003 by the
BRITISH FILM INSTITUTE
21 Stephen Street, London W1T 1LN

The British Film Institute is the UK national agency with responsibility for encouraging the arts of film
and television and preserving them in the national interest

Cover design by Ketchup
Cover illustrations: (front) Lars von Trier illustration by Lise Rønnebæk; (back) *The King is Alive*
(Kristian Levring, 2000), *Julien Donkey-Boy* (Harmony Korine, 1999)

Set by Fakenham Photosetting Limited, Fakenham, Norfolk
Printed in the UK by Cromwell Press, Trowbridge, Wiltshire

British Library Cataloguing-in-Publication Data
A catalogue record for this book is available from the British Library

ISBN 0–85170–952–4 (pbk)
ISBN 0–85170–951–6 (hbk)

Contents

In truth the prison unto which we doom
Ourselves no prison is: and hence for me,
In sundry moods, 'twas pastime to be bound
Within the Sonnet's scanty plot of ground;
Pleased if some souls (for such there needs must be)
Who have felt the weight of too much liberty,
Should find brief solace there, as I have found.

William Wordsworth

Acknowledgments

I would like to thank the University of Hong Kong for a Research Initiation Grant in support of my work on Dogma 95. I am also grateful to Pia Zeverin (Zentropa Films) for information related to Zentropa Real and for help in securing a copy of Lone Scherfig's *Italiensk for begyndere* (*Italian for Beginners*). Leila Vestgaard (Nimbus Film) provided images and information pertaining to Arthy's *Se til venstre der er en svensker* (*Old, New, Borrowed and Blue*). The project could not have been completed without the cheerful and efficient assistance of Vicki Synnott (Danish Film Institute), who kept a steady stream of films, facts and figures flowing from Copenhagen to Hong Kong. Jesper Jargil, Leif Tilden, Martin Rengel, Rick Schmidt, Antonio Domenici, Vincent Lannoo and Vincent Chui generously provided copies of their films and, in some cases, press kits. Thanks to Paisley Livingston for help with the preparation of the final manuscript, to Jonathan Chan (University of Hong Kong) for research assistance in the eleventh hour, and to Shu Kei for kindly agreeing to speak to the issue of Dogma's Hong Kong and Asian reception in an email interview. I am indebted to Ben Lee, Leo Ou-fan Lee, Ackbar Abbas, and especially Esther Cheung for organising a panel discussion on Dogma 95 and Hong Kong cinema at the University of Hong Kong in June 2002, and to film-makers Vincent Chui and Ann Hui for their insightful comments on the Dogma concept on that occasion. Esther Cheung's willingness to don the hat of ad hoc translator gave me access to relevant materials in Cantonese. My essay on Dogma has benefited from critical comments from audiences at the University of Aarhus, the University of Hong Kong, the University of Madison-Wisconsin and the University of Michigan. I am especially grateful to Morten Kyndrup, David Bordwell, Patrick Rumble and Tobin Siebers for making those conversations possible. Henning Hoeg Hansen kept me abreast of the discursive excesses surrounding the release of Jesper Jargil's *De lutrede* (*The Purified*) in Denmark in the summer of 2002. A special thanks to Ben Lee and Hamid Naficy for organising a discussion of Vincent Chui's *Leaving in Sorrow* at the University of Rice in the autumn of 2002. Ben's infectious enthusiasm for Dogma and insightful insistence on the relevance of performativity and cultural circulation helped push the project forward. Thanks also to Peter Schepelern for lending us his eagle eye. My gratitude to Cheng Kwok Hung and Jason Lau for their passionate contributions to our Dogma discussions in the classroom.

Mette Hjort

First of all, I should thank the British Academy for providing a research grant in support of my work on film manifestos and the public sphere, of which my work on Dogma is a small part. I would also like to thank the School of English and American Studies at the University of East Anglia for supporting my research on Dogma with a supplemental research grant allowing me to present my work at conferences. My colleagues in film and television studies at UEA – Justine Ashby, Charles Barr, Andrew Higson, Peter Krämer and Yvonne Tasker – also deserve thanks for the lively and challenging research culture that has developed in the film and television sector and that makes writing and working here such a pleasure. The graduate students at UEA are also a key part of this culture, and so thanks should go to Corin Depper, Neil Ewen, Martin Fradley, Kristian Moen, John Read and Silvia Barlaam for their enthusiasm, intellectual curiosity and friendship. Special thanks to Emma Bell, also of UEA, who went above and beyond the call of duty in tracking down Dogma-related material, and who also compiled the Dogma filmography. Claire Thomson, in the School of Languages and Literary Translation at UEA, also deserves thanks for sharing her thoughts on Dogma and on Danish cinema more generally. Finally, I should thank the audiences at the University of Kent-Canterbury, the Society for Cinema Studies conference in Washington D.C., and the University of Glasgow, whose comments on my presentations on Dogma greatly enhanced the work.

Scott MacKenzie

Joint thanks: Andrew Lockett and Sophia Contento, our editors at the British Film Institute, carefully shepherded the project through to completion. Thanks also to Werner Herzog, who graciously allowed us to reprint his Minnesota Declaration.

Notes on Contributors

Sally Banes is Marian Hannah Winter Professor of Theatre History and Dance at the University of Wisconsin, Madison. Her books include *Terpsichore in Sneakers: Post-Modern Dance* (Wesleyan University Press, 1986), *Greenwich Village 1963: Avant-Garde Performance and the Effervescent Body* (Duke University Press, 1993), *Writing Dance in the Age of Postmodernism* (Wesleyan University Press, 1994), *Democracy's Body: Judson Dance Theatre 1962–64* (Duke University Press, 1995), *Dancing Women: Female Bodies on Stage* (Routledge, 1998) and *Subversive Expectations: Performance Art and Paratheater in New York 1976–85* (University of Michigan Press, 1998).

Emma Bell is a doctoral candidate in the School of English and American Studies, University of East Anglia. She is currently writing her thesis on Dogma and its relationship with earlier avant-garde movements, such as Dadaism and Surrealism.

Ib Bondebjerg is Professor of Film & Media Studies at the University of Copenhagen, and former Chairman of the Board of the Danish Film Institute. He is co-director of the European research project *Changing Media – Changing Europe* (2000–04). His current book-length project focuses on Danish cinema from 1940 to 1972. He is the author of several books in Danish, the editor of *Moving Images, Culture and the Mind* (University of Luton Press, 2000) and co-editor of *The Danish Directors: Dialogues on a Contemporary National Cinema* (Intellect, 2001).

Noël Carroll is Monroe C. Beardsley Professor of the Philosophy of Art at the University of Wisconsin, Madison, and President of the American Society for Aesthetics. His many books include *Philosophical Problems of Classical Film Theory* (Princeton University Press, 1988), *Mystifying Movies: Fads and Fallacies in Contemporary Film Theory* (Columbia University Press, 1988), *The Philosophy of Horror, or Paradoxes of the Heart* (Routledge, 1990), *Theorizing the Moving Image* (Cambridge University Press, 1996), *A Philosophy of Mass Art* (Clarendon Press, 1997), *Interpreting the Moving Image* (Cambridge University Press, 1998), *Philosophy of Art: A Contemporary Introduction* (Routledge, 1999) and *Beyond Aesthetics: Philosophical Essays* (Cambridge University Press, 2001).

Claus Christensen is a freelance writer, and a frequent contributor to *Film*, a film journal published by the Danish Film Institute.

Mads Egmont Christensen holds an MA in Film Production from the University of Southern California. He was the Head of Production at Gutenberghus Film and TV

Production in the mid-1980s, and went on to become Managing Director of Metronome Productions. He was appointed Course Director at the European Film College in Ebeltoft in 1998. He is Assistant Director of *Pelle the Conqueror* (*Pelle Erobreren*) and producer of *Jerusalem* and *The Boys from St Petri* (*Drengene fra Sankt Petri*).

Berys Gaut teaches in the Department of Moral Philosophy at the University of St Andrews in Scotland. He has published widely on the philosophy of film, aesthetics and moral philosophy. He is currently writing a book entitled *Art, Emotion and Ethics*.

Mette Hjort is Head of Comparative Literature at Hong Kong University and Senior Lecturer in Languages and Intercultural Studies at Aalborg University. She was previously Associate Professor and Director of Cultural Studies at McGill University, Montreal, Canada. She is the author of *The Strategy of Letters* (Harvard University Press, 1993) and editor or co-editor of *Rules and Conventions* (Johns Hopkins University Press, 1992), *Emotion and the Arts* (Oxford University Press, 1997), *Cinema and Nation* (Routledge, 2000), *The Danish Directors: Dialogues on a Contemporary National Cinema* (Intellect Press, 2001) and *The Postnational Self* (University of Minnesota Press, 2002). She is currently completing a book-length study on contemporary Danish cinema, focusing on the challenges faced by a small nation in an age of globalisation.

Paisley Livingston was for many years Professor of English at McGill University. He is currently Senior Lecturer in the Department of Education, Philosophy and Rhetoric at the University of Copenhagen. He is the author of *Ingmar Bergman and the Rituals of Art* (Cornell University Press, 1982), *Literary Knowledge: Humanistic Inquiry and the Philosophy of Science* (Cornell University Press, 1988), *Literature and Rationality: Ideas of Agency in Theory and Fiction* (Cambridge University Press, 1991) and *Models of Desire: René Girard and the Psychology of Mimesis* (Johns Hopkins University Press, 1992). He is co-editor, with Berys Gaut, of *The Creation of Art* (Oxford University Press, 2003).

Scott MacKenzie is Lecturer in Film and Television Studies at the University of East Anglia. He is the author of *Screening Québec: Québécois Cinema, National Identity and the Public Sphere* (Manchester University Press, 2003) and co-editor of *Cinema and Nation* (Routledge, 2000). His articles have appeared in *CinéAction, Canadian Journal of Film Studies, Public* and *Screen*. He is currently writing a monograph on film manifestos. He previously taught at McGill University and the University of Glasgow.

Martin Roberts is a faculty member in the Media Studies Program at New School University, New York, and has taught at Harvard and MIT. After completing a PhD in French Studies at Cambridge University, his research interests have focused on ethnography, post-colonialism and transnational media studies, with a special interest in cinema and music. He is currently working on a book on cinema and globalisation.

Peter Schepelern is Senior Lecturer in Film and Media Studies at the University of Copenhagen. He is the author of *Lars von Trier's Elements* (*Lars von Triers Elementer*, Rosinante, 1997), editor of *Filmleksikon* (Rosinante, 1995), co-editor of *Danish Film 1972–1997* (*Dansk Film 1972–1997*, Rosinante, 1997) and editor of *100 years of Danish Cinema* (*100 års dansk film*, Rosinante, 2001).

Murray Smith is Professor of Film Studies at the University of Kent. He is the author of *Engaging Characters: Fiction, Emotion and the Cinema* (Clarendon Press, 1995) and *Trainspotting* (BFI, 2002). He has co-edited *Film Theory and Philosophy* (Clarendon Press, 1997) and *Contemporary Hollywood Cinema* (Routledge, 1998).

Ginette Vincendeau is Professor of Film at the University of Warwick. She is the author of *The Companion to French Cinema* (Cassell/BFI, 1996), *Pépé le Moko* (BFI, 1998) and *Stars and Stardom in French Cinema* (Continuum, 2000). She has edited or co-edited *La Vie est à nous: French Cinema and the Popular Front* (BFI, 1986), *French Film: Texts and Contexts* (1990; 2nd edn 2000), *Popular European Cinema* (Routledge, 1992), *The Encyclopedia of European Cinema* (Cassell/BFI, 1995) and *Film/Literature/Heritage: A Sight and Sound Reader* (Routledge, 2001).

Introduction

Mette Hjort and Scott MacKenzie

ORIGINS

Dogma 95 was flamboyantly institutionalised as public fact on 20 March 1995 in the Odéon Cinema in Paris, the venue for a conference celebrating the centenary of film.[1] With his characteristic sense of spectacle and provocation, the invited Danish film-maker, Lars von Trier, indicated a desire to depart from the programme, proceeded to read the Dogma 95 manifesto and so-called 'Vow of Chastity' aloud, threw copies of the red leaflet into the audience and, having declared himself unable to reveal any further details, left the theatre. The manifesto, it turned out, was signed by Lars von Trier and his young colleague Thomas Vinterberg on behalf of the Dogma film collective, which also includes Søren Kragh-Jacobsen and Kristian Levring.[2] The first Dogma film, *Festen* (*The Celebration*), was released in 1998 and attributed to Thomas Vinterberg. Since then von Trier, Kragh-Jacobsen and Levring have been identified, though not officially credited in any paratextual apparatus,[3] as the directors of Dogme #2: *Idioterne* (*The Idiots*, 1998), Dogme #3: *Mifunes sidste sang* (*Mifune*, 1999) and Dogme #4: *The King is Alive* (2000) respectively.[4] At this point, the term 'Dogma' refers not only to the Danish collective and films just mentioned, but to a significant number of cinematic works by Danish and non-Danish film-makers who have been able to convince the Dogma brethren of a given film's compliance with the ten specific rules identified in the Vow of Chastity.

Manifestos, as Peter Schepelern points out in his piece entitled 'Kill Your Darlings' (this volume, pages 58–9), had been a feature of Lars von Trier's film-making practice since *The Element of Crime* (1984), which won the Prix Technique at Cannes and effectively put the emerging director on the map of international art cinema. Yet it is important to recognise that in the case of Dogma 95 it was not a matter of accompanying an ambitious feature film with a somewhat cryptic manifesto designed to frame it in terms of a deeply personal and intentionally provocative vision.[5] Not only did the appearance of the Dogma 95 manifesto significantly predate the detailed conception, creation and release of von Trier's Dogma film, the tract itself spelt out, in detail, the rules that were to be followed if film-makers were to unite, as they were intended to do, around the vision on offer. In the context, then, of Lars von Trier's contributions to the manifesto genre, Dogma 95 marks a shift from self-reflexive criticism aimed at mediating works to art-house audiences to a form of genuinely collectivist instigation, a shift motivated in part, it would appear, by the director's changed sense of his desired role.

Whereas von Trier once cultivated the image of the internationally oriented loner of Danish film, his preferred persona is now that of 'the gentle, almost avuncular enabler'

(Hjort and Bondebjerg 2001: 209). While the film production company, Zentropa, was initially established by von Trier and his partner (the producer Peter Aalbæk Jensen) in order to guarantee the director full artistic control, at this point the company functions largely as 'an open-ended, collectivist and multifaceted project' (Hjort and Bondebjerg 2001: 209–10). In 1999 von Trier realised his plans to create a Danish Film Town in the former army barracks in Avedøre, on the outskirts of Copenhagen. Housing Zentropa alongside other innovative companies such as Nimbus Film (which produced Thomas Vinterberg's *The Celebration*), the Town quickly became a veritable engine of renewal within the context of Danish film-making. In the founding document accompanying the site's inauguration – 'Project "Open Film Town": Visions in Connection with the Film Town in Avedøre' (reprinted in Hjort and Bondebjerg 2001: 224–27) – von Trier made a passionate case for the democratisation of the cinematic medium, a case that resonates with the Dogma manifesto's critical reflections on globalisation and certain aesthetic practices allegedly rooted in bourgeois individualism.

Composed in a hybrid spirit of semi-drunken irony and high seriousness, the Dogma manifesto articulates a programme of action that is continuous with some of von Trier's earlier initiatives. What Dogma 95 reflects is von Trier's enduring commitment to a conception of film as formal innovation and compelling expression rather than standardised product. Yet, if 'art cinema' is a term that comes to mind here, it is important to realise that Dogma 95 reimagines the relevant phenomenon in a collectivist register, one shaped by a shrewd understanding of the economic and political realities of cultural production in an increasingly globalised world. Dogma 95 is motivated by idealism, but it is also a deeply pragmatic undertaking. It involves a mixture of elements that calls, not for exclusive description in terms of 'marketing strategy', 'public relations stunt', 'aesthetics of denial', 'low-budget film-making', 'art cinema' or 'vehicle for public criticism', but for a critical narrative that elucidates the deeper connections among these seemingly diverse characterisations.

That Dogma 95 was a proposal worth taking seriously as a potential path to artistic renewal, international recognition and economic growth was an idea clearly endorsed by Jytte Hilden, the Danish social democratic Minister of Culture in 1995. Hilden was willing to match words with monies and made a verbal promise to von Trier of 15 million kroner (derived from lottery sales) in support of the envisaged Danish Dogma films to be directed by the collective's members. Yet, as the temporal lag between the manifesto's initial public circulation and the release of the first Dogma film in 1998 suggests, circumstances arose that were to threaten the very existence of the project. Unexpectedly von Trier found himself embroiled in a controversy that involved questions of jurisdiction and control flavoured with some of the anti-meritocratic sentiment that has characterised Danish attitudes since at least the mid-19th century.[6] State support for Danish film-making is administered by the Danish Film Institute and allocated to specific projects following an assessment on artistic and other grounds by a consultant appointed for a three-year term. A grant flowing directly from the Ministry of Culture to the Dogma project would have violated the very mandate of the Danish Film Institute. As a result, the Danish Film Institute was allotted the 15 million kroner as an extra budget line designed to support low-budget films 'inspired', as Hilden put it, by 'Dogma 95' (Ahm 1996). Eager to protect its autonomy and especially the consultant's authority as the critical assessor and gatekeeper, the Danish Film Institute interpreted Hilden's statement quite literally as pointing to diffuse notions of inspiration rather than abidance by the manifesto's dicta or actual group belonging. The Dogma collective was informed that members were invited to apply for support for their proposed films, but that any application would be treated on a par with those from other film-makers. The result was that none of the brethren applied for funding, for as von Trier pointed out, the idea of isolated applications subject to discrete assessment undermined the very idea and practicability of an avant-gardist *movement*.

This was by no means the first time that von Trier had been at loggerheads with the Danish Film Institute. The DFI's initial refusal to fund *The Element of Crime* on the grounds that it made use of English and German rather than Danish was, for example, dramatically overturned by the Danish Parliament in the early 80s. In the case of Dogma 95, however, the Ministry of Culture decided to respect the autonomy of the relevant state institution, which meant that the collective's cinematic programme, announced with such provocative self-confidence in Paris, seemed destined to remain a mere blueprint.

That Dogma 95 is more than a suggestive idea today is largely due to the efforts of Bjørn Erichsen, the visionary director of the Danish Broadcasting Corporation. During a press conference held at the Banana Republic Café in Copenhagen on 8 April 1997, Erichsen, seated alongside the brethren, framed his project of revival in terms of an idea of civic duty. The claim, more specifically, was that Erichsen's concept of public service included support for cultural experiments, and especially for those initiated by the country's artistic elite. Erichsen's striking self-description as a grateful servant to the talented effectively foregrounded the appropriateness of special treatment based on merit and implicitly characterised the DFI's response to Dogma 95 as a churlish instance of misplaced egalitarianism and parochialism (Møller 1997). The collaborative agreement between DR TV and the film collective hinged on the question of holdback. Dogma films, Erichsen pointed out, would be shown on television after only three months, the normal holdback period being twenty-four months. Indeed, Erichsen and the brethren had managed to mobilise support for Dogma throughout the Nordic countries, with public service channels in Sweden, Norway, Finland and Iceland paying in advance for broadcast rights after the first quarter. Dogma 95 had not only been revived, but had been transformed into a clear example of the kind of successful collaboration between film and TV that politicians and administrators, including those at the DFI, so frequently had cited as desirable.

1998 saw the release of Dogme #1 and Dogme #2, both of which generated considerable interest in the Dogma concept at Cannes. Indeed, Thomas Vinterberg's *The Celebration*, an intense tale of child abuse and dysfunctional familial dynamics, was awarded the Jury's Special Prize. Dogme #3, Søren Kragh-Jacobsen's *Mifune*, which won the Silver Bear at the Berlin Film Festival in 1999, further confirmed the emerging view that the Dogma rules amounted to more than a cynical publicity stunt and instead reflected important insights into the very conditions that make creativity and innovation

possible. Reporting from Cannes in 1999, the respected film critic, Ebbe Iversen, identified the relevant festival as the site and moment of Dogma 95's internationalisation. The
basis for his statements about Dogma 95's transformation was the fact that Zentropa had
brokered agreements with a number of non-Danish producers to produce sixteen new
Dogma films, eight of which would be Scandinavian productions. That the boundary
between the national and the international is never unmarked and always a source of
intense concern in the small nation-state of Denmark is tellingly revealed by Iversen's
choice of title for his article: '*Danish* [emphasis added] agreement about 16 new Dogma
films' ('Dansk aftale om 16 nye Dogme-film').

If Dogma 95 to some extent expressed a wish, on the part of initiators and supporters
alike, to see a small nation take the lead internationally, the current state of the movement
would seem to bespeak a certain measure of success. In addition to the brethren's films,
the movement has generated a second wave of Danish Dogma films. Lone Scherfig was
the first Danish film-maker to take up the Dogma baton after it had been duly circulated
among members of the collective. In spite of understandable worries about whether she
would be able to meet the expectations surrounding Dogma following the successes of
The Celebration and *Mifune*, Scherfig's *Italiensk for begyndere* (*Italian for Beginners*, 2000)
was to become the second Dogma film to win the Silver Bear at Berlin. In 2001 the film
sold 700,000 tickets in Denmark out of a total of 2.1 million. Indeed, *Italian for Beginners*
was a major factor in the staggering 75 per cent increase in 2001 (compared to 2000) in
ticket sales for Danish films in Denmark (DFI 2001). Set in the lower-middle-class suburb
of Hvidovre, the film, as Bondebjerg points out, explores 'the depressing routine of daily
life', the joylessness of a modern, welfare-state Denmark. With its emphasis on psychologically damaged characters who, through a course in Italian, discover the lovers who can
somehow make them whole, the film has been classified as a romantic comedy that to a
certain extent violates the interdiction on genre films.

Et rigtigt menneske (*Truly Human*, 2001), directed by the Swedish graduate of the
Danish Film School, Åke Sandgren, is similarly part of the second wave of Danish
Dogma films. While the awards won by *Truly Human* are less prestigious than those garnered by *The Celebration*, *Mifune* and *Italian for Beginners*, Sandgren's film was fêted at
the Montevideo International Film Festival of Uruguay and at the Festival du Cinéma
Nordique in Rouen, and has enjoyed considerable success at more than twenty festivals
around the world. Sandgren's story is by no means without risks, for it involves the rather
fantastical transformation of 'P' (Nikolaj Lie Kaas), a character imagined by a lonely
seven-year-old child, into a real human being. In addition, the seven-year-old Lisa (Clara
Nepper Winther) is magically resurrected once her parents have learnt, through the grief
experienced on her death, just how much they in fact love her. Sandgren manages to get
the viewer to accept and even to be intrigued by these rather dramatic ontological shifts
in what is otherwise a universe governed by the laws of everyday reality.

Truly Human was followed by *En kærlighedshistorie* (*Kira's Reason: A Love Story*,
2001), directed by Ole Christian Madsen, a rapidly emerging figure and one of the first
Danish film-makers to focus the camera on the complexities of belonging in a Denmark
characterised by religious and ethnic diversity rather than genetic and cultural hom-

ogeneity. His Dogma film, *Kira's Reason*, presents the psychologically disturbed Kira (Stine Stengade) as a puzzle to be slowly solved by the unfolding narrative. In the concluding moments of the film, we discover that her institutionalisation, lack of self-control, lasciviousness and sense of despair can all be traced to the traumatic loss of her youngest child shortly after birth and, more importantly, to her husband Mads' (Lars Mikkelsen) failure adequately to support her at that time. Due in part to Christian Madsen's unorthodox approach to framing and the palpable rhythms of the hand-held camera, the film has the kind of psychological intensity that critics also noted in connection with *The Celebration*.

One of the most recent Danish Dogma films, Susanne Bier's *Elsker dig for evigt* (*Open Hearts*, 2002), focuses on the 'fragility of life' and is at some level a reflection of the film-maker's response to the events of 9/11 (Kjær 2002b: 1). With a script by Anders Thomas Jensen (who was the scriptwriter for *Mifune* and *The King is Alive*), and with Paprika Steen (*The Celebration*, *The Idiots*, *Mifune*), Nikolaj Lie Kaas (*The Idiots* and *Truly Human*) and Mads Mikkelsen (*Kira's Reason*) in leading roles, *Open Hearts* clearly draws on the cultural capital that Dogma's earlier Danish successes created. In *Open Hearts*, much as in Sandgren's *Truly Human*, the plot turns on the intervention of fate in the form of a car accident. In one fateful moment, the rosy future envisaged by Joachim (Nikolaj Lie Kaas) is transformed into a fantasy of the past as the young student is left to grapple with a permanent paralysis from the neck down. Traumatised by his changed life, Joachim breaks with his fiancée, Cecilie (Sonja Richter), who seeks solace from Niels (Mads Mikkelsen), a doctor who is not only married, but married to Marie (Paprika Steen), the negligent driver and cause of the accident. Drawing on the hand-held aesthetic that the Dogma rules encourage, and the sense of raw intimacy and probing honesty that this visual style is able to create, Bier engages viewers in a world of intense emotions that derive their force from the absolutely unanticipated nature of the events by which they are caused.

Open Hearts sold 45,000 tickets during its opening weekend in Denmark, a success by local standards which points both to Bier's public record as a film-maker with a broad popular appeal and to continued interest in the Dogma label. That we are dealing here with a convergence of popular opinion and critical assessment is clearly suggested by the film's many nominations for awards, including the first Nordic film prize and the Oscar for Best Foreign Film. Interestingly, the international reception of *Open Hearts* at the time of writing explained the film's strengths in terms of a combination of factors, only some of which are directly traceable to the Dogma equation. Indeed, *Open Hearts* was described by Steve Gravestock in the Toronto Film Festival programme as correcting certain false impressions created by Dogma 95 even as it breathed new life into the brethren's original project. The visibility of Dogma 95, he argued, allowed a standard account to emerge that construed contemporary Danish film as moribund prior to the brethren's salvage operation. Yet *Open Hearts* draws attention to the vibrancy of pre-existing national or indigenous tendencies, and thus to the fact that there was cinematic life in Denmark before the advent of Dogma. *Open Hearts*, the view is, takes Dogma in new directions that may well have the effect of deepening the movement's legitimacy and of prolonging its existence. The multiple reasons underwriting the film's reception at the national level resurface here with added significance within a context that marks the work's entry into an international or transnational public sphere. With *Open Hearts* Dogma 95 begins to fulfil its original potential as a vehicle for a fully blown politics of recognition, for in this case the Dogma effect functions as a leveraging device that allows Bier to lift certain popular traditions into the light of international visibility, and out of the obscurity that a purely national mode of reception ultimately constitutes.

That the second wave of Danish Dogma films, to which *Open Hearts* belongs, is far from exhausted is clearly suggested by an early 2003 release and a further projected Danish Dogma release later this year. Natasha Arthy's Dogma film, *Se til venstre der er en svensker* (*Old, New, Borrowed and Blue*, Nimbus Film), opened in Denmark on 31 January, 2003. A former children's television director, Arthy established herself with her first feature, the children's film *Mirakel* (*Miracle*), which did very well on the festival circuit. In *Old, New, Borrowed and Blue*, Arthy teams up with one of the most talented of Danish scriptwriters, Kim Fupz Aakeson, who described the intention motivating the work as follows: 'It'll be a feel-either-way film. We've picked some of melodrama's features. It'll be really serious and cruel in places, and very funny in others. We want to challenge the Dogme rules in the direction of realistic everyday portraits' (Kjær 2002a). Riding on the crest created by her debut film, *Små ulykker* (*Minor Mishaps*, 2002), Annette K. Olesen secured conditional funding in the autumn of 2002 from the DFI for a projected Dogma work entitled *Forbrydelser* (*Crimes*), to be produced by Zentropa's Ib Tardini. The project has been veiled in secrecy, not only as a means of generating public interest through mystery, but also in order to superimpose a further guiding principle on the rules specified by the brethren. Much as in the case of *Minor Mishaps*, the intention is to involve the actors in the development of their characters, without, however, disclosing information about the overall narrative development that is envisaged. In the context of the national cinema that Dogma was meant to revive, the making of a *bona fide* Dogma film, it would appear, has become virtually a point of honour among filmmakers who have already enjoyed a certain measure of success.

What is remarkable about Dogma 95, however, is the fact that it amounts to more than just a parochial effort on the part of a number of Danish film-makers to reinvent the cinema more generally and Danish cinema more specifically. Fuelled in part by the success of the Danish films, the Dogma initiative has itself been internationalised, resulting in what Ryan Gilbey calls 'the most radical film-making movement since the French new wave' (2002). Stated in this way, the point is hyperbolic and has the unfortunate effect of downplaying the very real contributions, aesthetic, artistic and other, that a strategic accommodation with, rather than a formal rejection of, the realities of commercial filmmaking have made possible in various contexts, the new Hong Kong cinema of the 80s and 90s being a noteworthy example. Yet, the characterisation is clearly prompted by what must be recognised as a cinematic initiative that is capable of generating significant cinematic works as well as the dynamics of a certain global mobilisation. Indeed, the list of foreign Dogma-certified productions now includes the French *Lovers* (1999), directed by Jean-Marc Barr, Harmony Korine's *Julien Donkey-Boy* (USA, 1999), the Korean

The poster for the most recent Danish Dogma film, Natasha Arthy's *Se til venstre der er en svensker* (*Old, New, Borrowed and Blue*) (courtesy of Nimbus Film)

Intyebyu (*Interview*, Daniel H. Byun, 2000), the clandestinely filmed *Fuckland* (2000) by Argentine film-maker José Luis Marquès, *Chetzemoka's Curse* (Rick Schmidt, USA, 2000), the Italian *Diapason* (Antonio Domenici, 2000), the Swiss *Joy Ride* (Martin Rengel, 2000), Richard Martini's *Camera* (USA, 2000), Shaun Monson's *Bad Actors* (USA, 2000), Mona J. Hoel's Norwegian *Når nettene bliver lange* (*Cabin Fever*, 2000), the Spanish *Era Outra Vez* (*Once Upon Another Time*, Juan Pinzás, 2000), Leif Tilden's *Big Chill*-inspired *Reunion* (USA, 2001), the Belgian *Strass* (Vincent Lannoo, 2001), Vladimir Gyorski's *Resin* (USA, 2001), James Merendino's *Amerikana* (USA, 2001) and Michael Sorenson's *Converging with Angels* (USA, 2002).

Admittedly, a number of the titles in this list have little to recommend them above and beyond the Dogma label. Yet, as Hjort argues ('The Globalisation of Dogma', this volume, pages 135–59), the lack of quality in the international films may ultimately be less significant than the dynamics of the Dogma concept's global circulation. Curiously, the line separating pedestrian from significant works virtually coincides with national boundaries, for, as critics have noted, the standard achieved by the Danish films by far surpasses that of the wave of international Dogma films. Critics have repeatedly noted the discrepancy (as have indeed the Dogma brethren themselves), but have had nothing particularly probing to say in the way of an explanation. In this connection it is helpful to refer to some remarks made by Mogens Rukov who taught both von Trier and Vinterberg during their years at the Danish Film School. In Jesper Jargil's documentary on Dogma 95, *De lutrede* (*The Purified*, 2002), Rukov points out that von Trier was a highly proficient film-maker with proven mastery of most of the technical aspects of his profession when he initiated Dogma 95. Von Trier's idea, in other words, was precisely to place a ban on the very techniques that he had spent years carefully mastering. Following Rukov, Dogma 95 makes most sense as a challenge to the expert film-maker rather than the novice, who, he argues, should be required to follow an entirely different set of rules. If Dogma 95 is a minimalist strategy aimed at a certain cinematic asceticism, then novices should be invited to adopt a maximalist strategy oriented towards a certain cinematic excess. Von Trier ultimately has a more inclusive conception of prospective Dogma film-makers, for he certainly envisages beginners profiting from the alternative aesthetic that the Dogma programme promotes and legitimates. The following excerpt from an interview with von Trier does, however, suggest that the film-maker supports Rukov's line of reasoning as at least a partial account of the impetus behind Dogma:

> I think the need to go back to basics, which the rules are a response to, is more urgent now than ever before. I would find it amusing if Dogme could continue to exist like a little pill you could take when there was too much of the other kind of thing, too much refinement and distanciation. You'd then take a little Dogme pill and feel much better afterwards, because you'd be grounded again (Hjort and Bondebjerg 2001: 222).

A plausible explanation, then, for the lack of quality in many of the works listed above is that Dogma has tended, outside Denmark, to appeal to film-makers who are still in the process of breaking into film-making. With its legitimation of low-budget film-making and non-mainstream aesthetics, Dogma 95 provides aspiring film-makers with a self-validating point of access to the world of independent film and, potentially, to the larger, pre-constituted audience that the recognition of earlier Dogma films at key festivals such as Cannes and Berlin helped to generate.[8]

The relatively high quality of the Danish Dogma films becomes less puzzling once one realises that in the Danish context Dogma 95 has functioned as precisely the kind of 'pill' that von Trier believes experienced film-makers accustomed to the complex apparatus of big-budget film-making should be required to swallow every now and again. In Denmark novices typically begin by making films within the context of the 'New Fiction Film Denmark' programme, which supports projects of a more limited scope and budget. Arguably novices have an easier time breaking into film-making in the Danish, state-supported system than they do in many other parts of the world. Indeed, the Danish Film Institute has put considerable effort into developing workshops and programmes where aspiring Danish film-makers can refine their film-making talents before undertaking feature-length projects. As a result, Dogma 95 has, to date, been the province of experienced Danish film-makers who have been tried and tested in various ways and who have clearly demonstrated talent and expertise. In this sense, an interesting process of pre-selection has been operative in the context of the Danish Dogma phenomenon, which cannot be said to have been the case on the international level. Jean-Marc Barr, for example, had considerable experience as an actor, but no background as a film-maker when he directed *Lovers*, which, in many ways, is characteristic of the weaker Dogma films. Here, clearly, the problem was not the lack of talent as such, but rather the lack of the right kind of talent. What was missing, precisely, was the know-how that is typically acquired through trial and error, through the time-consuming process of simply engaging in film-making. Compare this situation with that of Susanne Bier, director of *Open Hearts*. Born in 1960, Bier is one of Denmark's most successful female film-makers, with a long list of feature films to her name, including the box-office hit *The One and Only* (*Den eneste ene*, 1999), an energetic and focused attempt to reinvent the indigenous genre of the popular folk comedy in a modern idiom. Married to the talented Swedish actor and theatre director Philip Zandén, Bier has worked successfully, not only in Denmark, but also in Sweden. Inasmuch as many of Bier's films are co-productions involving the Nordic and in some cases other European countries, she has been grappling for some time now not only with the apparatus of mainstream film-making, but also with the intricacies that co-financing arrangements bring to the film-making process. Bier, it could be argued, is precisely the kind of film-maker who should be making a Dogma film, for in her case the notion of an ascetic shedding of ingrained habits, procedures and frameworks makes considerable sense.

While the internationalisation of Dogma 95 has not generated the volume of quality films that might have been hoped for, one title in particular merits attention. *Julien Donkey-Boy*, directed by the independent film-maker Harmony Korine, is a fascinating exploration of the mind of an adolescent schizophrenic caught in a dysfunctional family. The film casts Werner Herzog in the role of the abusive father with a mysterious past, a past that is evoked in part by means of a strong accent, but more importantly by regular bullying behaviour. The father, for example, forces his son, Julien, to wear the dresses of his deceased mother and to submit to being hosed down with cold water in the name of manliness and endurance. Julien, we are led to believe, is the father of his pregnant sister's baby, who is stillborn as a result of an ice-skating accident. The film includes harrowing scenes of Julien carrying the dead baby around in public, and much has been made of Korine's use of covert cameras in this connection:

> People didn't know they were being filmed. We had about eight or nine covert camera operators on the bus. Anthony was sitting there looking at a book, but he had a little camera in the palm of his hand, and a little monitor wired up inside a hole that he cut in the book. So he's watching. And there's a camera in a bag, and one in a hat, one on someone's glasses. We're presenting real people with a real dilemma: a kid gets on a bus with a dead baby wrapped up in a dirty old towel. It was a real liberty we were taking. And for an actor it's a moral dilemma to get into a situation like that. It's a terrible thing to do. People didn't know how to react. *I* wouldn't know how. In fact, the stuff they left in the finished film is the mildest stuff we got in terms of people's reactions (Ewen Bremner [Julien], interviewed in Kelly 2000: 187).

As in many of the other noteworthy Dogma films, the interest of *Julien Donkey-Boy* has to do with psychological depth and intensity, with the sense, to put it 'Dogmatically', that a certain inner truth or authenticity is being disclosed. What makes *Julien Donkey-Boy* unique in the context of Dogma's internationalisation is its status as the only non-Danish Dogma film to make use of the rules to reimagine a pre-existing cinema aesthetic, that of the American 'indie' film. Korine, who directed *Gummo* (1997) and co-wrote Larry Clark's youthful alienation 'indie' film *Kids* (1995), deploys the Dogma aesthetic to inject a sense of reality (if not realism) into the often hyper-kinetic visual style of American independent cinema. As a result, *Julien Donkey-Boy* stands out as one of the only non-Danish Dogma success stories in the United States.

To recapitulate, Dogma is a phenomenon that has developed in a series of partially overlapping stages. The first of these, spanning the period from 1998 to 2000, is defined by the release of the early Danish Dogma films produced by the brethren themselves. The second wave of Danish films, beginning with Lone Scherfig's *Italian for Beginners* in 2000, marks a new phase that is still ongoing. The internationalisation of Dogma begins with Jean-Marc Barr's *Lovers* in 1999 and continues today. In addition to these various cinematic trajectories, Dogma has involved a number of parodic elaborations as well as serious extensions to other domains, both artistic and non-artistic, all of which are described in detail by Hjort in 'The Globalisation of Dogma' (this volume, pages 143–8). In the present context, it is pertinent to point to the emergence of a fourth cinematic stage. We have in mind here the production of works that are only loosely inspired by the Dogma programme, a form of appropriation that could well become definitive of a new phase for the movement. At the time of writing, Vincent Chui Wan-shun's *Leaving in Sorrow* (2002), a moving and significant film about Hong Kong just before and soon after the handover in 1997, provided a telling example of a more piece-meal approach that, by virtue precisely of the emphasis on only partial or selective rule following, necessarily involved a renunciation of any and all aspirations to formal certi-fication. Released during the 26th Hong Kong International Film Festival, the film drew attention to Dogma's oppositional stance and its enabling effects, in this instance within the context of the Hong Kong independent cinema for which Chui has been a passion-ate spokesperson: 'Hollywood's studio system creates an artificial reality, but Dogma 95 looks for reality,' Chui said. 'My film has taken stories from real life and that's ideal for the Dogma style' (Chow 2002). Chui forges a link here between the aesthetic towards which Dogma would appear to incline and the telling of stories that seek to clarify the experiences of contemporary Hong Kong citizens. What is thus rejected is the idea that the aim of film-making should be to transport viewers into the convention-driven fic-tional worlds of the kind of commercial, studio-based genre cinemas that are characteristic of Hollywood, but also Hong Kong. *Leaving in Sorrow* is a clear instance of informal and partial, yet publicly acknowledged appropriation. Strict abidance by the letter of an invented and collectively imposed law is no longer all-important in this fourth phase, where the overarching question concerns the pay-offs of the Dogma con-cept in a particular context of appropriation and production. A fifth stage, defined by a more fluid notion of influence devoid of any explicit rhetorical link to the Dogma pro-

Chris breaks down when Hong takes her back to Beijing to confront the past: Vincent Chui's *Leaving in Sorrow*

gramme, would no doubt have to be included in an exhaustive account of the movement's effective history. Relevant in this connection is the way in which the hand-held aesthetic that Dogma helped to legitimate in an oppositional gesture is finding its way into the Hollywood mainstream.

Indeed, the impact of the Dogma manifesto within the public sphere has not gone unnoticed by Hollywood, even if top-ranking directors are not jumping on the Dogma bandwagon. Von Trier notes that Dogma is not just about following rules, but about setting limits, and through that process, liberating oneself from another set of rules (the conventionalised practices of Hollywood). The idea is to come up with *new* rules that, by virtue of their novelty, can play a role quite different from that of the established conventions. Referring to film-makers who might contest the value of the Dogma rules, von Trier makes the following point: 'you might argue that they could just as easily profit from a different set of rules. Yes, of course. But then go ahead and formulate them. Ours are just a proposal' (Hjort and Bondebjerg 2001: 222). As if by way of response, Steven Soderbergh came up with a manifesto, not for film-makers, but for actors thinking of working on his film *Full Frontal* (2001), which eventually featured Hollywood stars such as Julia Roberts, David Duchovny and David Hyde-Pierce, and was distributed by Miramax. The 'rules' read as follows:

Important

If you are an actor considering a role in this film, please note the following:

1. All sets are practical locations.
2. You will drive yourself to the set. If you are unable to drive yourself to the set, a driver will pick you up, but you will probably become the subject of ridicule. Either way, you arrive alone.
3. There will be no craft service, so you should arrive on set 'having had.' Meals will vary in quality.
4. You will pick, provide, and maintain your own wardrobe.
5. You will create and maintain your hair and make-up.
6. There will be no trailers. The company will attempt to provide holding areas near a given location, but don't count on it. If you need to be alone a lot, you're pretty much screwed.
7. Improvisation will be encouraged.

8. You will be interviewed about your character. This material may end up in the finished film.

9. You will be interviewed about the other characters. This material may end up in the finished film.

10. You will have fun whether you want to or not.

If any of these guidelines are problematic for you, stop reading now and send this screenplay back to where it came from. (Hunter 2002).[9]

While Hollywood may have refused explicitly to take up the particular challenge that the brethren's dicta entail, opting instead for more fluid patterns of influence, we find here a gesture that effectively incorporates Dogma into the institutional context of Hollywood. There is, in Soderbergh's serio-comic spin-off manifesto, an attempt to take issue with a different aspect of Hollywood's cumbersome apparatus, and to do so from within the lion's den, so to speak.

MODES OF DISTRIBUTION

While the Dogma manifesto foregrounds the need for a viable alternative film practice, the films themselves must circulate through traditional routes of distribution. In some ways the Dogma movement follows the distribution patterns first established by Roger Corman's New World Pictures in the 70s (which, in addition to producing and distributing B-movies and exploitation films such as *Night Call Nurses* [1972], also distributed Ingmar Bergman's *Cries and Whispers* [1972], Federico Fellini's *Amarcord* [1973] and Alain Resnais' *Mon oncle d'Amérique* [1980]). It is important to draw attention to the way in which the first few Danish Dogma films were distributed in the United States. At first blush, the situation would appear to be one of independent distributors negotiating the rights for art-house films for limited release. Yet, as Andrew Higson (2003) points out in his recent study of the British heritage film, the relationship between major and minor film distributors changed drastically in the 80s and 90s, with some major corporations buying out smaller, independent distributors and other major production and distribution companies setting up their own 'prestige' or art-house subsidiaries. The distribution patterns of many of the first internationally successful Dogma films reflect this trend. For instance, in the United States *The Celebration* was distributed by October Films and *The Idiots* by USA Films, both independent distribution companies now owned by the Hollywood conglomerate Universal Pictures. *The King is Alive* was distributed by IFC Releasing (the Independent Film Channel, which also released Richard Kelly's documentary on Dogma; see below), a subsidiary of the cable company Bravo Networks. *Mifune* was released by Sony Pictures Classics, the 'prestige' line of Sony Films. *Italian for Beginners* was released by Miramax, which followed in the footsteps of Corman by pioneering the independent, art-cinema crossover hit, and which is now a subsidiary of the Disney Corporation. The most successful of the American, 'indie' Dogma films, Harmony Korine's *Julien Donkey-Boy,* was released by Fine Line Features, the art-house wing of New Line Pictures. These 'prestige' distributors emerge in connection with the studios' desires to target specific markets, often with foreign releases that demonstrate a 'crossover' potential. The gamble is a worthwhile one for companies that are typically associated with Hollywood cinema, for it only takes one hit the size of *La vita è bella* (*Life is Beautiful*, Roberto Benigni, Italy, 1997) or *My Big, Fat Greek Wedding* (Joel Zwick, USA, 2002) to offset the losses that tend to be incurred as a result of distributing art-house films. It is, however, interesting to note that the Dogma films that acquired this kind of 'prestige', art-house label in the United States were all Danish in origin – with the exception of *Julien Donkey-Boy*. What is apparent here, it would seem, is the extent to which Dogma remains a Danish movement in the American mind, although Dogma is very much about rethinking art cinema in ways that might loosen the latter's traditional ties to concepts of nationhood and nationality.

DOGMA AND ITS COMMENTATORS

While opinions may diverge about the ultimate value and significance of the Dogma films as individual works of cinematic art, as well as about the directors' deeper motivations for making films under the Dogma banner, there can be little doubt at this point that the Dogma phenomenon warrants critical attention, at least from film scholars, but arguably also from the many thinkers in various disciplines who have an interest in understanding the realities of globalisation. Interestingly, the most visible attempts so far to come to grips with the originating intentions behind Dogma 95 and its impact as a movement take the form, not of scholarly works, but documentaries. Richard Kelly's *The Name of this Film is Dogme95* (2000), produced for the Independent Film Channel (US) and FilmFour (UK), provides interviews with key directors, producers and actors, as well as witty scenes with Kelly himself preaching the rules from a pulpit and enacting their implications through a series of genre-based shots followed by their Dogmatic versions, with the 'subtractions' clearly highlighted. Jesper Jargil has directed two Dogma-related films, *De ydmygede* (*The Humiliated*, 1998) and *De lutrede* (*The Purified*). The first is a subtle account of the making of von Trier's *The Idiots*, focusing on the director's deep commitment to his rule-governed project and on his growing alienation from his actors as a result of his inability to come to grips with his unrequited feelings for the actress Anne Louise Hassing. In *The Purified* Jargil brings together the four brethren to discuss the current state of the Dogma movement and to confront each of them with scenes that in some way are controversial in connection with the rules. Thus, for example, Kragh-Jacobsen is shown giving Sofie Gråbøl detailed instructions on how to play the wedding night scene in *Mifune*, and this clip generates a heated discussion among the brethren about the extent to which Dogma is intended to rule out *mise-en-scène*. Von Trier is similarly confronted with shots of himself manipulating an extension cord in order to produce the needed light for an attic scene. And Vinterberg is reminded of the dishcloths that were hung in a window so that they could dry but which ended up functioning as a kind of lighting arrangement during the shooting of *The Celebration*.

While the documentaries identified above provide insightful portraits of Dogma 95, they are no substitute for fully blown scholarly analysis. Yet, with the exception of a special issue of editor Richard Raskin's *p.o.v.: A Danish Journal of Film Studies* (2000), the English-language discussion of Dogma 95 has been left largely to journalists who, understandably enough, have foregrounded only some of the more obviously tellable aspects of the phenomenon. Jack Stevenson's *Lars von Trier* (2002) includes a helpful, but for the most part anecdotal account of Dogma, while Shari Roman's edited volume subtitled *Hollywood, Indiewood & Dogme 95* (2001) functions primarily as an archive of interview materials, the significance of which has yet to be spelt out. Hjort and Bondebjerg's interview book, *The Danish Directors* (2001), provides exchanges about Dogma with von Trier, Vinterberg and Kragh-Jacobsen, but does not attempt a deeper analysis. While Danish film scholars have been intrigued by Dogma 95, their publications on the topic tend to be descriptive, rather than analytic. What is more, there is little interest in the Danish context in the specific details of Dogma's internationalisation or appropriation in areas other than the cinematic. Nor is there any recognition of the way in which the term 'Dogma' has come to function as a vehicle for what Hjort, following Leo Ou-fan Lee, calls 'public criticism' ('The Globalisation of Dogma', this volume, p.135). *Purity and Provocation* draws, then, on philosophers, film theorists, established scholars of various national cinemas, a well-known dance theorist and a successful producer to tease out the various conceptual bases and more general implications of Dogma as a cinematic programme, a corpus of works and a network of interconnected discourses with global effects.

PURITY AND PROVOCATION: THE CONTRIBUTIONS AND APPENDICES

The critical essays are divided into three sections with distinct foci. The first section encompasses contributions that aim to shed light on what might be called the 'origins' of Dogma 95. It is a matter here of reflecting on some of the broad social tendencies to which Dogma 95 is a response, on the place of the Dogma initiative within a larger tradition of cinematic manifesto writing, and on the continuities between this collectivist, rule-governed project and Lars von Trier's earlier and ongoing endeavours. A quite different approach characterises the second section, where close analysis of individual films is the preferred means of making sense of the hermeneutic conundra of the movement's founding documents and of assessing the coherence and ultimate value of the Dogma proposal. Fine-grained discussions of some of the more 'canonical', as well as of one of the less successful Dogma films, are followed by analyses in the third section of the Dogma concept's marketability and extension beyond its original cinematic boundaries. The first of three appendices offers easy access to the Dogma movement's manifesto and Vow of Chastity and to most of the English-language spin-off manifestos. A second appendix comprises filmographies for all Dogma films, while a third provides information on Dogma-related films. *Purity and Provocation* is a co-ordinated attempt, then, to point to ways of understanding the motivational complexities of the Dogma movement, to assess the artistic, political or film-theoretic significance of a number of individual works, and to furnish tools for further research on the individual works that sustain the cinematic movement, as well as on the circulation of the Dogma concept within a global media culture.

In 'Dogma 95: A Small Nation's Response to Globalisation', Mette Hjort takes issue with a number of influential views on Dogma 95 that construe the movement as apolitical, as an ingenious marketing exercise, and as an experiment in enhancing creativity through the imposition of *arbitrary* constraints. Dogma 95, Hjort contends, is in fact politically motivated inasmuch as it represents a small nation's response to the pressures of globalisation, understood as a form of convergence on cost-intensive aesthetic norms with the effect of aggravating existing problems of access. Following Hjort the political thrust of Dogma 95 becomes clear once we grasp the extent to which the rules are not in fact arbitrary but constitute a direct response to the institutional features of small-nation film-making.

In 'Manifest Destinies: Dogma 95 and the Future of the Film Manifesto', Scott MacKenzie explores the connections between Dogma 95 and earlier cinematic movements originating in, or associated with, manifestos or manifesto-like statements. His view is that Dogma 95 most closely resembles the Free Cinema movement initiated by Lindsay Anderson on account of the way in which it combines elements of a novel approach to film-making with an understanding of the workings of publicity. The global reach of Dogma 95, MacKenzie suggests, has to do with the founding manifesto's divergence from the modernist manifesto as analysed by Janet Lyon (1999). More specifically, a certain systematic separation of 'form and content' provides the key to understanding the efficacies of the Dogma programme.

The larger context evoked by Peter Schepelern as a way of coming to grips with Dogma 95 is neither globalisation nor the history of cinematic movements, but the oeuvre of Lars von Trier. Schepelern makes a case for seeing the idea of self-imposed rules as a guiding principle in almost all of von Trier's productions, from his early diploma film entitled *Befrielsesbilleder* (*Images of a Relief*, 1982) to his most recent feature, *Dogville* (2003). Schepelern's view is that while von Trier's self-imposed rules serve a range of functions, their ultimate basis is an essentially ludic conception of film-making. A wide range of examples is mobilised in support of this contention, with special emphasis on the relatively unknown theatre experiment known as *Psykomobile #1: Verdensuret* (*Psychomobile #1: The World Clock*, 1996).

Ib Bondebjerg's critical strategy is to highlight divergences among the Danish Dogma films and similarities between these same works and other non-Dogma films produced in Denmark in the course of the 90s. The point is not to diminish Dogma 95, but to valorise a more general cinematic trend that characterises Danish film-making in the 90s. The suggestion is that the role played by Dogma in a Danish context has little to do with the widely discussed rules and the artistic consequences of the behaviours that they do or do not allow, and far more to do with the profiling of a pre-existing tendency.

In 'Naked Film: Dogma and its Limits', close analysis of the first two Dogma films (Vinterberg's *The Celebration* and von Trier's *The Idiots*) becomes a means of clarifying the aims specified in the movement's founding documents, for it is Berys Gaut's view that, in addition to being 'instances of the rules and their (main) point', these films are also '*about* the rules and their point'. Gaut initially considers the idea that Dogma 95 might be understood as a marketing device or as an attempt to enhance creativity through the imposition of constraints, but he goes on to argue that Dogma's foundational texts support neither of these interpretations. The task, he claims, is to understand what is meant by 'film of illusion' and 'individual film', for the *stated* point of the kind of rule-governed activity that Dogma prescribes is to combat these related phenomena. Gaut's detailed account of what might be meant by these terms allows him to conclude that the main target of the critique that Dogma launches against mainstream film-making is the 'film of illusion', opposition to the idea of the 'individual film' being a 'sub-ordinate goal' within the Dogma scheme of things. Gaut's verdict is that Dogma 95 offers 'an interesting account of what is wrong with mainstream cinema today, and how to combat it', but he also points to a number of conceptual problems with the move-ment's rationale. A helpful distinction between content realism and perceptual realism allows Gaut to expose the rather arbitrary way in which the Dogma rules support a basic commitment to realism. The oppositions between individual vision and truth, and between art and truth, on which Dogma relies are further identified as overly 'crude'. In Gaut's mind the real significance of Dogma 95 may well lie in its validation of low-budget film-making.

Paisley Livingston's argument in 'Artistic Self-Reflexivity in *The King is Alive* and *Strass*' pursues a similar tack. It is Livingston's hypothesis that at least some of the Dogma films, and particularly Dogme #4 and Dogme #20, support the idea that the critique of illusionistic film-making is directed at films that reduce 'imaginative fiction to certain forms of fantasy'. Cinematic fantasy, in Livingston's account, is defined as films where 'the medium's representational techniques – its "illusionistic" devices – are employed to guide, stimulate, and enable the spectator's pleasurable imaginings', the hedonic pay-offs in question being crucially linked to 'events which are deemed by the fantasiser to be out of reach' in the sense of being either transgressive or impossible in the fantasiser's opinion. The critique of cinematic fantasy in this sense sheds light on key aspects of the Dogma manifesto and Vow of Chastity. Livingston's interpretation of the significance of the staging of *King Lear* by tourists stranded in the Namibian desert in *The King is Alive* construes Levring's film as a meta-cinematic reflection on the ills of fantasy, as does his reading of the role of Pierre Radowsky's (Pierre Lekeux) theories of acting in Vincent Lannoo's film, *Strass*.

Murray Smith's analysis of *The Idiots* in terms of the kinds of issues of engagement and alignment that form the core of his groundbreaking book, *Engaging Characters* (1995), identifies the character Karen (Bodil Jørgensen) as a central figure whose basic stance towards the project of 'spassing' points to the deeper commitments of the Dogma brethren as expressed in the movement's founding texts.

Ginette Vincendeau's contribution on Jean-Marc Barr's directorial debut, *Lovers*, speaks to the issue of national cinema and Dogma's relation to the conceptual framework in question. Vincendeau characterises *Lovers* as a mode of hybrid expression drawing on 'the techniques of Dogma and the aesthetics and themes of the New Wave'. Her assump-tion is that the New Wave and Dogma represent strategies for reinventing national cinema in a French and Danish context respectively. *Lovers* is interpreted as occupying 'an inter-national media space' that problematises the very category of national cinema on which Dogma 95 continues somehow, at least in its founding moments, to rely. Vincendeau's suggestive conclusion is that Barr's internationalist work ultimately 'allegorises the diffi-culties in conceptualising the "new Europe" which the film means to celebrate'.

'The Globalisation of Dogma: The Dynamics of Metaculture and Counter-Publicity' is the first of several contributions dealing with the extension of the Dogma concept beyond the sphere of feature film-making. It is Hjort's contention that while Dogma is a response to globalisation it also qualifies as an instance of what Arjun Appadurai calls 'globalization from below' (2001: 3). Metaculture and counter-publicity, she claims, provide the key to understanding the dynamics of Dogma's globalisation.

In 'Decoding *D-Day*: Multi-Channel Television at the Millennium', Martin Roberts focuses on one of the ways in which the Dogma brethren themselves have extended the Dogma concept to other areas, in this instance TV. *D-Day* refers to the brethren's millennium project, which has been characterised by Vinterberg as a continuation of the game of Dogma, albeit by other means, i.e. other rules. The fact that *D-Day* tends to be discussed in terms of what might be called a 'Dogma ethos' (although the website dedicated to the experiment in multi-channel broadcasting explicitly states that *D-Day* does not conform to the relevant rules) provides clear evidence of the intended and actual circulatory efficacity of Dogma as a concept. Roberts' understanding of *D-Day* as a kind of 'symbolic invasion' of Denmark on the part of the Dogma brethren hinges in large measure on the very concept of play or game behaviour to which Schepelern also attributes special importance. Whereas any concept of the national was merely implicit in the original Dogma proposal, national imaginaries are central to *D-Day*, which Roberts construes as a kind of 'collective video game' allowing players to 'participate, on a symbolic level, in the "game" of the nation itself'.

'Dogma Dance' by Sally Banes and Noël Carroll deals intensively with an initiative aimed at a hybrid art form, that of film dance. While film-making practices thus remain central, the regulation of these practices through a new Dogma-inspired manifesto with a different set of rules no longer serves to distance film from the illusionistic practices of a Hollywood mainstream, but to defend an ideal hybridity of film dance from the totalising encroachments of film, on the one hand, and dance, on the other. The aim, interestingly, is not to create a cinematic sub-genre within the genre that Dogma has been held to circumscribe (Seßlen 1999), for the Dogma Dance manifesto makes a point of ensuring that none of the dance films made according to its prescriptions could ever achieve certification from the Dogma 95 collective. Banes and Carroll rightly suggest that this kind of codified departure from a founding Dogma practice expresses an intention genuinely and creatively to *extend* the Dogma concept in various ways. The gesture of creative appropriation in a new founding document effectively charts a trajectory 'from Denmark to Great Britain' and 'from narrative film to screen dance', thereby allowing Dogma to travel across 'national and artistic borders'. 'Dogma Dance' explores a fascinating instance of appropriation and begins to speak to the more general question of what, precisely, it is that has allowed Dogma to make its way so effectively around the globe.

Claus Christensen's 'Documentary Gets the Dogma Treatment' is a largely descriptive account of Lars von Trier's formulation, prompted by the journalists Klaus Birch and Michael Klint, of Dogma rules for documentary film-making. Much as in the case of Dogma 95, which was conceived as a mini-movement involving the production of at least four films by the Dogma brethren, the 'dogumentary' initiative envisages a certain initial volume by projecting the production of at least six films. These documentaries are to be directed by four Danes (Klaus Birch, Michael Klint, Bente Milton and Sami Saif), one Norwegian (Margreth Olin) and one Swede (Pål Hollender). Drawing on conversations with Birch, Klint, Milton and Saif, Christensen's discussion provides valuable information about the intentions and expectations of the first 'dogumentarists'. References to statements made by the producer Carsten Holst help to shed light on the effectiveness of Dogma as a marketing device that, somewhat unusually, is linked to considerations of a deeper or more substantive nature: 'The novelty is that we're selling each film on the basis of Lars von Trier's idea instead of a particular story … By doing so we give our directors the freedom to tell stories they're really passionate about.' The 'dogumentary' manifesto emerges as yet another example of agents converging on the Dogma concept with mixed intentions aimed at exploring matters of genuine concern, but in a manner that maximises the probability of an audience. Lars von Trier's role in this instance is that of originator, but also that of authoritative custodian, for his reconceptualisation of Dogma along documentary lines effectively revives the original Dogma concept while carving out a path for its extension to other areas. If Dogma manages to inscribe itself in lasting cultural memory, it will likely, and somewhat predictably, be remembered on account of a handful of provocative films. More interesting, perhaps, is the idea of a lasting narrative about the circulatory efficacities that the originator of the movement clearly understands so well. A concluding essay by the producer Mads Egmont Christensen provides an industry-based perspective on the success and promise of Dogma in the context not only of Danish film, but European film more generally.

THE FILMS

The most influential Dogma films have been discussed briefly above and are examined in greater detail in the essays that make up *Purity and Provocation*. What follows, then, is a series of brief descriptions, organised according to geographical regions, of most of the Dogma films that do not receive extensive analysis in the contributions. The emphasis on countries of origin is intended to highlight the globalised nature of the movement, but it also reflects the difficulties involved in providing a purely chronological account of the Dogma films. More specifically, a chronology that simply follows the order of certification based on stated intent (Dogme #1, Dogme #2, etc.) would not follow the order of release (for instance, Dogme #5 was released before Dogme #4, and Dogme #28 is now released, but Dogme #27 is still in production). It should be noted that a brief discussion of *Lovers* is included here in order fully to chart the geography of Dogma's circulation, although the film is ably discussed by Ginette Vincendeau in her contribution.

EUROPE
Lovers (France)
Jean-Marc Barr's *Lovers* was the first of the non-Danish Dogma films. Barr, who has appeared in several of Lars von Trier's films, made this film with his now frequent collaborator, Pascal Arnold. *Lovers*, which is about an illegal immigrant from the former Yugoslavia who falls in love with a French woman in Paris, was nowhere nearly as well

received as the Dogma films made by the Danish brethren. Part of the explanation has to do with the fact that the film was not that easy to categorise in terms of contemporary trends in European cinema. *Lovers*, while sharing some thematic concerns with the earlier Dogma films, has far more in common with the French *cinéma-vérité* tradition. As such, while the film is in some ways a stylistic throwback to classics of the *nouvelle vague*, such as *Chronique d'un été* (Jean Rouch and Edgar Morin, France, 1961) and *Le Joli mai* (Chris Marker, France, 1962), it falls outside the mainstream of current French cinema. Nevertheless, *Lovers* did have some festival successes, winning prizes at the Cottus Festival of Young East European Cinema and the Munich Film Festival. A retrospective of Barr's work was also shown at the Montreal World Film Festival in 2002. Undaunted by negative reviews and having achieved some festival acclaim, Barr and Arnold proclaimed that *Lovers* was the first part of a trilogy, which also included *Too Much Flesh* (Jean-Marc Barr and Pascal Arnold, France/USA, 2000) – about sexual repression in small-town America – and *Being Light* (Jean-Marc Barr and Pascal Arnold, France/Germany, 2001) – a film about travel as a means of self-discovery. Neither of these films are Dogma films, although there are some aesthetic similarities. They named the trilogy the 'freetrilogy' and came up with a manifesto of their own to accompany the films. The manifesto begins by stating that 'Collective freedom flourishes with the freedom of each of its individuals, as long as one's actions don't infringe upon the freedom of others', and continues as follows:

> The three films have been recorded digitally and then transferred onto 35mm film. By reducing large crews, heavy machinery and ultimately the budget, this permits the creator's freedom to pursue subjects on an intimate basis and with more humanity. Adapting to this new way of filming is NOT for purely financial reasons but instead the new way of filming is taken into account when in the writing process.
>
> More importantly there is a state of mind, an attitude that navigates this new way of filming, a dynamic that allows for an openness of spirit that at the same time respects an economic reality, which if mastered, permits even more freedom. We hope to encourage other filmmakers to get their films made in this way.
>
> This trilogy of freedom, in it's [sic] content and its fabrication is our message of hope for this new century (Barr and Arnold 2002).

Lovers was then repositioned as being not only a Dogma film but also a part of the 'freetrilogy'. Indeed, it was described by the film-makers as being about 'the Freedom for every individual in Europe to love whom they want, where they want, whatever their nationality'. Following this theme, *Too Much Flesh* was construed as being about 'the freedom to pursue one's sexuality within the context of a community where hypocritical values reign'. *Being Light*, the closing film in the trilogy, was held to address 'Freedom of thought and spirit in a world that is veering towards the standardisation of ideas and behaviours'. In theme, if not in aesthetic achievement, the 'freetrilogy' manifesto and films call to mind Krzysztof Kieślowski's *Three Colours* trilogy (1993–94), which was based on the founding motto of modern France: 'liberty, equality and fraternity'. While

Barr and Arnold's two subsequent films have also been critically panned (and less well received by festival audiences), it is interesting to see how the Dogma manifesto prompted Barr and Pascal to come up with their own statement of purpose. Indeed, *Lovers* is probably the only film in the history of cinema to ascribe to two different film manifestos at the same time.

Diapason (Italy)

Directed by Antonio Domenici, this film follows the nocturnal strivings of an unusual assortment of contemporary Rome's denizens, including a wealthy young film producer, an ageing movie production manager who boasts of having once worked with Fellini, a vain and beautiful American actress, a sleazy art dealer and his drug-addict minions, and finally, a group of immigrants from the Ivory Coast who make their living by various criminal means, including drug-dealing, prostitution and theft. This odd collection of marginal individuals are out to realise various interconnecting and conflicting goals as they range about late into the Roman night. The production manager must convince the actress to take a role in a film he is supervising; a young painter wants to distract the art dealer with a black prostitute so that he can steal a painting from him and sell it to the film producer; one of the crooks, who procures the prostitute, has stolen a Volvo and hopes to get enough money to buy himself a van and begin a stable and ordinary life with a family. Sordid and unstable coalitions are formed and broken. The artist takes his girl-friend who is suffering from an overdose to a veterinarian, who exploits her sexually while she is unconscious; the film producer seduces the actress and sends the production manager home alone; the hapless small-time crook suddenly loses all of his money when the police impound the stolen Volvo. A few moments of beauty emerge against this back-ground of sordid and cynical dealings: the leader of the immigrant crooks expresses his joy at the birth of a daughter; the veteran producer speaks with poetic eloquence about his love for the city; and the young artist finds a moment to paint with febrile intensity. This contemporary response to *La Dolce Vita* (1960) maintains its pace and vigour throughout, and is consistently convincing in its depiction of these marginal beings.

Joy Ride (Switzerland)

Martin Rengel's film focuses on a group of uninspired and massively inarticulate German Swiss youths in their early twenties, who share a routine of killing their free time together by drinking beer and tequila, and smoking hashish. This pattern is dis-turbed, however, when a young woman attaches herself to the group. She lends them money when they are broke, and has a seemingly endless supply of drugs. The boys are ambivalent about her, however, as each apparently asks himself whether the other males find her sufficiently attractive. One of them, who may well have been rejected by her, crudely labels her 'the rake'. In spite of their age, the boys' code seems to be that it is 'uncool' to be interested in women, unless, perhaps, they have large breasts. Yet one of the lads ends up spending some time alone with the young woman as a result of her advances. It appears as though something resembling a romance is blossoming – though the film is elliptical in its presentation of the events. For reasons that remain unstated, the other boys nastily oppose this relationship, and do everything they can to convince their comrade to drop her. As he is weak, immature and strangely ambivalent, their boorish tactics succeed, and he stifles whatever fond inclinations he may have had. In an unexpected and inordinately brutal turn of events, the young men take the young woman for a ride and strangle her. In the final scene, the mother of the victim visits the principal culprit in prison and we see him break down in remorse. An initial title shot informs us that this sad story was based on an actual incident, and though the film does have a kind of ethnographic quality – especially with regard to these youths' brutish language – it lacks the explanatory dimension that would make it a significant statement. Instead, its sordid subject matter has the dubious virtue of giving the phrase 'Eurotrash' new meaning.

Era Outra Vez (Once Upon Another Time, Spain)

This first Spanish Dogma film tells the story of a group of people gathering in northern Spain for their tenth anniversary reunion after graduating from college together. Released in Spain, the film has since played on the festival circuit, most notably in Moscow where it was nominated for a prize. It premiered in the US at the Miami Hispanic Film Festival. The film, which is shot in Galician, shares certain features with Vinterberg's *Festen*, and also, strangely enough, John Sayles' *The Return of the Secaucus Seven* (USA, 1980) and Lawrence Kasdan's *The Big Chill* (USA, 1983). What is interesting about the film, in addition to the Galician, is the way in which its abidance by the Dogma rules helps to set it apart from much of what an international audience would expect from contemporary Spanish cinema. *Era Outra Vez* is a compelling example of how Dogma is interfacing with international cinema trends. On the one hand, the film avoids the bright, saturated aesthetic of Pedro Almodóvar or the languid pacing of Manuel Oliveira. Yet, director Juan Pinzás' use of Galician gives the film a cultural specificity it otherwise would not have, and delivers a Galician film to an international audience (albeit only one that attends festivals). This tension between the local and the international is one of the appeals of Dogma, as the publicity generated through strategies of association or yoking can have an impact outside the confines of political debates within any given nation-state.

SOUTH AMERICA

Fuckland (Argentina)

The relationship between European art cinemas and the Third cinemas of South America has always been one fraught with problems. While a film such as *Hour of the Furnaces* (*La hora de los hornos*, Fernando Solanas and Octavio Getino, Argentina, 1968) was in many ways tied to the revolutionary aesthetic to be found in the works of Jean-Luc Godard, Bernardo Bertolucci and Andrzej Wajda, to name but a few, financial limitations and the struggle for political liberation made European art cinema and Third cinema uneasy allies. This uneasiness still obtains today. For instance, in a recent article chron-icling the ups and downs of Brazilian cinema, Carlos Diegues notes with irony that: 'We never have had huge budgets ... We were making Dogma films before Dogma existed. For us Dogma is not a theory but a necessity. In Brazil we never make the films we dream of making; we make the films we *can* make. We don't make the ideal films; we make the *possible* films. It's a kind of style' (Williams 2002: 20). José Luis Marquès' *Fuckland* can thus be seen, not only as an element in the Dogma movement, but as coming out of the history and traditions of the Third cinemas that precede Dogma and claim some of Dogma's aesthetic innovations as their own.

Fuckland was a *cause célèbre* at the London Film Festival – so popular, in fact, that extra screenings were added – but the film has yet to receive widespread distribution in the UK or North America. *Fuckland* was shot over the period of a week in the Falkland Islands. Marquès, an Argentine, arrived on the island with his crew and one British actor, shortly after the travelling embargo between Argentina and the islands was lifted. Armed with a hidden video camera, the main character, Fabián Stratas (played by Fabián Stratas), goes to the islands to reclaim them in his own way: through reproduction. He argues that if enough Argentines can impregnate islanders, then the reconquest of the island would finally come about. What is interesting about this film is the way in which it takes the Dogma aesthetic to one of its logical conclusions: if Dogma is more 'real' and 'immediate' than mainstream cinema, then it is the job of the director actively to engage with the reality surrounding his or her shoot. Following this premise, the handheld camera was hidden so that the locals would not know they were participating in a film, just as the female lead, Camilla Heaney, was not told the plot of the film, other than the most basic details (she is a nurse and she is an islander), before shooting began. Heaney improvised her character in response to Fabián's actions, without knowing about his plan to begin his 'conquest through impregnation' with her. The audience finds out at the end of the film, through a video recording left by the angry nurse, that she knew what was taking place and that Fabián's plot is foiled. Yet, the message never reaches its intended audience, as the only people who see this message are the film's spectators, and not Fabián himself. More so than any other Dogma film, *Fuckland* plays with the viewer's assumptions about what the video image connotes (one reviewer likened the film to watching a friend's travel videos), with the profound effect that the use of hand-held camera has on how one reads the image. In this context, one can trace the genealogy of this preoccupation back to the South American films of the 60s and 70s, which, once again, points to *Fuckland* as an amalgamation of Dogma and Third cinema aesthetics. But one can also see *Fuckland* as a return to the realist tradition of cinematic culture, with its emphasis on the camera's ability to provide access to the 'real' (Bazin, Kracauer et al.). The film does this by blurring the boundaries between fiction and reality, leaving the viewer in a quandary as to which parts of the film are staged, and which parts are not.

ASIA

Intyebyu (Interview, Korea)

Daniel Byun's Dogma contribution is a film about the making of a film based on interviews dealing with memories of love, desire and relationships. The story unfolds in Seoul in the spring of '99, with a brief flashback sequence to scenes of the director Eun-sok

(Lee Jung Jae) at work in Paris in '98. The focus is on the evolving relationship between Eun-sok and the young woman (Shim Eun-ha), who identifies herself as Young-hee. A photograph of Andrei Tarkovsky's grave, taken by Eun-sok while filming in Paris, links the project of the represented, but also the implied director, to an ideal of truth. Eun-sok is shown writing 'Tarkovsky's grave' on the Polaroid, and to this he later adds the question: 'Are you searching for the truth?' Indeed, a key shift from impersonation to the revelation of true identity as a result of a relationship mediated by interviews on camera establishes truth as the film's central theme. Young-hee, it turns out, has adopted the identity of a hairstylist she happens to encounter following the traumatic loss of her lover, who was also her professional dance partner. Having led Eun-sok to her lover's grave in a moment of sincerity, Young-hee subsequently records the narrative of her true identity with the camera that the director left her. The film concludes with Eun-sok watching images of a now truthful Young-hee that suggest that she has come to reciprocate his love. Stylistically, the most remarkable feature of the film in a Dogma context is the proscribed yet repeated use of music for atmospheric purposes and without any diegetic justification.

NORTH AMERICA
Chetzemoka's Curse (USA)
The title of Rick Schmidt's film refers to a legendary curse on the small town where this dull drama unfolds. The curse is simple but effective: small-town *ennui* provokes departures in a vain quest for something better, but sooner or later the victims long to return. The story centres on a twenty-something woman who works as a hotel receptionist and maid. She is unhappy in love. Her smug boyfriend has already announced his plan to take off on a trip on his own. He is still willing to have sex with her, but will not make the commitment she desires. In lengthy pre- and post-coital dialogues she tries to persuade him otherwise, but unsurprisingly this does not do the trick. Hoping to stimulate some jealousy, she seduces a middle-aged family man and proposes that he drop everything and go to Thailand with her. He agrees, but stalls until the girl shows up unannounced at his home and provokes a violent confrontation with his wife. The two adulterers head off together, but as Chetzemoka's curse would have it, we surmise that they will be back. The slow working out of this tedious drama is interlarded with lengthy, home-movie soliloquies in which the characters privately tell us more about themselves than we wanted to know, the end result being that viewers may begin to imagine that this very film is part of the curse.

Camera (USA)
Richard Martini's Dogme #15 is an incredibly low-budget independent film, so low in fact that its premiere was as a video release. This is unfortunate, as *Camera* takes the rules of Dogma and applies them in an ingenious and engaging manner. Essentially, the main character in *Camera* is a digital video recorder. While *Fuckland* blurs the boundaries between fiction and reality, *Camera* turns the camera itself into the protagonist of the film; in some ways the film foreshadows Steven Soderbergh's recent film (which has an

accompanying manifesto) *Full Frontal*. Throughout the course of *Camera*, this DV camera-protagonist is bought, stolen and pawned. It records moments in the lives of its many temporary owners. It is used to make commercials, document lives and, generally, to perform the many functions that a DV camera can be made to perform. *Camera* also breaks down barriers between the private and public spheres, demonstrating both the intimacy and the voyeurism that a portable camera allows. Perversely, despite its low-budget status, the film has the biggest stars of any Dogma film, with cameo appearances by Angie Everhart, Oliver Stone, Jack Nicholson, Phillip Noyce and Rebecca Broussard. Unlike some of the later US 'indie' Dogma films, *Camera* demonstrates how Dogma can be deployed to reimagine independent film along aesthetic lines that diverge significantly from those explored by the Danish Dogma films.

Bad Actors (USA)

Bad Actors, much like *Camera*, uses the improvisational spirit of Dogma as the catalyst for the film. The story of *Bad Actors* is exceedingly straightforward: the film depicts ten actors, none of whom are very good, in an acting class with an old, drunken drama teacher (played by Cissy Wellman). The director of the film, Shaun Monson, has written the following about the genesis of the film:

> I contacted some friends of mine who are actors and asked them if they would star in an experimental film that we would shoot in a single day. No script. No rehearsals. Totally improvised. They would also use their real names (which was the toughest thing I asked of them because the movie was called *Bad Actors*). All I told them was that it centred on an acting class and they had to be 'drama queens', and I told them to prepare a monologue, but surprise me with it. Our producer, Nicole Visram, asked five more friends of ours to come out and operate the cameras. We used five Canon XL-1s simultaneously to shoot the movie. We owned one already and simply rented four more for the weekend. We paid for all this, which wasn't that much (a few thousand), on a credit card. The camera operators were positioned around the room, so as to get angles of all the actors and not shoot each other. We provided earpieces for each of them, which they wore snugly beneath their headphones, and then I sat in an adjacent room and watched via five monitors. By radio I could tell the operators to push in or pull out on whomever was speaking at the time.
>
> The only outline of a script that I provided for anyone was the class instructor, played by Cissy Wellman (a regular on the hit 70s show *The Waltons*, and daughter of legendary film director William Wellman). This outline was her so-called 'notes' during class, and it was full of material that made improvising easier on the other actors. We shot the entire film once before lunch, and again afterward. I spent the next two months editing it together, before we submitted it to the Dogme 95 committee for certification. In August 2000, they officially certified the film #16. Once we received our Dogme certification, an investor came forward to transfer the film to 35mm. This was an individual we had worked with once before on a web site, so that's how we found her. The 35mm print was completed in January 2001, and we began submitting it to festivals (Monson 2002).

What is evident here is the way in which Monson adapted Dogma to his own ends: the improvisational style makes possible an inexpensive shoot, abidance by the ten rules allows *Bad Actors* to become a Dogma film, and this in turn releases the capital to produce a 35mm print. Monson amalgamates the 'credit-card ethos' of 90s independent film-making, most often championed by Roberto Rodriguez, with an acute sense of marketing possibilities. While *Bad Actors* does not presently have a distributor, the Dogma label has given it access to festivals that otherwise would have remained out of reach.

Reunion (USA)

Leif Tilden's debut portrays the interactions of seven characters who meet on their way to a high-school reunion in a small town in California. The story is on the whole a drab and low-key affair that underscores the continuities and changes characteristic of twenty years of everyday life. One classmate arrives reeling from a divorce, while another is overjoyed at having become the town mayor. The most popular and charming high-school boy turns out to have led a humdrum existence as a bus driver, while the girl everyone thought of as a hopeless wallflower has become a wealthy, self-confident and glamorous photographer. These two momentarily find each other attractive and have a fling in the bushes. Some of the events depicted and recounted in the classmates' meetings are, however, a tad less banal. A black musician has a tense and disappointing first encounter with the son he fathered in a short-lived affair with a high-school classmate. In spite of this biological father's expectations and worries, the neglected fact of cross-racial paternity does not really mean much to the young man. Another classmate must tell his stiff and disapproving father that he has come out of the closet and has had to resign from the army as a result. Meeting, finally, at a classmate's pizzeria, the seven participants in the reunion have some drinks, make confessions, quarrel and attempt to generalise about life, their mildly tempestuous encounter ending on an implausibly upbeat note. Like beer gone flat, *Reunion* lacks the dramatic effervescence and talent of such reunion films as *The Big Chill*, and suffers from a slow pace and banal dialogue and characterisation.

Resin (USA)

Some Dogma film-makers have used the public recognition that the manifesto brings as a means of engaging in political debates within the public sphere. Vladimir Gyorski's *Resin* deals with the notorious Californian anti-drug legislation known as 'three strikes' (allowing courts to give three-time felony offenders a life sentence) and is a clear example of a film-maker deploying the Dogma rules to both aesthetic and political effect. After its festival run (it premiered at the Chicago Underground Film Festival and won the Audience Choice award), the film was screened at a number of events in order to raise awareness about the Draconian measures taken by the California legislature with the alleged intent to promote 'law and order'. As a result of screenings at 'legalise pot' demonstrations, the film garnered a much larger audience than the non-Danish Dogma film typically receives. The 'immediacy' of the pseudo-documentary aesthetic in *Resin* accentuates the plight of the main character Zeke as an individual left in the uncaring hands of the US legal system. A key intertext for *Resin* is that of the *cinéma direct* movement of the 50s and 60s, where hand-held cameras and direct sound were supposed to provide more direct access to the real world, unmediated by the film-maker's biases and point of view. To this extent, *Resin* in many ways echoes the films of Fred Wiseman. Documentaries such as *Titticut Follies* (USA, 1968), *High School* (USA, 1969), *Law and Order* (USA, 1971) and *Juvenile Court* (USA, 1972) all explore the often oppressive and alienated nature of institutions in a manner that *Resin*, consciously or not, also deploys.

At fundraising screenings, *Resin* was used as a starting point for debates about the repressive nature of California's 'three strikes' law and of the American 'war on drugs'. Here, then, a fictional film becomes a catalyst for extra-diegetic arguments about political culture. Yet, it is important to note that the political ambition of the film is combined with marketing strategies; it is precisely the Dogma label that delivers the theatre viewers who otherwise would not be there. 'Dogma' functions in this instance as an art-cinema brand name that separates *Resin* from any number of other cheaply produced, politically engaged, independent films. If the original Danish Dogma films can be understood, in part, as the revitalisation of a national cinema through a 'brand-naming' of a country's art cinema, then we can see in *Resin*, and other international Dogma films, the deployment of that very process of 'brand-naming' to attract new audiences. In some respects, then, Dogma can be understood as the globalisation of an art-cinema movement as a product line.

Converging with Angels (USA)

The most recent non-Danish Dogma film is in many ways a slight effort, and certainly one that would not garner much critical attention without the Dogma label attached to it. The film tells the story of two characters: a male prostitute named Dylan Thomas, who, while enjoying the money he receives, is alienated from his job, and a woman, Alison Campbell, who after being coerced into an unwanted sexual relationship with her boyfriend and some others, goes to a pub and gets quite drunk. Dylan sees her lying in the gutter, brings her home and lets her sleep in his high-rise apartment. She at first thinks he will take advantage of her, and when he doesn't she begins to fall for him, makes him dinner and then seduces him. While they both feel something for each other, he only tells her of his occupation on the way to a party together to meet 'clients'. His 'madam' coerces Alison into prostitution and she leaves in disgust. Try as they might to connect up again, their lives fall apart, with Alison in a coma and Dylan back plying his trade. At the world premiere of *Converging with Angels* at the Montreal World Film Festival, director Michael Sorenson proclaimed that 'Dogma was dead', a comment attributable perhaps to the fact that his film still lacks a distributor. If nothing else, *Converging with Angels* demonstrates that the publicity that can be obtained by making a Dogma film becomes one of diminishing returns if the film itself is only there to play out a formula. While the first Dogma films displayed stylistic audacity by harkening back to earlier cinematic movements and by reinvigorating debates about European new waves, some of the American Dogma films (such as *Chetzemoka's Curse* and *Reunion*) have demonstrated a profound lack of vision, at least to the extent that they have failed to rethink or recast American 'indie' cinema in ways that might parallel the dialogic dimensions of the European Dogma films.

REFERENCES

Ahm, L., 'Filminstitut afviser penge: Vil ikke tage imod politisk diktat', *Politiken*, 21 December, 1996.

Appadurai, A., 'Grassroots Globalization and the Research Imagination', in A. Appadurai (ed.), *Globalization* (Durham: Duke University Press, 2001), pp. 1–21.

Barr, J.-M. and P. Arnold, <www.jeanmarcbarr.cinephiles.net/freetrilogy/manifesto.html> (2002).

Chow, V., 'Faith, Hope and Chastity', *South China Morning Post*, 28 March, 2002.

DFI, 'Pressemeddelelse: 75% flere solgte billetter til danske film', 20 December, 2001.

Gilbey, R., 'Dogme is Dead. Long Live Dogme', *The Guardian*, 18 April, 2002.

Higson, A., *English Heritage, English Cinema* (Oxford: Oxford University Press, 2003).

Hjort, M. and I. Bondebjerg (eds), *The Danish Directors: Dialogues on a Contemporary National Cinema* (Bristol: Intellect Press, 2001).

Hunter, S., 'Simply Soderbergh', *Washington Post*, 2 August, 2002.

Iversen, E., 'Dansk aftale om 16 nye Dogme-film', *Berlingske Tidende*, 20 May, 1999.

Kelly, R., *The Name of this Book is Dogme95* (London: Faber and Faber, 2000).

Kjær, M., 'A Cold Shower', Danish Film Institute, <www.dfi.dk/sitemod/moduler/index_english.asp?pid=9220> (2002a).

Kjær, M., 'When Life Has a Will of Its Own', Danish Film Institute, <www.dfi.dk/sitemod/moduler/index_english.asp?pid=9110> (2002b).

Lyon, J., *Manifestos: Provocations of the Modern* (Ithaca, NY: Cornell University Press, 1999).

Møller, H. J., 'Dogme 95 en naturlig udfordring', *Politiken*, 9 April, 1997.

Monson, S., <www.projectgreenlight.liveplanet.com/news/comm_news_article.jsp?> (2002).

Raskin, R. (ed.), *Aspects of Dogma, p.o.v.: A Danish Journal of Film Studies* no. 10, 2000.

Roman, S. (ed.), *Digital Babylon: Hollywood, Indiewood & Dogme 95* (Hollywood: Lone Eagle Publishing Company, 2001).

Seßlen, G., 'Oprør i blindgyden: De danske Dogme-film, Radikal dilettantisme eller utopiforrœderi?', *Kritik* no. 14, 1999, pp. 57–60, translation of 'Aufbruch in die Sackgasse', *Die Zeit*, no. 28, 1999.

Smith, M. (ed.), *Engaging Characters: Fiction, Emotion and the Cinema* (Oxford: Clarendon Press, 1995).

Stevenson, J., *Lars von Trier* (London: BFI, 2002).

Williams, P., 'Rebirth in Brazil', *Moviemaker* no. 47, <www.moviemaker.com/issues/47/wc.html> (2002).

NOTES

1. Entitled *Le Cinéma vers son deuxième siècle*, the conference was jointly organised by the French Ministry of Culture and the film society, *Ier siècle du cinéma*.

2. The established documentary film-maker, Anne Wivel, was originally also to have been part of the collective.

3. Dogma rule number 10 specifies that 'the director must not be credited'.

4. The dates indicated here refer to the Danish premieres. Levring's film premiered in Denmark significantly after its festival release elsewhere.

5. In the manifesto accompanying *The Element of Crime* von Trier makes the following

provocative claims: 'We won't settle for "well-meaning films with a humanistic message". We want more – the real thing, the fascination, the experience – childlike and pure as true art. We want to go back to the time when love between film-maker and film was young, when the joy of creating oozed out of every frame. Substitutes cannot satisfy us any more. We want to see religion on the screen. We want to see mistresses of the screen vibrant with life: unreasonable, stupid, stubborn, ecstatic, repulsive, wonderful, but *not* tamed and made sexless by a moralising grumpy film-maker, a stinking puritan, cultivating the moronic virtues of the nice façade' (cited in Hjort and Bondebjerg, 2001: 216–17).

6. Writer Aksel Sandemose's concept of a 'Law of Jante', understood as a form of tyrannical levelling, is frequently used to identify the negative effects of an otherwise important commitment in contemporary Denmark to equality as a foundational norm.

7. Thanks to Shu Kei for this reference.

8. See S. Roman (2001) for an exploration of the impact of Dogma's legitimation of digital video on 'indie' film-making milieus.

9. <www.soderbergh.net/simply/rules.htm> provides a set of sycophantic 'Rules for Fan Listing', any reference to Dogma being interestingly and conspicuously absent.

PART ONE

1

Dogma 95:
A Small Nation's Response to Globalisation

Mette Hjort

When the competition is spending US$40 million on marketing a film in the United States alone, the time, it would appear, has come radically to change the rules of the game of cinema. The originally Danish cinematic project and now transnational movement known as Dogma 95 mobilises a manifesto form and practice of rule-following to articulate and circulate a stripped-down and hence widely affordable concept of film-making. While the aims of Dogma 95 may be multiple, an all-important ambition is to unsettle an increasingly dominant film-making reality characterised by astronomical budgets and by marketing and distribution strategies based, among other things, on vertical integration, stardom and technology-intensive special effects. What motivates this move, I shall argue, is a probing understanding of the implications of Hollywood-style globalisation for small nations and the minor cinemas they produce.

The release of a Dogma film is typically followed by a spate of articles discussing the extent to which the film in question did or did not abide by the very rules that must be observed if the film is to qualify as a *bona fide* Dogma work. Violations, it would appear, abound, and this has led many a journalist to conclude that the emphasis on rule-following is ultimately a hoax, a largely cynical means of generating publicity. This sceptical line of reasoning puts the question of the brethren's deeper intentions on the agenda for discussion, and what I want to do here is develop a rather different account of their motivations. I begin by considering a non-sceptical explanation for the insistence on rules, namely the idea that creativity is enhanced by the imposition of constraints. While it is interesting to note this connection, I conclude that it leaves important aspects of the Dogma puzzle untouched. My own reading of the deeper aims behind Dogma 95 involves taking issue with a common misapprehension of the movement as profoundly apolitical. What commentators have systematically overlooked, I argue, is the connection between Dogma 95 and small nationhood, which is where the politics of Dogma lie. My claim, in brief, is that the rules imposed by Dogma 95 amount to a novel and insightful response to the inequities of globalising processes. Dogma 95, then, is best thought of as a form of cinematic expression that comes to us from, and as a defence of, the margins of cinematic production that small nations and minor cinemas inevitably are.

DOGMA 95 AND RULE-FOLLOWING

In an article acerbically entitled 'The Danish Dogme Films: Radical Dilettantism or
Betrayal of Utopia', the German film critic, Georg Seßlen, suggests that Dogma 95 in
fact amounts to a form of genre construction, although one of its dicta explicitly pro-
scribes genre films (Seßlen 1999: 60). Dogma certainly seems to involve something like
a blueprint, a label and a contract, three of the four elements that Rick Altman (1999:
14) identifies as central to the phenomenon of genre. Yet it is difficult to identify the
'whatness' of Dogma films in terms of the kinds of discernible regularities that Bordwell
and Thompson (1997: 53–4), for example, associate with genres. It is one of the great
ironies of Dogma 95, as a bemused von Trier points out, that the gesture of 'putting film
into uniform' results in anything but standardised products:

> It's easy to see who's made what. That's the paradox. We talk about putting the films in
> uniform and we create uniform rules, but the paradox is – and this is also the point – that the
> first three Dogme films very much reflect their individual directors. It's amusing that this
> should be the case, but then why would talk of uniformity destroy individual qualities? That's
> precisely what hasn't happened although there's been an imposition of uniformity and an
> emphasis on the collective (Hjort and Bondebjerg 2001: 221).

The rule proscribing geographical and temporal alienation does, of course, have the
effect of linking Dogma to contemporary story worlds. Also, the interdiction on special
lighting and on optical work and filters, combined with the requirement that the camera
be hand-held, does tend to favour a certain aesthetic style centred around an instability
and obscurity of the image. And, as critics have noted, the best of the Dogma films are
characterised by compelling stories and outstanding performances. Yet, it is important to
note that we are not dealing here with the kinds of fully blown regularities of theme,
iconography, mode of presentation or visual style that are constitutive of genre in the
standard sense of the term. Nor do all of the films begin to conform to the quasi-regu-
larities just identified. Harmony Korine, for example, devised an additional rule directed
against the very concept of a well-told story: 'In a way, I added a Rule to the Manifesto
just for myself: I wouldn't allow any kind of a plot to seep through. I don't like plot-
oriented movies. I like things that kind of evolve, or just begin and end – like life does'
(Kelly 2000: 196).

The ultimate basis for a given film's inclusion or non-inclusion in the Dogma category
is to be sought at the level of authorial intention and conditions of production. A film,
after all, is a Dogma film by virtue of its having been intentionally made in accordance
with the ten rules specified in the manifesto's Vow of Chastity (see Appendix I). In this
sense Dogma 95 imposes a dual interpretive task, for in addition to providing a reasoned account of *why* the Dogma brethren might have chosen to articulate their
cinematic project in terms of a concept of rules, the critic also owes the reader an analysis of what, exactly, is involved in following the Dogma rules. How, for example, does
one know whether one is following the rule that requires the camera to be hand-held?
If the camera simply rests on an immobile hand which itself rests on the floor, can the

rule be said to have been observed? In Jesper Jargil's documentary, *The Purified*, von Trier is shown responding to precisely this question with a categorical 'no', while Søren Kragh-Jacobsen insists that the answer is 'yes'.

There are many different ways of getting at the deeper, non-cynical, reasons for a 'Dogmatic' insistence on rule-governed activity. A promising approach is the one developed over many years by the prolific philosopher and political theorist, Jon Elster. The idea that an imposition of constraints can help to enhance creativity was first explored by Elster in 'Conventions, Creativity, Originality' (1992), where Elster distinguishes among a number of different kinds of constraints that might arise in the context of art. An artist's activities may, for example, be constrained by the particular *technology* that he or she chooses to work with at a given moment in time – by the immobility of the camera, for example, in the case of the earliest silent films. In addition, most artists will have to frame their activities in relation to available *monies*, and are thus subject to certain economic constraints. As Elster points out, this may, in the context of film, mean that a director has to sacrifice 'the big battle scenes' (32). A third kind of limitation is *temporal* in nature. Films are due to be released by certain deadlines, publishers expect manuscripts to be delivered on or around the date agreed upon in a contract, and so on. The effects of these kinds of constraints, claims Elster, are by no means always negative. On the contrary, the challenges they represent for the artist can stimulate precisely the kinds of creative problem-solving, flow and insight that are needed to produce valuable new works. It is to this connection between constraint and creativity that we must look, Elster argues, if we wish to understand a fourth category of constraints in the context of the production of art: those that are self-imposed. In *Ulysses Unbound: Studies in Rationality, Precommitment, and Constraints* (2000), Elster reconsiders the terms of his discussion, opting to speak of 'imposed', 'invented' and 'chosen' constraints. Interestingly, the first three kinds of constraints identified in the discussion of the 1992 article are all subsumed beneath the new category of 'imposed' constraints.

In Elster's refined account, the fourth category of 'self-imposed' constraints divides into constraints that are *invented* and those that are *chosen* by the artist from amid existing constraints. The history of art abounds with examples of artists setting limits on their own activities. In the 1992 discussion of self-imposed constraints, Elster, not surprisingly, refers to Georges Perec's well-known decision to write *La Disparition* (*A Void*) without once using the letter 'e', but he also points to certain generic conventions, to the 4–4–3–3 rhyming scheme, for example, that characterises the sonnet form (32, 38). In the refined account, the former becomes an example of an invented constraint and the latter an example of a chosen constraint. Now, in Elster's mind both of these rule-governed activities involve *arbitrary* constraints, for in each case an entirely different constraint would allegedly have served the intended purpose equally well, which is simply to stimulate creativity (1992) or to maximise '*aesthetic value*', creativity being 'the ability to succeed in this endeavor' (emphasis in the original, 2000: 200). The idea, following this line of reasoning, is not for the artist to be constrained by a *particular* constraint, but simply to be somehow constrained.

In the case of Dogma 95 we appear to have a clear example of *invented* self-imposed rules or constraints. Yet, are the rules as arbitrary as Elster's account would have us believe? And is enhanced creativity (and the maximisation of aesthetic or artistic value that such enhancement affords) the *sole* reason for adopting these constraints? Here a comparison with Perec's experiments is helpful. While Perec's decision to avoid the letter 'e' may seem arbitrary at first blush, the choice was in fact a reasoned one.[1] That is, it was the ubiquity and apparent indispensability of the letter 'e' in the French language that made Perec opt for this letter rather than one of the remaining twenty-five alternatives. The point, precisely, was to stimulate creativity by depriving oneself of one of the most basic tools of linguistic expression. The letter 'z' would simply not have involved the same level of constraint or the same kind of challenge; eliminating its use, in short, would not have inspired the same level of creativity.

According to the Dogma brethren, the self-imposed rules were anything but a matter of arbitrary choices. Indeed, von Trier and Vinterberg claim to have generated the rules by following a simple maxim: 'Identify the very means of cinematic expression on which you habitually rely and then make the technique or technology in question the object of an interdiction' (*The Purified*). In the case of Vinterberg, the application of this maxim led to a rule that was originally intended to place a ban on the use of non-diegetic music. Von Trier, on the other hand, decided to rule out the elaborate lighting arrangements and camera movements in which he had invested so heavily in earlier films. The constraints, then, we can conclude, are at once self-imposed and invented but by no means arbitrary, for the rules reflect the film-makers' conception of what, in their minds, had been the very basis, the very essence, of their prior film-making practices.

The question at this point is: why did the Dogma brethren decide to pull the rug out from underneath their own feet, so to speak? There can be no doubt that Elster's insight into the internal connection between creativity and constraint is part of the picture here. This, for example, is how the Nimbus Film producer, Lars Bredo Rahbek, describes Thomas Vinterberg's reactions to a one-minute film student production entitled *Dogme2000*: 'Ah! This is one of the few guys who has understood what Dogme is really about.' What the student had grasped, following Rahbek, was that 'Dogme is not about following the Brothers' Rules: it's simply about setting some rules and some limitations, and these can be any. The idea is simply to gain creativity through self-imposition' (Kelly 2000: 80). In a more recent interview conducted by Claus Christensen from the Danish Film Institute, Vinterberg confirms the idea that the premise of Dogma 95 was that constraint fosters creativity: 'one of the sterling qualities of Dogme was innovation and in that way my new film is completely in keeping with the spirit of Dogme. You may say that I've invented a new set of rules that has forced me to innovate' (Christensen 2002: 3). The context here is a discussion of Vinterberg's *All About Love* (2002), a big-budget co-production involving an international cast and the intention to do the exact opposite of what the Dogma rules required: 'For Dogme the camera had to be hand-held and the scenes had to be shot on location, so this time I went in for tripods and sets and studios. Joaquin Phoenix and Claire Danes' escape through the streets of New York was shot in the car park at

Filmbyen. I spat in Dogme's face' (Christensen 2002: 2). The point here is not to explore Vinterberg's most recent work, but to establish the extent to which the Dogma brethren's self-understandings support some of Elster's basic claims about the value of inventing aesthetic or artistic constraints. In this connection it is worth noting that Elster's suggestive view to the effect that 'The creation of a work of art can ... be envisaged as a two-step process' involving an initial *'choice of constraints* followed by *choice within constraints'* sheds a certain light on the very nature of the Dogma rules. Elster's intuition is that 'Constraints must leave room for choice' (emphasis in the original; 2000: 176) if they are to stimulate creativity. In the context of Dogma 95, this line of reasoning suggests that the conundra of interpretation and followability to be explored at length below are the result, not of some mere failure to articulate sufficiently precise rules, but rather of the need to make room for the very indeterminacy that makes choice, and hence creativity, possible.

While Elster's account of constraints helps us to make sense of important aspects of the Dogma project, it is important to note that there is more at stake in the rules than enhanced creativity. Understanding this involves seeing to what extent the term 'arbitrary' is inappropriate in the context of Dogma's invented constraints. The practices that the film-makers rule out have a dual aspect, for they are not merely personally favoured approaches to film-making, but precisely the techniques that a certain increasingly dominant, cost-intensive conception of film narrative and film aesthetics requires. In the case of Dogma, the invented self-imposed constraints are indeed meant to stimulate creativity, but they are also intended to redefine film aesthetics in such a way as to somehow level the playing field. The point, we shall see, is to create the conditions that enable citizens from small nations to participate in the game of cinematic art. The rules of Dogma 95, it turns out, are *multiply motivated*, rather than arbitrary, choices.

To claim that constraints in the form of rules promote creativity is to adopt a realist perspective that presupposes the very possibility of rule-following. What is interesting, however, is the curiously overlooked fact that many of the Dogma directors' statements about the relevant rules resonate with precisely the kind of scepticism that has informed much of the philosophical discussion of rule-following in the wake of Saul Kripke's *Wittgenstein on Rules and Private Language* (1982) and Nelson Goodman's *Fact, Fiction, and Forecast* (1965). In philosophical contexts, the sceptical account of rule-following centres around two key issues: the problem of inference and the inscrutability of intention. The claim, more specifically, is that any sequence of actions can be construed in terms of a variety of rules. What, then, warrants the inference, at any given moment, that the agent in question is following rule x as opposed to rule y? What is more, how can an agent be sure that his or her attempt to follow a given rule is not in fact better described in terms of a quite different rule?[2]

There are, it is true, certain differences between the kind of context that Dogma 95 engenders and the examples that are the basis for the philosophers' sceptical positions. Goodman's new riddle of induction foregrounds the possibility of new input disconfirming an initial inference about the nature of the rule being followed. In the case of a Dogma film, however, we are dealing with a closed system, in the sense that the film

comes to us as a definitive expression. In addition, informed viewers have prior knowledge of the rules allegedly governing the production of the audiovisual material on
which inferences are to be based. That these differences by no means nullify, but merely
attenuate the force of the sceptical challenge in the context of Dogma 95 is, however,
amply evidenced by the brethren's concerns about questions of both inference and
interpretation.

A film, we know, qualifies for inclusion in the Dogma category if and only if it has been
certified by the brethren and has received the Dogma certificate that is a paratextual feature of all Dogma films. How, then, is Dogma certification achieved? Up until the
autumn of 1999 certification presupposed a critical assessment by the brethren with the
intent of confirming abidance by the rules. The process involved in certifying Harmony
Korine's *Julien Donkey-Boy* was, however, to motivate a radical change of policy, a shift
from vetting to self-scrutiny:

> To the best of our knowledge, *Julien Donkey-Boy* does, indeed, observe the Dogme criteria
> to a satisfactory extent. Our judgment is based on an actual review of the film as well as an
> interview with the director ... Considering the fact that there are numerous practical
> problems connected with our review of aspiring Dogme films, we have decided on a
> change of practice when issuing Dogme certificates. In the future the director himself is
> solemnly to declare his adherence to the Dogme 95 Manifesto (cited in Kelly 2000: 33).

The problem, as Kristian Levring pointed out, was that inferring rule abidance from the
finished film was an impossibility: 'you can easily shoot in slow motion without breaking
the Rules. But you'll still have people saying, "Is it Dogme?" Harmony's film looked to
me like it had been shot according to the Rules. But if you really want to enforce this,
you have to go on the shoot' (Kelly 2000: 56). What is abandoned, in other words, is the
original conception of a Dogma film as a cinematic work that is *manifestly* governed by
the specified rules. At this point a statement of intent suffices for certification purposes:
'Dogme certificates shall be issued solely on the basis of a signed and sworn statement to
the effect that the Vow of Chastity has been adhered to in full and without any review of
the applicants' films.'

The problems posed by Dogma 95 are not limited to issues of evidence and inference, for many of the rules have been experienced as essentially non-followable, even
with the best of intentions. Knowing, for example, whether one is actually following
the rule proscribing taste or genre is ultimately impossible since what is *entailed* by
these rules is underspecified. Levring, for example, is eloquent about the difficulties
posed by the ban on aesthetics: 'I think one of the Rules that I find very, very difficult
is that the film must have no "aesthetics". If I tell the DP I want a close-up, that's
taste. That's how I want to see it. If I frame it like this or like that, that's an aesthetic
choice. When you write a script, every line in there is taste' (Kelly 2000: 54).
Vinterberg's account of his attempts to respect the genre interdiction is also instructive, for it points to key differences among the rules with respect to their followability:

I thought a lot about this genre Rule. And I found it a bad Rule, actually. Because it's very difficult to avoid genre. And somehow it's not very creative, because it's very unspecific. Creatively, I found the best Rules were the most specific ones. 'You have to hold the camera in your hand.' 'You cannot bring props with you.' But not being able to make a genre, or not being allowed to have 'taste' is, in a way, impossible (Kelly 2000: 117).

Yet it is perhaps von Trier's articulation of the basic problem that is most poignant: 'Many of the rules can't be kept or are as impossible to keep as the commandment "Love your neighbour like yourself"' (Rundle 1999: 1). Dogma 95, it would seem, is a cinematic movement that constitutes its distinctive identity in terms of a concept of rule abidance only to encounter the sceptical challenge to naive conceptions of rule-following.

It is important, however, not to overstate the sceptical point, for the fact remains that Dogma directors take themselves to be working within the confines of the specified rules – even in the absence of non-controversial evidence to that effect or of absolute certainty about the rules' entailments. Indeed, the directors' confessions, mock-serious in tone, serve only to stage an authorial self-conception as a humble observer of rules. Harmony Korine, for example, is forgiven the use of props to create the illusion of Chloë Sevigny's pregnancy, particularly since he claims to have tried hard to impregnate her prior to shooting. Kragh-Jacobsen humbly confesses to having draped a black cloth over a window, thereby momentarily overriding the interdiction on lighting arrangements. Vinterberg admits to having constructed the reception desk in the manor house, but believes the use of on-site materials attenuates the extent of the transgression. The emphasis in these meta-discourses on certain fleeting audiovisual moments and minute production details has the performative effect of reinforcing the idea, if not the unquestionable reality, of an overall abidance by rules. More importantly, the true significance of the rules lies not in the extent to which they, each individually, are followed at a micro-level, but rather in their larger systemic effect. I want to turn, then, to the non-arbitrary connection between the rules and film-making conditions in the context of small nations.

SMALL NATIONS AND GLOBALISATION

My aim here is to mount a case for seeing Dogma 95 – and its insistence on what would appear to be multiply motivated rules – as a political and rather unique response to cinematic globalisation. Hollywood's globalising practices have to date been countered in Denmark by two nationally motivated initiatives – the transnationally oriented Nordic Film and TV Fund (NFTF) and Dogma 95. Now, it is true that the Danish Dogma films have received subsidies from the NFTF due to the Danish Broadcasting Corporation's involvement in the project following von Trier's dispute in 1995 with the Danish Film Institute over funding for the Dogma project. The point is, however, that the NFTF's original commitment to 'locomotive films' capable of galvanising the Nordic film industries and of appealing to pan-Nordic audiences amounts to a radically different diagnosis of and cure for the ills of globalisation than those articulated by the Dogma collective. Elsewhere I look carefully at the ways in which the *original* vision for the NFTF supported the production of Nordic heritage films. What interests me in this context is the fact that Dogma 95 avoids the kind of nostalgic investment in the local that is a feature of dominant types of heritage film and thus emerges as an appealing non-nationalist response to globalisation. The discussion of Dogma 95 *qua* response to globalisation involves, then, an implicit contrast with Danish and Nordic heritage films. Whereas the heritage films belonging to a tradition of 'quality' film-making foreground *national* or *transnational belonging*, Dogma 95 insists on *national participation* in the art world and on the renewal of international art traditions. A key difference has to do with *participation* as opposed to *belonging*, with access to the world of film-making rather than some first-order semantic content. Dogma 95, I shall argue, is an attempt to resist the dynamics of an intensified localism fuelled by globalism by focusing attention, not on heritage and ethnicity, but on the very definition of cinematic art and on the conditions of that art's production.

THE DEFENCE OF AESTHETIC DIVERGENCE

Interpretations of what Dogma 95 amounts to are remarkably diverse and include characterisations such as 'cynical, yet successful marketing strategy', 'serious aesthetic experimentation', 'playful transgression' and 'reconceptualisation of film along collectivist lines'. Critics have been quick to point out that the attention generated by Dogma 95 is disproportionate to its degree of originality. After all, critics have argued, key features of the manifesto and Vow of Chastity resonate with earlier avant-gardist experimentations, be it a matter of the cinematic innovations of *cinéma direct* and Italian neo-realism, or the various visions for the seventh art associated with Lindsay Anderson, Dziga Vertov and Jean-Luc Godard. Indeed, Leif Tilden, the Swedish-born American director of Dogme #17: *Reunion*, points out that 'without the banner of "Dogma filmmaking", many directors such as indie legend John Cassavetes have been making Dogme-style films for years' ('*Reunion* Presskit', 10). Yet, to focus exclusively on such moments of partial precedence is to overlook the true originality of Dogma 95, which lies, not in any one recommendation or procedure, but in the articulation of a viable response to globalisation, one that reflects a genuine understanding of the specific dilemmas and vulnerabilities of minor cinemas as well as a desire to identify something other than ethnic nationalism as a means of resisting homogenisation.[3] That there is a non-trivial connection between Dogma 95 and globalisation becomes apparent, I believe, once we grasp the extent to which the relevant proposal rests on concepts of small nationhood and picks up on debates about the very definition of art.

In an exchange with the Swedish film-maker and critic, Stig Björkman, Lars von Trier clearly suggests that Dogma 95 should be thought of as a polemical response to the phenomenon of Hollywood globalisation:

> Stig Björkman: So Dogma 95 didn't emerge as a protest against Danish film and film production?
> Von Trier: No, I stopped protesting against Danish film a long time ago. If you want to articulate a protest it has to be directed against something that has a certain kind of

authority. And if you feel that something lacks authority, then there's really no point in protesting against it. If there's anything in the world of film that has authority, it's American film, because of the money it has at its disposal and its phenomenal dominance on the world market (Björkman 1998).

It is in this context of an increasingly globalised American film industry that Dogma 95's alleged 'rescue action', which involves a somewhat cryptic and hyperbolic critique of illusionism, makes sense. For the point is not simply to reject mainstream film-making in an American vein, but to mount a genuine challenge to the ever-narrowing conception of what constitutes viable or legitimate film-making that is the direct result of the relevant kind of market dominance.

An important feature of Dogma's critique of illusionism is that it allows for a reconceptualisation of the economics of film-making, and thereby, as we shall see, for the legitimation of non-convergent aesthetic practices. 'The use of cosmetics', we are told in the manifesto, 'has exploded' since 1960. Indeed, 'decadent' film-makers now hold sway, and such individuals aspire primarily 'to fool the audience'. The ills allegedly inflicted on audiences by these decadent film-makers include 'emotions' generated by 'illusion', 'superficial action' and illusions of 'pathos' and 'love'. Dogma 95, the brethren claim, is committed to the view that film 'is not illusion', and the Vow of Chastity thus rules out mainstream genre films, prime manifestations, it would seem, of nefarious illusionist practices. The effect of rule number 8 ('genre movies are not acceptable') and related rules ('special lighting is not acceptable' and 'optical work and filters are forbidden') is to free the prospective film-maker from an increasingly naturalised obligation to see film as necessarily yoked to the cumbersome and, more importantly, expensive apparatus of mainstream film-making, Hollywood style. What is established by the same token is a counter-practice that significantly changes the economic requirements for participation in the world of film-making. This counter-practice was further reinforced when the Dogma brethren agreed, with a vote of three to one, that rule number 9 (which speci-fies that 'The film format must be Academy 35mm') should be interpreted as a distribution rather than a production requirement. The resulting emphasis on digital video has clear economic implications, as von Trier points out:

> Mainly it [the interpretation of rule 9] has made the process much cheaper which of course also pleases me. And it has led to a trend where people around the world have started making these cheap, cheap Dogme films ... people who used to be limited by a notion of how a proper film should be ... now feel that they can make films (Rundle 1999).

While the term 'people' here picks out individual independent film-makers operating within large nations (such as Harmony Korine), an equally important referent, I contend, is aspiring film-makers in their capacity as citizens of small nations.

That small-nation status is an indispensable factor in the Dogma equation has been systematically overlooked by critics who have been content to characterise Dogma 95 as wholly apolitical on account of a conspicuous absence in the manifesto of the kind of explicit sloganising that tends to figure centrally in the relevant programmatic literature. An early spokesperson for this account of Dogma is John Roberts in his piece entitled 'Dogme 95':

> What is significant about this list [of rules] is its largely technical and formal character; there are no political exhortations, or denunciations of other film makers; it is, rather, a kind of low-key DIY guide for aspirant amateurs; the fire of the 1960s avant-garde is tempered by an earnest practicality (cited in MacKenzie 2000: 164).

Yet, to resist aesthetic convergence on certain cost-intensive styles, effects, images, sounds and framings is precisely to defend film as a viable medium of expression for citizens of small nations. The political thrust of the brethren's project is to be sought, then, in the way in which the rule-governed activities promote conditions of production that are feasible within the context of small nations.

The literature on small nations is voluminous and in this context I can only state that my understanding of the relevance of the concept for Danish realities involves privileging factors such as geographic size, linguistic reach, population size and the impact of what Steven Borish has called 'long-term territorial loss' (1999: 28). Interviews with filmmakers, producers and consultants from the Danish Film Institute clearly confirm that Dogma 95 was originally motivated by a belief that if small nations are to compete successfully with Hollywood in an era of globalisation they somehow have to change the very rules of the game, to challenge increasingly entrenched views of what counts as a film. Lars von Trier puts the point as follows:

> But then I'm very glad that some people in Argentina, I think, have suddenly done a whole lot of Dogme films – ten, I think. One of them in just two days. Just like, 'Let's go', you know? And if that is the only thing that comes out of these Rules, then I think it's fantastic – that people in countries like Estonia or wherever can suddenly make films, you know? Because they look at Dogme and think, 'If *that*'s a film, then we can make films too.' Instead of just thinking, 'Oh, if it doesn't look like *Star Wars*, then we can't make a film' (Kelly 2000: 145–46).

Interestingly, the countries referred to here – Argentina and Estonia – both qualify as small nations following Miroslav Hroch's (1985) influential account, which emphasises rule by non-co-nationals over a considerable period of time. In addition, Estonia meets a number of the other criteria of small nationhood (such as geographical size) that Ernest Gellner (1996) identifies as key in his debate with Hroch.

Richard Kelly's Channel 4 documentary, *The Name of this Film is Dogme95*, features an equally striking pronouncement by the other co-founder of the Dogma 95 movement, Thomas Vinterberg:

> The reason for hitting the table so hard is of course that when you're a small country you have to yell to get heard. It's the same thing as a person with a small penis wanting a huge motor bike [cut to Zentropa producer, Peter Aalbæk Jensen, on his motor bike]. I think part of the arrogance behind Dogme 95 is that we represent a very small country with very small penises.

The physical size of an organ (belonging to a particular producer who has even staged its exposure to the media in swimming pools at Cannes) becomes a symbol here for defining features of the Danish nation, for various forms of smallness.

Inasmuch as Dogma 95 is informed by a concept of small nations, it presents itself as a national moment in the logic of globalism/localism that globalisation unleashes.[4] Yet, in spite of its clear implications for Danish film-making, Dogma 95 is anything but a national or nationalist undertaking. Indeed, the manifesto clearly situates Dogma 95 within an international art-cinema tradition in which meta-level reflection on art and notions of authenticity and innovation figure centrally. In this case, then, a focal awareness of certain national predicaments and challenges becomes the basis, not for various localist vocabularies, but for a vigorously renewed artistic internationalism.

I have been suggesting that, as a response to globalisation, Dogma 95 is importantly linked to the concept of art, and it is time now to begin to make good on this claim. Let us begin by noting the consensus view (held by viewers, critics, film-makers and policymakers) that the success of especially the Danish Dogma films has to do with the privileging of content over form, of story and characterisation over the virtuosities of technical modes of audiovisual presentation. It is true, of course, that the Dogma rules do not prohibit what might be referred to as the 'technically well-made film'. Indeed, to some extent the challenge posed by these rules is a matter of reducing the available means of cinematic creation while targeting expectations centred around dominant norms of cinematic expression. Søren Kragh-Jacobsen certainly seems to have been operating with this kind of take on the rules when he opted to have cinematographer Anthony Dod Mantle shoot *Mifune* with a 16mm camera, and without aiming at a hand-held visual aesthetic. For the most part, however, there has been a tendency to interpret the rules as providing a licence to set aside a number of norms related to the clarity and relevance of images, and to gravitate instead towards an aesthetics of the image that privileges instability, obscurity and even, at times, apparent irrelevance, in the sense that it is a matter of including within the frame what would normally be excluded, of excluding what would normally be included. Referring to his role as cinematographer for Korine's *Julien Donkey-Boy*, Dod Mantle makes the following remark: 'Again, it was all about decomposing the image: breaking down the official, conventional sharpness we're so used to, losing some detail but finding a texture' (Kelly 2000: 107). Strikingly, *Julien Donkey-Boy* opens with a twenty-second shot of solid black. This is followed by blurred images of a woman skating on an ice rink. An image of some unidentifiable brown substance then appears briefly on the screen as a kind of puzzling and unmotivated transition to the next sequence, which focuses on Julien in a wintry forest setting. Julien is shown interacting with a young boy and there is some virtually incomprehensible discussion of the turtle that they have found. The child with whom Julien is talking is off screen most of the time and the object of their conversation – the turtle – figures only briefly on screen. There are no establishing shots to orient the viewer. There are no close-ups of what focuses the characters' attention. The images are wobbly, blurred and at times filled with apparently irrelevant visual input. It is indeed appropriate, with reference to these opening sequences, to talk, not only of a 'decomposition' of images, but of a dissolution of the most basic narrative principles allowing viewers to make sense of stories.

That the stripped-down minimalism of Dogma's proposed project of purity and constraint encourages, or at least allows, an exploration of the very boundaries between visibility and invisibility is also clearly evident in Antonio Domenici's *Diapason*, which privileges night shooting in a context where lighting is ruled out and concludes with a lengthy shot of solid black. Equally telling in this connection is the fact that Aalbæk Jensen and Vibeke Windeløv, producers of Lars von Trier's *The Idiots*, decided to transgress rule number 5 (proscribing optical work during post-production) because they deemed certain images to be unacceptably dark, verging on the non-visible.[5] Referring to her own experience of following the Dogma rules while directing *Open Hearts*, Susanne Bier points to an anti-aesthetic that nonetheless emerges as a defining aesthetic: 'You can't superimpose an aesthetic approach on reality. You have to film in the street and accept the way it looks. This prevents you from putting aesthetics ahead of the plot and the characters. But although on the face of it the Dogma rules are anti-aesthetic the overall aesthetic is that they all more or less resemble documentaries' (Kjær 2002: 2). The point is that Dogma 95 is an invitation to question and refuse the force, be it normative or other, of some of the regularities that are constitutive of dominant narrative and visual conventions. The best of the Dogma films polemically reinstate the idea of stories with psychological depth and intensity, while many challenge influential visual norms in the area of fiction film-making through a self-conscious hand-held camera aesthetic. Making sense of these shifts necessarily involves viewers making comparisons with forms of mainstream cinematic narration.

Dogma 95 is precisely a kind of *marked* cinema, one that brings to light the otherwise largely *unmarked* nature of the Hollywood mainstream. Hamid Naficy's masterful work, *An Accented Cinema* (2001), draws attention to the counterhegemonic thrust of diasporic films which 'signify and signify upon cinematic traditions by means of their artisanal and collective production modes, [and] their aesthetics and politics of smallness and imperfection' (2001: 4–5). In addition, claims Naficy, this accented cinema is 'deeply concerned with territory and territoriality', precisely because the directors in question themselves are deterritorialised. While the Dogma movement does not find its origin in exile, it does find a starting point in reflections on small nations and marginality. Like so much contemporary art, Dogma 95 is also a theory about art, an invitation to theorise, from a position of marginality, the art of cinema in an increasingly monocultural age. The idea is formally to 'mark' a certain oppositionality without, however, having recourse to various rhetorics of territoriality and deep belonging. It is a question of turning the very constraints that are constitutive of a marginal positioning into a source of creativity and innovation, and to do this, not individually, but collectively, as part of a movement.

Yet, if Dogma 95 is a theory of, and prescription for, cinematic art, then what are we to make of the Vow of Chastity's concluding phrases: 'I swear as a director to refrain from personal taste! I am no longer an artist. I swear to refrain from creating a "work", as I regard the instant as more important than the whole. My supreme goal is to force the truth out of my characters and settings. I swear to do so by all the means available and at the cost of any good taste and any aesthetic considerations.' The question, of course, is whether this statement amounts to a rejection of the very concept of art, or whether it is a matter, rather, of taking issue with a particular under-standing of what cinematic art is. Even the former interpretation does not guarantee an escape from art, because, as we know, a refusal of the concept of art is itself a well-established artistic move within the modern art world and even definitive of the avant-garde (Bürger 1984). What is more, the idea that a preference for the transient over the enduring or monumental would make concepts of art irrelevant to the Dogma project is nonsensical, for the prioritisation in question recalls a clearly defined position in the philosophy of art, as readers of Jean-François Lyotard's enthu-siastic commentary on Theodor W. Adorno's aesthetic theory (and its putative appreciation of pyrotechnics as the ultimate art form) well know (Hjort 1987). To interpret the proscription of taste and aesthetic considerations literally, as an injunc-tion with general rather than specific address, is, as Thomas Vinterberg, Kristian Levring and Leif Tilden were to discover, to involve oneself in what Jürgen Habermas (1990: 77–9) has called 'performative self-contradictions'. The point made by these directors was that the rule in question simply cannot be followed.[6] To create a Dogma film, it would appear, is necessarily to make choices that express aesthetic prefer-ences, that is, judgments of taste. That concepts of art remain highly relevant in the context of Dogma 95 is clearly suggested by Jesper Jargil as he reflects on his docu-mentary about the brethren's initiative:

> The interesting thing about Lars von Trier is that he makes public commitments. He
> draws up manifestos and sets of rules, thus involving everyone else. He gives us the
> chance to learn about an act, which is usually kept secret and shrouded in mystery.
> Von Trier opens the door into art's secret chamber; it's absolutely fascinating. Just what
> governs the process of *artistic creation*? Some think we destroy art if we reveal the
> mechanisms behind it. I don't feel that way at all. I think it just reveals even more layers.
> We enter new layers of magic that are even more fascinating (my emphasis; Christensen
> and Michelsen 2002: 4).

The tendentious statements about art are, then, best interpreted as part of the mani-festo's polemic with the French New Wave and its auteurist and allegedly bourgeois artistic legacy. On this reading Dogma 95 cannot be said to amount to a rejection of the concept of art as such, but should be viewed rather as a politically and artistically motiv-ated intervention in the world of art. Indeed, Dogma 95 makes most sense as a defence of cinematic art, one designed, among other things, to resist the ongoing globalisation of certain mainstream 'art regards', to borrow Jerrold Levinson's term. This line of reasoning presupposes a broad, inclusive sense of the term 'art', for Dogma 95 cannot be read as defending the same conception of cinematic art as that endorsed by the French New Wave.

Understanding exactly how Dogma's response to globalisation hinges on a concept of art requires, then, an elucidation of the notion in question. A helpful definition that does not involve stipulations about the nature of aesthetic experience or the defining features of aesthetic objects is the historical one proposed by Levinson: 'A work of art is a thing intended for regard-as-a-work-of-art, regard in any of the ways works of art existing prior to it have been correctly regarded' (1990a: 6).[7] There is no privileging here of one taste culture over another, for the definition allows the products of popular, middle-brow and high-brow taste cultures to count equally as art as long as the condition of relevant intentions is satisfied. The term 'regard' picks out an approach, a particular stance or way of looking, or a cluster of concerns or interests; and relevant art regards may, for example, include 'regarding an artefact as an expression of feeling, as a representation, as a display of form, as an articulation of cultural ideals, [and] as a reflection upon the nature of art' (Carroll 1999: 241). The central intuition is that something qualifies as art by virtue of a certain relation to earlier works of art. Following Levinson (1996) a given artwork can be connected to earlier artworks in two distinct ways. In the case of a so-called 'relational' connection, the artist actually articulates his or her work with reference to earlier works and art regards. In the case of an 'intrinsical' connection, on the other hand, the artist just happens to intend his or her work to be regarded in a way that corresponds to an already established art regard.

Now, what is interesting for present purposes is the fact that this inclusive, historical definition of art effectively allows us to register the main impact of globalisation on film, namely, the tendency to shift the balance decisively in favour of a cluster of art regards that emerge within, and help to sustain, popular and middle-brow taste cultures where facile entertainment rules supreme. What is contested by Dogma 95 is precisely the resulting marginalisation of other kinds of art regards that involve seeing the cinematic work as an instance of formal experimentation, as meta-reflection, as a transgression of norms and as a vehicle for truth and insight, to name only some of the candidate art regards. Levinson's discussion of revolutionary artworks is also instructive, for it helps to get at the polemical thrust of Dogma 95. What is particularly useful in the following reconstruction of revolutionary artistic intent is the distinction between a primary and secondary intention: 'My object is for regarding in any way artworks have been regarded in the past (but with the expectation that this will prove frustrating or unrewarding, thus prodding the spectator to adopt some other point of view – this being my ultimate intention).' The secondary intention, Levinson goes on to claim, 'embodies the true aim of such art, but the primary intention must be present to make it art at all' (1990a: 15). Dogma 95, we note, cannot be characterised as revolutionary in Levinson's sense since at least some of the intended art regards are established ones. At the same time, the polemical nature of Dogma 95 involves viewers coming to understand that dominant art regards having to do, for example, with costly and technology-intensive production values, are not only unrewarding but irrelevant. In this sense, the logic embedded in the reconstruction above plays a key role in the Dogma 95 phenomenon.

The concept of art regards allows us to see just how different the brethren's response to globalisation is from that underwriting the kind of quality, heritage film production that the NFTF originally envisaged as a solution to audience problems in the Nordic countries. What might be called the 'reactive globalisation' of the NFTF is based on the assumption that globalisation is a form of Americanisation, a process involving *cultural* homogenisation. Cinematic transnationalism in the North is crucially concerned, then, with one particular art regard, namely, the idea of art as cultural expression. The aim, more specifically, is to protect or create the conditions that make diversity of cultural expression through art possible, where 'culture' is understood to pick out the salient ways in which a given (trans)national community has imagined itself, linguistically, artistically, politically and historically. The renewed internationalism of Dogma 95, on the other hand, singles out American-style film-making for critique, but does so without targeting the national content of the films in question. What is resisted is not so much *cultural* convergence as *aesthetic* convergence. Globalisation is implicitly understood as a systematic gravitation towards one kind of art regard, a middle-brow or popular view of art as standardised entertainment involving cost-intensive visual and narrative styles.[8] The renewed internationalism of Dogma 95 aims, then, at a quite different kind of diversity, for it is a matter of fostering, not deep cultural divergence, but aesthetic differentiation as a value in and of itself. The point quite simply is to ensure that ongoing cinematic production is fuelled by a wide range of art regards. Whether these art regards are coupled with one kind of national cultural *content* or another seems to be of little or no concern. What *is* important, however, is that cinematic art not be reduced to the kind of expensive spectacle that is unfeasible in certain national contexts of cinematic production. The homogenisation of art regards is thus considered a threat, not so much to national culture as such, as to various nationals' active participation in the art world as producers of art.

CONCLUSION

Whether Dogma 95 will persist in the form of ever-growing numbers of Dogma films is at some level irrelevant, for some of the important lessons that Dogma teaches us can already be drawn. The sense of empowerment that surrounds Dogma 95 has to do in large measure with a realisation that marginality of various kinds need not be synonymous with the impossibility of participation, the absence of recognition, a systematic experience of global indifference and imprisonment within a demoralising, stultifying and claustrophobic geographical and cultural locale. Dogma 95 demonstrates that the local need not be framed in terms of primordial belonging or heritage. It establishes that if the goal is to develop a distinctive voice and vision that will be met, not with indifference, but with recognition, within the larger sphere of things, then an important first step may well be to understand and embrace the limitations of the local as a kind of inevitable standpoint or starting framework. To do so, it would appear, may well be to allow the power of practice and discourse to work its magic, to produce conditions that ultimately enable because they limit, rather than limiting *simpliciter*.

REFERENCES

Altman, R., *Film/Genre* (London: BFI, 1999).

Björkman, S., 'Den nøgne kyskhed', *Politiken*, 10 May, 1998.

Bordwell, D. and K. Thompson, *Film Art* (New York: McGraw-Hill, 1997).

Borish, S. M., *The Land of the Living: The Danish Folk High School and Denmark's Non-Violent Path to Modernization* (Århus: Blue Dolphin, 1999).

Bourdieu, P., *Distinction: A Social Critique of the Judgement of Taste*, trans. R. Nice (Cambridge, MA: Harvard University Press, 1987).

Bürger, P., *Theory of the Avant-Garde*, trans. M. Shaw (Minneapolis: University of Minnesota Press, 1984).

Carroll, N., *A Philosophy of Mass Art* (Oxford: Clarendon Press, 1998).

Carroll, N., *Philosophy of Art* (London: Routledge, 1999).

Christensen, C., 'It's All About Taking Chances', Danish Film Institute, <www.dfi.dk/sitemod/moduler/index_english.asp?pid=9100> (2002).

Christensen, C. and L. Michelsen, 'The Purified', Danish Film Institute, <www.dfi.dk/sitemod/moduler/index_english.asp?pid=9240> (2002).

DFI, 'Pressemeddelelse: 75% flere solgte billetter til danske film', 20 December, 2001.

Elster, J., 'Conventions, Creativity, Originality', in M. Hjort (ed.), *Rules and Conventions: Literature, Philosophy, Social Theory* (Baltimore: The Johns Hopkins University Press, 1992).

Elster, J., *Ulysses Unbound: Studies in Rationality, Precommitment, and Constraints* (Cambridge: Cambridge University Press, 2000).

Gellner, E., 'The Coming of Nationalism and its Interpretation: The Myths of Nation and Class', in G. Balakrishnan (ed.), *Mapping the Nation* (London: Verso, 1996).

Goodman, N., *Fact, Fiction, and Forecast* (New York: Bobbs-Merrill Company, Inc, 1965).

Habermas, J., 'Discourse Ethics: Notes on a Program of Philosophical Justification', in S. Benhabib and F. Dallmayr (eds), *The Communicative Ethics Controversy* (Boston: MIT Press, 1990).

Hjort, M., 'Lars von Trier', in Y. Tasker (ed.), *Fifty Contemporary Film-Makers* (London: Routledge, 2002).

Hjort, M., 'Danish Cinema and the Politics of Recognition', in N. Carroll and D. Bordwell (eds), *Post-Theory* (Madison: University of Wisconsin Press, 1996).

Hjort, M., 'Quasi una amicizia: Adorno and Philosophical Postmodernism', *New Orleans Review* no. 14, 1987, pp. 74–80.

Hjort, M. and I. Bondebjerg (eds), *The Danish Directors: Dialogues on a Contemporary National Cinema* (Bristol: Intellect Press, 2001).

Hroch, M., *The Social Preconditions of National Revival in Europe* (Cambridge: Cambridge University Press, 1985).

Kelly, R., *The Name of this Book is Dogme95* (London: Faber and Faber, 2000).

Kick, M., 'Hot New Swedish Directors Break Through', *Screentalk*, <www.screentalk.org> (2001).

Kjær, M., 'When Life Has a Will of Its Own', Danish Film Institute, <www.dfi.dk/sitemod/moduler/index_english.asp?pid=9110> (2002).

Kripke, S., *Wittgenstein on Rules and Private Language: An Elementary Exposition* (Oxford: Basil Blackwell, 1982).

Levinson, J., 'Defining Art Historically', in *Music, Art & Metaphysics: Essays in Philosophical Aesthetics* (Ithaca, NY: Cornell University Press, 1990a).

Levinson, J., 'Refining Art Historically', in *Music, Art & Metaphysics*, 1990b.

Levinson, J., 'Extending Art Historically', in *The Pleasures of Aesthetics: Philosophical Essays* (Ithaca, NY: Cornell University Press, 1996).

Levinson, J., 'Elster on Artistic Creativity', in P. Livingston and B. Gaut (eds), *The Creation of Art: New Essays in Philosophical Aesthetics* (New York: Cambridge University Press, 2003).

MacKenzie, S., 'Direct Dogma: Film Manifestos and the *fin de siècle*', *p.o.v.: A Danish Journal of Film Studies* no. 10, 2000, pp. 159–70.

McGinn, C., *Wittgenstein on Meaning* (Oxford: Basil Blackwell, 1984).

Naficy, H., *An Accented Cinema: Exilic and Diasporic Filmmaking* (Princeton, NJ: Princeton University Press, 2001).

Nordic Council, 'Undersøgelse af film og TV distribution i Norden', *TemaNord* 589, Copenhagen, 1994.

Rundle, P., 'We Are All Sinners: Interview with Lars von Trier', <www.dogme95.dk/news/interview/trier_interview2.htm> (1999).

Seßlen, G., 'Oprør i blindgyden: De danske Dogme-film, Radikal dilettantisme eller utopi-forrœderi?', *Kritik* no. 14, 1999, pp. 57–60, translation of 'Aufbruch in die Sackgasse', *Die Zeit*, no. 28, 1999.

Tilden, L., Press package, *Reunion* (2001).

Wilson, R. and W. Dissanayake (eds), *Global/Local: Cultural Production and the Transnational Imaginary* (Durham, NC: Duke University Press, 1996).

NOTES

1. In 'Elster on Artistic Creativity', Jerrold Levinson considers the Perec example in some detail and suggests a line of reasoning that is consistent with the basic point I am making here.

2. The emphasis on the inscrutability of intention and problem of inference is more central to Kripke's interpretation of Wittgenstein than it is to other accounts of the Viennese philosopher. See McGinn (1984). My thanks to Ben Lee for drawing attention to this point.

3. For a discussion of contemporary Danish cinema as a 'minor cinema', see Hjort (1996) and the first of the two introductions to Hjort and Bondebjerg (2001).

4. See Wilson and Dissanayake (1996) on the dynamics of the global and local.

5. Von Trier had not been informed and a much-publicised crisis ensued.

6. Leif Tilden: 'I broke Commandment number 10 … *The Director must refrain from personal taste*. I believe *everything* is personal. How can one refrain from personal taste when it comes to storytelling?' (see Kick 2001).

7. This key article was first published in 1979 and has generated a number of critical responses that have prompted Levinson to further defend and refine his views. See, for example, 'Refining Art Historically', published in the same collection of essays, and 'Extending Art Historically' (1996). Levinson has, in particular, been taken to task for his concept of 'Ur-art'. While probing, these criticisms are not relevant to the use of Levinson's definition of art in this context.

8. For a defence of popular mass entertainment as art, see Noël Carroll (1998).

2

Manifest Destinies:
Dogma 95 and the Future of the Film Manifesto

Scott MacKenzie

At first glance, one can state quite simply that the history of film manifestos represents a history of one unmitigated failure after another. Indeed, one must wonder why film-makers, theorists and radicals of all stripes continue to produce film manifestos at such a manic and prodigious rate. From the early 1900s to the early 2000s, the proliferation of film, video and television manifestos has been immense, while their 'effects', on the whole, are quite minimal. Are the writers of film manifestos manic-depressive masochists, continually setting themselves up only to fail on a grand scale, or are the effects of film manifestos more diverse than a hard-line instrumental or intentionalist account would lead one to believe? It is this question that I wish to consider, through an examination of Dogma 95, and the Vow of Chastity manifesto produced by Danish film-makers Lars von Trier and Thomas Vinterberg.

To understand the ways in which Dogma differs from previous manifesto movements, one must come to terms with a series of questions. For instance, one of the striking features of Dogma is its international appeal. This process of internationalisation is a break from the way in which moving-image manifestos have, for the most part, functioned and circulated in the past. Indeed, its internationalism makes the Dogma movement relevant to many current debates in film studies. Not only does Dogma 95 raise salient questions about national cinemas, film aesthetics and the role of the film manifesto in cinema culture, it also functions as a focal point for the debates surrounding the history of the cinema in its 100th year. Questions about the relationship between the avant-garde and the popular cinema, the role of 'minor cinemas' and the dominance of Hollywood, and the history and future of art cinema as a means of cultural exchange between national cultures are all of relevance to the debates surrounding Dogma.

Given the internationalisation of Dogma, how does the movement's set of aesthetic constraints 'translate' into other cinema cultures? Is Dogma a response to Danish cinema, to Hollywood cinema, or to the failures of previous art-cinema movements? As a call to arms, is the Dogma manifesto read and interpolated differently in different cultural, political and aesthetic contexts? Some would argue that Dogma's focus on aesthetic concerns allows for the movement's transnational appeal. Others, such as Richard Kelly, have argued that the Dogma rules are best understood as a recasting of

Danish author Aksel Sandemose's ten Jante rules (Kelly 2000: 207). In this light, the questions raised by Dogma, whether inadvertently or not, have far more to do with the ways in which the relationship between film, minority cultures and globalisation can be understood at the cinema's centenary, than with the simple 'conforming to the rules' version of the manifesto put forth in most journalistic accounts.

One must also address the profound sense of irony that permeates Dogma. The traditional, modernist manifesto, as Janet Lyon points out, is both an exhortation to action and a simultaneous attempt to eradicate dissent and debate. She writes:

> The literary and political manifestos that flag the history of modernity are usually taken to be transparent public expressions of pure will: whoever its author and whatever its subject, a manifesto is understood as the testimony of a historical present tense spoken in the impassioned voice of its participants. The form's capacity for rhetorical trompe l'oeil tends to shape its wide intelligibility: the syntax of a manifesto is so narrowly controlled by exhortation, its style so insistently unmediated, that it appears to say only what it means, and to mean only what it says. The manifesto declares a position; the manifesto refuses dialogue or discussion; the manifesto fosters antagonism and scorns conciliation. It is univocal, unilateral, single-minded. It conveys resolute oppositionality and indulges no tolerance for the faint hearted (Lyon 1999: 9).

Here is where Dogma's irony becomes paramount. While the Dogma manifesto's rhetoric conforms to that of the modernist manifesto that Lyon outlines, interviews with Vinterberg and von Trier foreground that conforming to a set of rules is not the whole, or even major, goal. For the Dogma brethren, the purpose of the manifesto is to provoke, and almost any response, other than the status quo, will do. The challenge is not to produce Dogma film after Dogma film; instead it is to challenge conformity. This is a break with other kinds of manifesto writing. How, then, does the Dogma 95 manifesto – and the films produced under its rubric – relate to the historical trajectory of the cinema manifesto? To examine whether or not Dogma constitutes a paradigm shift in the history of film manifesto writing, we must begin by considering the history of film manifestos themselves.

MANIFESTOS AND FILM HISTORY

Throughout the history of the cinema, radicals and reactionaries alike have used the film manifesto as a means of stating their key aesthetic and political goals. Indeed, film manifestos are almost as old as the cinema itself. By the early 10s and 20s, Italian Futurists, French Dadaists and Surrealists and German Expressionists were all producing manifestos, stating their political, aesthetic and philosophical principles. In most cases, these texts were calls to revolution – a revolution of consciousness, of political hierarchies and of aesthetic practices, which all bled together in an attempt radically to redefine the cinema and the culture in which it existed. Luis Buñuel's famous claim that the film *Un chien andalou* (France, 1928) was a call to murder is only the most infamous of the statements in circulation at the time;[1] many others framed the ways in which avant-garde, experimental and alternative film (and later, television and video) came to be understood

throughout the history of cinema. Furthermore, film manifestos can be seen as constituting the earliest form of film theory: for instance, Ricciotto Canudo's 'Manifesto for
the Sixth Art' in many ways marks the beginnings of a theory of radical film practice.[2]
Similarly, Sergei Eisenstein, Vsevolod Pudovkin and Grigori Alexandrov's Soviet manifesto on sound marks the beginnings of critical discussions on the relations between
image and sound in the cinema.[3] Surrealism, Free Cinema and the rise of educational
films were all framed, to varying degrees, by manifestos. In subsequent years, virtually
every artistic and political movement existing outside mainstream, narrative cinema sal-
lied forth with a manifesto, proclaiming the end of the old regimes of representation and
the need to wipe the slate clean and begin anew. Here, the slicing open of the eye in *Un
chien andalou* again stands as a nodal point, encapsulating the preferred mode of address
adopted by manifesto scribes.

Despite the wide variety of ideological and political points of view put forth in film manifestos, the rhetorical stances adopted by the writers – which foregrounded both an urgent
call to arms and a profoundly undialectical form of argumentation – led to a certain similarity in the cinematic manifesto genre. Because of the programmatic, proclamatory nature
of most manifesto writing – which is an unavoidable occurrence, precisely because of the
inflammatory nature of the discourse involved – the intended outcomes of manifestos
were, for the most part, hopelessly doomed; yet this hopelessness added to the nihilistic
romance of dramatic intervention in the public sphere. This romance was fortified by the
fact that manifestos were most often texts of the moment. Intrinsically tied not only to the
cinema, but the immediate world surrounding the authors, manifestos have had, in most
cases, quite short lifespans; they quickly left the world of political intervention and became
that most aberrant thing (at least in the eyes of the writers themselves), a declawed aesthetic text. This led to the need to write and rewrite basic principles, either by design, in
order to maintain relevance, or by force, because of political pressures; one only has to look
at the ways in which André Breton continually rewrote his manifestos of surrealism as an
example of the former, or the ways in which the fundamental, guiding principles underlying the cinema of Sergei Eisenstein necessarily shifted as intellectual montage and Lenin
led to Stalin and Socialist Realism – a sad but inevitable example of the latter.[4]

Thus far, I have painted a fairly dismal image of the effectivity of the film manifesto in
cinema culture. And, while one could argue that far more work needs to be done to elu-
cidate, within a historical framework, how these texts circulated within the public sphere,
the generalised failure of film manifestos points to the fact that the cinema scholar's
interest in them as texts, and as statements of purpose, is as tied to their extremism, and
the possibility they offer the reader to reimagine the cinema, as it is to any capacity they
might actually have to initiate change. Indeed, the cinema one imagines while reading
these texts is often far more interesting than some of the films produced under the aus-
pices of their influences. In many ways, therefore, it is the extremism of most manifestos
that gives them, if not their political foundation, then their intellectual appeal. From Luis
Buñuel and Dziga Vertov, from Stan Brakhage and Guy Debord, and from Jean-Luc
Godard to Laura Mulvey, the basis of the manifesto is precisely to provoke not only a
new form of cinema, but also a way of reimagining the cinema itself.

FREE CINEMA AND TO FREE THE CINEMA

In many ways, the manifesto movement that foreshadows Dogma to the greatest degree is Britain's Free Cinema. Like Dogma, Free Cinema functioned both as a new way to make films and as a publicity stunt in order to garner recognition within the public sphere. The aesthetic similarity is that both movements reimagine cinematic form. Films such as Lindsay Anderson's *O Dreamland* (UK, 1953) and Karel Reisz's *We Are the Lambeth Boys* (UK, 1959) are as decisive a break from the dominant, Griersonian mode of documentary prevalent in Great Britain in the 50s as Dogma is a break from contemporary art-cinema practices today. Furthermore, like Dogma, Free Cinema was – to the extent that Anderson programmed a wide variety of films – an international movement, including works such as Georges Franju's *Le Sang des bêtes* (France, 1949) and Norman McLaren's *Neighbours* (Canada, 1953). Yet it is the combination of aesthetic and publicity strategies that unites the two movements. As Lindsay Anderson says about the origins of Free Cinema:

> What happened with Free Cinema is quite interesting. Free Cinema was created for practical reasons: the films existed before the group … We asked ourselves – 'What are we going to do when we've finished these films?' because we knew nobody would want to see them; there was no way of showing them. I think I got the idea: 'Well, let's make a movement.' For journalistic reasons as much as anything, because journalists won't write about an independently made 16mm film of 20 minutes or about a 50 minute film about two deaf mutes in the East End. But if you put your films together and make a manifesto and call yourself 'Free Cinema' and make a lot of very challenging statements – then of course you write the articles for them, and they're very happy to print them. You do their work for them (Orbanz 1977: 46–47).

He goes on to state that: 'I've told young film-makers many times "Make Free Cinema. Make yourselves a movement, even if you're not one really. Pretend to be, get together". But they won't do it and they insist on their isolation. So it's very difficult to get their films shown or noticed' (1977: 51). Here, Anderson is being both earnest and ironic in accessing the strategic possibilities of manifesto writing, and this kind of instrumentality is also at work in Dogma.

How, then, does Dogma fit into the paradigms of film manifestos delineated above? The international popularity of the Dogma films raises interesting questions about these issues. Why would films such as *Festen* (*The Celebration*, Thomas Vinterberg), *Idioterne* (*The Idiots*, Lars von Trier) and *Mifunes sidste sang* (*Mifune,* Søren Kragh-Jacobsen) have such an international appeal, when most films made in the shadow of manifestos have existed in relative obscurity? One of the key issues may be a shift in emphasis in the kind of manifesto offered by the so-called Dogma brothers; one which shifts from a properly ideological critique of cinematic production and its relation to the non-diegetical world, to a rhetoric which only addresses modes of production, and does so without offering an ideological critique as a necessary corollary to the goals of the aesthetic renunciations at the heart of the Dogma project. As John Roberts notes:

Like many cinematic manifestos this century, Dogme 95's edicts emphasise the paralysis and decadence of commercial cinema in terms of its corrupting illusionism, trickery and sentimentality. As with the New Realism of the 1950s, Godard's Dziga-Vertov group in the late 1960s and the cinemas of national liberation of the 1970s, the relationship between social experience and the dominant forms of cinematic narration is challenged on the grounds of its loss of authentic speech and agency (1999: 141).

Yet despite these parallels with past manifesto manifestations, Roberts goes on to note that: 'What is significant about this list [of rules] is its largely technical and formal character; there are no political exhortations, or denunciations of other film makers; it is, rather, a kind of low-key DIY guide for aspirant amateurs; the fire of the 1960s avant-garde is tempered by an earnest practicality' (1999: 142). To the extent that the Dogma brothers do indeed attack the French *nouvelle vague*, Roberts is wrong about the lack of retrospective negation of prior cinematic movements. Nevertheless, we can see that formal experimentation and the content of the films themselves are understood to be divorced. It is this disjunctive relation between form and content that I wish to address presently, through an examination of the tenets put forth in the Dogma 95 manifesto. It is this thematic divorce of form from content that I contend represents the decisive break from the majority of cinematic manifesto writing of the past.

DOGMA AND *LA NOUVELLE VAGUE*

If there is a key historical antecedent and cinematic intertext invoked by Lars von Trier and Thomas Vinterberg in the Dogma 95 manifesto, it is the arrival of the French *nouvelle vague* in 1960. Von Trier and Vinterberg contend that Jean-Luc Godard, François Truffaut, Claude Chabrol, Eric Rohmer and Jacques Rivette were all for the overthrowing of the cinema of the past, but did not make anywhere near a decisive enough break with the past to bring about a new cinema. The Dogma brothers write:

> DOGMA 95 is a rescue action!
>
> In 1960 enough was enough! The movie was dead and called for resurrection. The goal was correct but the means were not! The new wave proved to be a ripple that washed ashore and turned to muck.
>
> Slogans of individualism and freedom created works for a while, but no changes. The wave was up for grabs, like the directors themselves. The wave was never stronger than the men behind it. The anti-bourgeois cinema itself became bourgeois, because the foundations upon which its theories were based was the bourgeois perception of art. The auteur concept was bourgeois romanticism from the very start and thereby … false!

Yet, the *auteur* cinema of *la nouvelle vague* was not a consolidated film style; it did not follow uniform rules of cinematic evolution or revolution, in the manner implied by the Dogma brothers. Truffaut himself put this vision of *la nouvelle vague* to rest twenty-eight years earlier, when he stated:

People who say 'The New Wave has failed' without defining what they mean by that, I suppose they're thinking of 'intellectual' films which were not successful at the box-office, and with this in mind they refuse to 'label' films which pleased them or were successful – an arbitrary division since the New Wave is just as much *L'Homme de Rio* as *L'Immortelle*, *Le Vieil homme et l'enfant* as *La Musica*, *Les Cœurs verts* as *Un Homme et une femme* ... The New Wave did not have an aesthetic programme, it was simply an attempt to rediscover a certain independence which was lost somewhere around 1924, when films became too expensive, a little before the talkies (Hillier 1986: 107).

It is individualism that the Dogma brethren see as the failure of *la nouvelle vague*, yet as Truffaut points out, it is precisely the individual visions of numerous dissimilar *auteurs* that was the backbone of New Wave cinema. Nevertheless, it is the received idea that post-1960 cinema movements (New German Cinema, *cinéma direct*, British 'kitchen sink' films) stultified their radical possibilities by adopting 'styles' of their own. Therefore, it is this kind of stylistic individualism which Dogma contends was the downfall of art cinemas following in the wake of *la nouvelle vague*:

> For the first time, anyone can make movies. But the more accessible the medium becomes, the more important the avant-garde ...
>
> In 1960 enough was enough! The movie had been cosmeticised to death, they said; yet since then the use of cosmetics has exploded.
>
> The 'supreme' task of the decadent film-makers is to fool the audience. Is that what we are so proud of? Is that what the '100 years' have brought us? Illusions via which emotions can be communicated? ... By the individual artist's free choice of trickery?

There are many parallels between this document and the kinds of manifestos that came before; the past is decried and a new form of cinema is celebrated as a way out of the abysmal quagmire brought about by the mainstream. Yet, it is the Vow of Chastity, attached to the manifesto itself, that shifts the dogma of Dogma away from the manifestos of the past. The need to return to a cinema of truth is underlined by the key tenets in the Vow of Chastity, the ten key aims of Dogma, which include: shooting must be done on location; the sound must never be produced apart from the images or vice versa; the camera must be hand-held (any movement or immobility attainable in the hand is permitted); the film must be in colour (special lighting is not acceptable); optical work and filters are forbidden; the film must not contain superficial action; temporal and geographical alienation are forbidden; genre movies are not acceptable; and the film format must be Academy 35mm.

IRONY AND REDEMPTION

The directors also refrain from 'good taste'. There are many interesting aspects to the Vow of Chastity; the first thing that springs to mind is the self-conscious religiosity of the language. Yet, combined with this unholy marriage of the spirit of the Protestant work ethic and Catholic flagellation, one finds that the vows themselves are pervaded with an irony that is typically missing in the modernist manifesto. As Vinterberg states: 'I think … Dogma is in the area between a very solemn thing and deep irony' (Wood 1998: 50). Indeed, the name of the movement – Dogma – is self-reflexively ironic in and of itself. There is also a reflexive self-consciousness lurking behind the film-makers' assumptions about their own cinematic past; it is not only the 'others' who need to reform their truant ways. For instance, in relation to his own film-making, Vinterberg notes that:

> We also wanted to break with the convention of filmmaking, first of all with the convention within our own filmmaking – force ourselves to try something new, due to the fact that there should be some sort of risk connected to making art. So from that aspect it's very solemn, and not rigid. On the other hand, it is a game, as it's defined in the manifesto, which is a bit arrogant, and of course, ironic also (Wood 1998: 50).

It is this irony that allows the directors to believe in both the solemnity of Dogma and in its irony as an act of provocation. Moreover, it seems that the rhetorical provocation within the public sphere brought on by the writing of a 'manifesto' is as much about opening up a critical discussion about the state of the cinema as it is about following rules while producing films. Lars von Trier echoes these assumptions when he states:

> I don't think it's necessarily crucial that the Dogme rules be followed. I think the issue of whether you can gain something by throwing away total freedom in exchange for a set of rules is worth discussing. And it's interesting to see whether some of those rules might be of use to others. I've created rules before, so I think I've demonstrated that they can lead to something positive. I think the need to go back to basics, which the rules are a response to, is more urgent now than ever before. I would find it amusing if Dogme could continue to exist like a little pill you could take when there was too much of the other kind of thing, too much refinement and distanciation … But I don't know what will happen to the Dogme concept (Hjort and Bondebjerg 2001: 222).

Von Trier also applies the Dogma ethos to the diary he kept while making *The Idiots*. His preface to the diary reads: 'The following is a kind of diary which I recorded in a dicta-phone throughout a period from just before the start of production until well into the editing stage. In keeping with the spirit of Dogma, I have neither read through nor cor-rected the text' (von Trier 2001: 2). In all of these discussions of Dogma as film practice, it is key to note that what Vinterberg and von Trier propose is not the only way to make film. As Vinterberg notes: 'I think to make another Dogme film right now would be suici-dal, because the fine thing about Dogme is to create renewal, and to do another Dogme film right after would be creating another convention, which would be very oppressive' (Wood 1998: 51). It is the process of reimagining film-making that is paramount.

SINS AND CONFESSIONS
Another level of irony, mixed in with the guilt of the Protestant work ethic, is the repenting of sins that the film-makers undertake when they break their own, self-pre-scribed rules. The role played by sin in this instance is quite curious, as it has no moral

content, only form. Or more precisely, one can only sin in connection with the form of the film itself. However, the Dogma directors do not look at the manifesto as simply a formal challenge. Von Trier, the *agent provocateur* of the new Danish cinema, takes a less ironic tone when dealing with the implications of the Dogma directives, and feels there are moral issues at stake behind the formal claims made in the Vow of Chastity. Further, he takes issue with those who see Dogma as an empty formal exercise:

> But there have been a number of crises and the idea of my having full control over my films has at times been a total lie. For example, Aalbæk and Vibeke Windeløv allowed filters to be used in connection with *The Idiots*. That was an insane cock-up, but it may have involved a break-down in communication on my part. Part of the problem with the Dogme concept has been that nobody has taken it completely seriously. It's been viewed as a bit of a joke … Why would anyone in his right mind impose such ridiculous restrictions on himself? (Hjort and Bondebjerg 2001: 210).

The irony and the overriding concern with form found in the Dogma 95 manifesto and in the often-conflicting ways in which it is understood by its 'authors' have not been ignored by other film-makers. As if by way of answering von Trier's question about 'ridiculous restrictions', both Vinterberg and Harmony Korine have published their own confessions. While Vinterberg's list is quite short (Wood 1998: 50), Korine's list, written after the completion of his Dogma film, *Julien Donkey-Boy*, is extensive, and related his need to make a Dogma film to both his formative years and his current relationship. Again, one can see the connection between irony and solemnity in the following 'confessions', which are worth quoting at length:

> In joining the Dogme brotherhood, something that I am staunch about, in a belief in making a film under God, forsaking convention and abiding strongly in its conviction, I proudly abandoned those cinema tactics that I had been brought up in. And in doing this, I succumbed to a religious-like, semi-Calvinist fervor. But as when I was a child, the temptation to sin was always a romantic option …
>
> To love the manifesto is the only way I could make it through, not to question it, but to give in as you would blindly give yourself to a higher power. But with that said, I must confess with little shame and a redemptive sorrow to my few sins against my brethren. As when I was a nine year old child and I burnt my mother's garden down with matches and dry grass while Mother trusted me enough to leave me alone at home for the first time, I was to tend to my younger siblings while she went shopping for a winter coat. But I started a fire instead. And the fire consumed more than her flowers. She smashed my bare ass with a yellow wiffle ball bat till the welts on my ass made a brutal enough impression for her to stop. Needless to say the lesson was learned and my vandalization ceased, at least for a while …
>
> I confess to Chloë Sevigny's pregnant belly not being truly pregnant. I tried to impregnate her myself, but there wasn't enough time. Plus she felt not ready to carry a child for nine months. I did try though. Perhaps it was my fault. Perhaps I am shooting blanks. And loving

her the way I do, I did not want another man to give it a try. So we used a round foam pillow
that was present on location in my grandmother's bedroom closet (Korine 1999).

In these three excerpts, the relationship between irony and solemnity is clear. In discussing Sevigny's 'pregnancy' Korine foregrounds the limits of realism and his 'inability'
to follow the rules to their logical extreme. Yet it is the extremity of the relationship
between the ironic and the solemn in Korine's text that forces the reader to consider the
cinema's modes of production and the ways in which the Dogma rules undermine the
shortcuts directors can easily take on the route to 'realism'.

Korine's concentration on family life is also of interest, given some of the recurring
themes found in Dogma films. Despite the hyperbole found in von Trier's many pronouncements about Dogma, it is indeed the case that, perhaps against the wishes of the
Dogma brothers, the aesthetics of the manifesto have lent themselves to films that often
share broadly similar concerns: those of the dysfunctional family and the ways in which
the psychical and mental harm done by families needs to be sorted out. Many Dogma
films have characters that are the agents responsible for the reimagining of the family: in
The Celebration, it is Christian (Ulrich Thomsen); in *The Idiots*, both Karen (Bodil
Jørgensen) and Stoffer (Jens Albinus) play this role, albeit in strikingly different ways; in
Mifune, the surrogate family constructed by Kresten (Anders Berthelsen) and Liva (Iben
Hjejle) compares favourably to Kresten's 'traditional' family back in Copenhagen; in *The
King is Alive* (Kristian Levring) the stranded group becomes a reconfigured, if dysfunc-
tional, family; *Julien Donkey-Boy* portrays the effects of schizophrenia on a family; and in
Fuckland (José Luis Marquès) a main character attempts to 'repopulate' the Falkland
Islands as a means of de-colonialisation.

CONCLUSION

Do Dogma's restrictions and abstinences lead to a revitalised form of cinema for the
second century? It is possible that Dogma was a moment in the sun, whose glory days
are, like all film manifestos before it, already fading. Despite the call for permanent
change, von Trier is already talking wistfully about the Dogma past:

> But I still think that Dogme might persist in the sense that a director would be able to say, 'I
> feel like making that kind of film'. I think that would be amusing. I'm sure a lot of people
> could profit from that. At which point you might argue that they could just as easily profit
> from a different set of rules. Yes, of course. But then go ahead and formulate them. Ours are
> just a proposal (Hjort and Bondebjerg 2001: 222).

Yet it is this proposal that has reinvigorated debates around the nature of both art and
political films at the end of the first century of the cinema. Furthermore, by embedding
within the modernist film manifesto a profound sense of irony, the Dogma brothers have
revitalised, for a short while, the notion of the film manifesto and its function within both
the cinema and the public sphere.

REFERENCES

Breton, A., *Manifestos on Surrealism* (Ann Arbor: University of Michigan Press, 1969).

Canudo, R., 'The Birth of a Sixth Art (1911)', *Framework* no. 13, 1980, pp. 3–7.

Hjort, M. and I. Bondebjerg (eds), *The Danish Directors: Dialogues on a Contemporary National Cinema* (Bristol: Intellect Press, 2001).

Kelly, R., *The Name of this Book is Dogme95* (London: Faber and Faber, 2000).

Korine, H., 'The Confession of *Julien Donkey-Boy*', <www.angelfire.com/ab/harmonykorine/confession.html> (1999).

Lyon, J., *Manifestos: Provocations of the Modern* (Ithaca, NY: Cornell University Press, 1999).

MacKenzie, S., 'Direct Dogma: Film Manifestos and the *fin de siècle*', *p.o.v.: A Danish Journal of Film Studies* no. 10, 2000, pp. 159–70.

Orbanz, E., *Journey to a Legend and Back: The British Realistic Film* (Berlin: Verlag Volker Spiess, 1977).

Roberts, J., 'Dogme 95', *New Left Review* no. 238, 1999, pp. 141–49.

Talens, J., *The Branded Eye: Buñuel's 'Un chien andalou'* (Minneapolis: University of Minnesota Press, 1993).

Taylor, R. and I. Christie (eds), *The Film Factory: Russian and Soviet Documents, 1896–1939* (Cambridge, MA: Harvard University Press, 1988).

Truffaut, F., ' "The Evolution of the New Wave": Truffaut in Interview with Jean-Louis Comolli, Jean Narboni (extracts)', in J. Hillier (ed.), *Cahiers du Cinéma: The 1960s – New Wave, New Cinema, Reevaluating Hollywood* (Cambridge, MA: Harvard University Press, 1986).

von Trier, L., 'Extracts from *The Idiots*: A Film Diary', trans. Peter Holm-Jensen, *Pretext* no. 4, 2001, pp. 1–16.

Wood, R., 'Humble Guests at the Celebration: An Interview with Thomas Vinterberg and Ulrich Thomsen', *Cinéaction* no. 48, 1998, pp. 47–54.

NOTES

Part of this essay, in a quite different form, originally appeared as Scott MacKenzie, 'Direct Dogma: Film Manifestos and the *fin de siècle*', *p.o.v.: A Danish Journal of Film Studies* no. 10, 2000, pp. 159–70.

1. See Buñuel's preface to the script of *Un chien andalou*, originally published in La *Révolution Surréaliste* 12 (1929), reprinted and translated in Talens (1993): 89.
2. See Canudo (1980): 3–7.
3. See Sergei Eisenstein, Vsevolod Pudovkin and Grigori Alexandrov, 'Statement on Sound', reprinted and translated in Taylor and Christie, eds (1988): 234–5.
4. For Breton's versions of the surrealist manifesto, see Breton (1969); the primary statement documenting the aesthetic renunciations of the Soviet Formalists is 'For a Great Cinema Art: Speeches to the All-Union Creative Conference of the Workers in Soviet Cinema', in Taylor and Christie, eds (1988): 348–55.

3

'Kill Your Darlings':
Lars von Trier and the Origin of Dogma 95

Peter Schepelern

Dogma 95, as presented in the manifesto by Lars von Trier and Thomas Vinterberg, is a movement with obvious parallels to earlier movements and initiatives in the cinema. Parallels can be drawn to Vertov's *Kino Pravda*, Italian neo-realism, the French *nouvelle vague*, the West German *Oberhausen* Group, Jean-Luc Godard's *Groupe Dziga Vertov*, as well as to individual artists such as John Cassavetes and Andy Warhol. Links can also be made to the art style of *Arte Povera* and to Jerzy Grotowski's Poor Theatre. Like most of these manifestations, Dogma – with its ten rules of cinematic abstinence – is also an anti-establishment reaction, an initiative taken to counter the trend towards bourgeois and superficial entertainment. Instead there is a search for reality, for the truth without illusions, and a movement towards the genuine and the humane. But all these historical similarities and connections should not obscure the fact that Dogma 95 first and foremost has its roots in Lars von Trier's own work and artistic expressions. This article will comment on von Trier's influence, with special reference to some of his less known accomplishments and projects.

HOMO LUDENS

Von Trier once stated that he has 'a very technical relationship to film' (although he underlines that it is not *only* technique that interests him). The obvious fascination with technique exhibited in his work can be seen as a symptom of a fundamental inclination to playfulness as an artistic method. He seems to confirm the theory that the process of artistic creativity is linked to the ability to maintain contact with one's inner child – the artist as *homo ludens* (to use the Dutch scholar Johan Huizinga's term). 'I bought myself a lot of funny technical toys' (Schepelern 2000: 265), von Trier said of *Europa* (1991), his technically most complex production and one of the technically most innovative works in recent cinema. His approach to film-making accords with Orson Welles' famous definition of film as 'the biggest toy train set any boy ever had' (Halliwell 1989: 1140). Already in von Trier's actual childhood, the camera was important to him. 'Playing with the camera was a good game, and I still think so,' he has said.

It is also in this context that von Trier's use of, or rather his obsession with, rules can be understood. Throughout his career, von Trier has set special rules for each production. The rules were usually a kind of production code used on the set and would typically establish some technical or aesthetic line to be followed. All of his major films have been accompanied by manifestos in which a more general attitude to the state of film art according to von Trier is expressed, often in a polemical and challenging form. 'I have always been crazy about manifestos. I read the Surrealist Manifesto as a young man and was impressed by it. I have also been a communist, and I believe, as far as I recall, that there is also a manifesto there. Manifestos are a good thing,' says von Trier (Monggaard Christensen 2000: 100).

RULES OF THE GAME

In the graduation film *Befrielsesbilleder* (*Images of a Relief*), the shots are extraordinarily long (with reference to Dreyer, Tarkovsky, Cassavetes), and von Trier has explained that the film has an 'incredible, and almost hysterical structure. It is in three parts where each shot refers to a shot in the next part' (Schepelern 2000: 63). In his feature debut, *The Element of Crime* (1984), the colours are reduced to a yellowish hue (partly by using natrium light). Cross-cutting is omitted on principle and is replaced by long complicated shots (the entire film has only approximately 150 shots where a typical contemporary film will have ten times that number). In *Epidemic* (1987), the systematic working principles are even more dominant. The film divides into two parts. About two-thirds of the film consists of scenes with Lars von Trier and his scriptwriter Niels Vørsel improvising in the roles as director Lars and writer Niels. The film is shot with a stationary 16mm camera by either von Trier or Vørsel or, in scenes where both are present, without a camera operator or cinematographer as a kind of demonstration against the meticulous and time-consuming methods of the professional cinematographer. The remaining one-third of the film constitutes a film within the film and is made in the style of a distinguished art film on 35mm with Dreyer's former cinematographer Henning Bendtsen behind the camera. What is more, the entire film was the result of von Trier's bet with Film Institute consultant Claes Kastholm Hansen as to whether the director could shoot a feature film for only one million kroner (approximately £90,000). The whole enterprise could be considered a kind of game. And the film 'tallies well with the idea of a more primitive film', as von Trier states in the press book (von Trier 1987: 7). The film is also an early example of von Trier controlling all aspects of the film as director, writer, actor and cameraman … with all shots filmed on authentic locations.

In the TV film *Medea* (1988), the image was deliberately given a 'muddy' patina by copying from video to film and back to video. In *Europa*, there is the refined use of front and back projection (the actors were never in Poland where the exteriors were shot – projections were used throughout), and the film shifts constantly from black and white, to black and white with a single colour element, and to shots in full colour. There are also camera stunts of great virtuosity such as the camera movement from the loving couple in the attic, through the hole in the roof and further on into the night, and finally into the compartment of a passing train, all in a single travelling shot.

In the hospital ghost story *Riget* (*The Kingdom*, 1994), a television serial made for Danish State Television (Danmarks Radio), the rules were dictated not only by aesthetics, but also by pragmatism. In order to simplify the technical working methods (and thereby speed up the shooting process), von Trier decided that a majority of scenes (the exception being the flashback scenes to the horror story set in the early 1900s) should be shot with only the available lighting, with hand-held cameras in all office and conference scenes and using a Steadicam in all corridor scenes. The resulting style was sketchy and coarse-grained, with distorted colours, a shaky documentary/news camera style, and a disregard for normal film language conventions such as the 180-degree line and the logic of eye-line match. This style confirmed that seemingly sloppy and faulty filming and editing did not bother the public as long as the plot and the characters were interesting. On the other hand, the style seemed attractive as a nonchalant contrast to the perfectionist and polished film style that was, and still is, so dominant in contemporary mainstream film (and television). The technique also led to excellent acting because the actors were allowed to act their scenes in long uninterrupted takes. And it gave von Trier, who in his earlier work had not been particularly comfortable directing actors, a new freshness and a more relaxed attitude. Thus, *The Kingdom* marks a decisive new direction in von Trier's career, as well as in Danish film more generally.

It was undoubtedly the positive results from this experience that made von Trier canonise the various ad hoc rules of *The Kingdom* in the codified rules of the Dogma manifesto, put together by von Trier (with some input from Vinterberg) in early 1995 shortly after the production of *The Kingdom*. However, it took three years before Dogma could move from theory to practice. And from the years before and around Dogma, there are two interesting von Trier projects (both more or less unknown outside Denmark) that illustrate his obsession with bizarre rules and the conviction that self-imposed obs-tacles and constraints intensify artistic creativity.

THE FUTURE HAS ALREADY BEGUN

In March 1991 von Trier, together with his co-author Niels Vørsel and producer Peter Aalbæk Jensen, announced a new and secretive feature film project called *Dimension*. Its special organisational rule was that it should be shot over thirty years. Shooting started in 1991 and the plan was to shoot for two or three days a year, producing approximately three minutes of the projected film's net duration each time. Shooting was to be completed in 2022 and the premiere was scheduled for 30 April 2024, von Trier's sixty-eighth birthday. *Dimension* was envisaged as a 90–100 minute colour feature film, organised through the Foundation *Dimension* and supported by von Trier and Aalbæk Jensen's company Zentropa and the Danish Film Institute. Because of the long production period the project has been secured with 'a last will and testament attached to the final contracts that transfer to others the responsibility for those posts in the production crew that become vacant due to death or serious disability'. Von Trier got the inspiration for the project in Berlin when the Wall fell:

> When I saw all the Trabants and Skodas puffing their way across the border, something happened. The powerlessness I saw in the eyes of the customs officers spoke to me and the idea came to me to let a European film collage – a kind of monument of the future – start there (Schepelern 2000: 156).

Von Trier and Vørsel's press release states:

> However omnipresent time may be as the so-called fourth dimension we refer to, and perhaps
> experience it as, it is however in itself invisible and immediately non-depictible …
>
> It is our idea and aim to produce a feature film with the flow of time as the all dominant
> cross-current. A feature film that uses the passage of time as a kind of documentary-esque
> innate entity and a decoration for the staged plot of the film and that uses time as the
> suspense-generating entity as the 'pursuer of all living things' (Schepelern 2000: 157).

The first three minutes were shot in May 1991 in Cannes where von Trier was visiting in connection with the presentation of *Europa*. One sees Eddie Constantine fly over the Croisette with a helicopter and land on an airfield. Since then scenes have been made starring Udo Kier, Jean-Marc Barr, Jens Okking and Baard Owe (1994) as well as Stellan Skarsgård and Katrin Cartlidge (1996). 'The important thing is the idea of shooting a film over thirty years. It is a minor plus that we can see people get older and that time goes by, but the idea itself is the most important thing,' von Trier has said in a TV programme that showed the first scenes. There is a short, confidential synopsis, but no manuscript. In the press release, von Trier and Vørsel explain:

> We have sketched the start of a 'poetic gangster story'. With the old man who during the first
> three minutes of the film dies of old age. He 'narrates' the film about his family and about the
> continuation of his work through the decades. We will use the film cliché with the old
> gangster to introduce an important entertainment element in the film. The film can thus be
> seen (and that is important) as a suspenseful gangster film about the next generation. About
> the decline of good manners and of families.
>
> The intention is gradually to introduce the social dimension. After the introductions … the
> characters gradually move out amongst the people. We started with a scene at an airfield on
> the Côte d'Azur and continue with shots from an apartment in Wiesbaden. The story will then
> take us around Europe and take place in and among current events and hot spots. We will
> experience Europe in front of TV monitors as well as 'live'. And it is clear that more and more
> we will be interested in change.
>
> In order to capture change, it is important that we do not stick to a script from year to year. We
> will only have a sketch in our pocket when we go out to face time (Schepelern 2000: 157–58).

The concept of shooting over a long period is known from Michael Apted's British TV documentaries *7 Up* (1963), *7 Plus 7* (1970), *21 Up* (1977), *28 Up* (1984), *35 Up* (1991) and *42 Up* (1998), in which the same people are followed once every seventh year from the age of seven. In feature films it has rarely been used, if at all. However, in recent years *Dimension* has come to a standstill as von Trier seems to have lost interest in the project. There is a plan that some of the actors should continue it on their own. Perhaps *Dimension* is best understood as conceptual art, where the concept is more important than the actual realisation. That also goes for the second project conceived of during or around the writing of the Dogma manifesto.

THE SPIRIT OF THE ANT-HILL

Psykomobile #1: Verdensuret (Psychomobile #1: The World Clock), a performance project presented in the autumn of 1996 in conjunction with Culture City Copenhagen, began as an invitation from the venerable institution *Kunstforeningen*, a Copenhagen art society established in 1825. The director Helle Behrndt had seen Peter Greenaway's exhibition *Le Bruit des nuages* (1992–93) in Paris, where the film director portrayed the history of the dream of flight through works from the Louvre's Graphic Arts Collection, and she wanted to present a similar encounter among several media. The dramaturge Lene Nørgaard Mikkelsen persuaded von Trier to join the project and in May 1995, a few months after the presentation of the Dogma 95 manifesto in Paris, he had come up with a concept that is described in three documents focusing on rules.

The plan was to people the nineteen rooms in *Kunstforeningen* with fifty-three prede-fined characters who, following different instructions, should improvise on the basis of the plot lines provided. What was unique in this case was that the actors received orders to change their attitudes from four different coloured lamps that were activated by computer impulses which in turn were controlled via satellite by ants! One could easily have filmed an ant-hill in von Trier's backyard in Lyngby, north of Copenhagen, or used a nature film about the life of insects. But this would have been too obvious and not nearly as interest-ing or funny enough. With the help of American ant specialist Richard Fagerlund, a large ant-hill was found in a desert close to a telephone exchange in a tiny town outside El Paso, Texas. The location also had to support a video camera which for three hours on all the fifty days of the show sent live footage of ant movements via satellite to Copenhagen, Denmark, where a computer registered the ants' movements in relation to a diagram that turned the lamps on or off in the nineteen rooms. So it was the ants in the desert outside El Paso that regulated all patterns of reaction and mood changes among the fifty-three characters 13,000 kilometres away in the art society in Copenhagen!

Jesper Jargil's *De udstillede* (*The Exhibited*) documents *Psychomobile #1: The World Clock* (© Jesper Jargil Film)

Von Trier's Document I, *Psychomobile #1: The World Clock* (twenty-four pages) contains a short description of the fifty-three characters and the nineteen rooms; Document II (three pages) sets up 'Rules and Instructions for the World Clock'; and Document III, 'The Practice and Placing of the World Clock in the Art Society' (three pages), provides other, more technical instructions. On this basis, Niels Vørsel wrote the 'script', a 270-page manual, which he completed in June 1996. Here, the fifty-three characters are analysed in individual schemes that summarily describe the relationship of one character to each of the other fifty-two characters (with the categories: no relation, distant relation, close relation, with commentaries) and to the nineteen rooms, including the significance of the four lamps for each character. Each actor was given only his or her own scheme and had to piece the character together based on the limited information it provided.

Document I, for example, describes 'Person No. 2, or Albert' as follows: 'Male. 45 years old. Counterfeiter. Prints money and lives well off of it. Aesthete. Spends lots of money on vanity. Nonsexual. Has 100,000 Crowns in counterfeit bills.' 'Person No. 32, called AA', is identified as 'Female. 18 years old. Aggressive attitude, noisy, maladjusted. Owns nothing.' In the scheme for Albert the actor is told (confidentially) that he has a distant relationship to Petite 1 (but 'Petite 1 leaves him cold'), a relationship to Postman ('Albert likes to make fun of Postman'), with Dr Magnus ('Albert finds Dr Magnus ridiculous') and with Smuck ('Smuck is Albert's enemy'). He also has a close relationship to the Mongrel ('Albert's helper. Is arrogant and has a superior attitude towards the Mongrel and always teases him for his lack of taste and refinement'). It is also made clear, for instance, that Room No. 3, the Blue Room, is his 'Study', that Room No. 12, the Rose Garden, is his 'Leisure Room', that Room No. 18, the Balcony, is his 'Starting Room'. And finally, the document spells out how he must react to the four colours of the lamps: 'Red – Tries to sell everything he has. Do not mind violent help from the Mongrel. Green – Does everything to help the last person who has approached him with a problem. Blue – Loses all faith in himself. Yellow – Organizes things, contributions or promises of contributions to anybody who might have something to offer, in an increasingly hysterical manner' (Schepelern 2000: 161).

Von Trier did not want to direct the performance himself (he has never directed for the theatre, although it has been announced that he will stage Richard Wagner's *Der Ring des Nibelungen* in Bayreuth in 2006), and after several crises the project was entrusted to Morten Arnfred, von Trier's co-director on *The Kingdom* and assistant director on *Breaking the Waves* (1996). The show was performed daily for two months from October to December 1996. It was enthusiastically received by the critics and was sold out the entire time it ran.

The World Clock is difficult to define more closely in relationship to genre and medium. The show has affinities with a contemporary theatre experiment by the Canadian John Krizanc – *Tamara* (1984) – which was staged in a whole villa. The audience had to walk from room to room and choose what part/corner of the story about the Italian writer Gabriele d'Annunzio and the Polish painter Tamara de Lempicka they wished to follow as told by the masters, the servants and the guests. But *The World Clock* is also an installation, a live exhibition, performance theatre, a kind of manifestation of a computer game and TV-zapper culture accompanied by a veritable chaos theory. Film is about the only thing that it is not. But *The World Clock* has clear connections to von Trier's other work. In this project, however, the interest in far-fetched rules of the game reaches new heights. Here we have arbitrary rule fulfilment in an intricate form of co-operation. *The World Clock* also circles around the phobias for elevators, hospitals and airports that are typical of von Trier.

Von Trier visited the rooms at *Kunstforeningen* and met the actors the evening before the opening. But he never saw a performance! Document III makes a key point: '*The World Clock* consists of three documents, and its realisation is a reproduction, not the work of art itself!' (Schepelern 2000: 164). Jesper Jargil shot seventy hours of video footage from which he made the documentary *De udstillede* (*The Exhibited*, 2000). But the entire complex of improvised, yet subtly controlled stories and actions – three hours a day for fifty days in nineteen different rooms – amounts to at least 3,000 hours of human drama. Once again the project was an experiment with rules but it was also about the artist's absence and withdrawal. Although von Trier was absent, there was no doubt that he was the spirit of the ant-hill.

RULES OF PUNISHMENT

Von Trier's early films, squarely situated within the domain of the experimental and eccentric art-film genre, focused on bizarre methods related to literary experiments found in writers like Raymond Roussel (whom Vørsel had read) and the Oulipo Group with Italo Calvino, Raymond Queneau and Georges Perec. Von Trier succeeded in creating a totally artificial artistic universe where everything was under the absolute control of the *auteur* artist who functioned as God or a puppeteer. Control is the key word here, and there can be no doubt that the question of control is crucial to von Trier's universe and to his personality more generally:

> My greatest problem in life is control versus chaos. I can get extremely afraid of not having control when I want it. The best situation I can imagine would be to accept the lack of control – but that's nearly a masochistic thought for me. All my worst anxieties are about losing control (Schepelern 2000: 282).

As a control freak who had gone all the way with *Europa*, von Trier now had no other option than to test the possibilities in deliberately abstaining from control, that is, systematically to prevent himself from doing what he most wanted to do. This was the tease in *The Kingdom* (where it also saved the production a lot of money) but in his later work the idea is pursued more and more seriously. The method, which combines personal therapy with artistic discipline, is a kind of aesthetic masochism. It is a form of self-imposed punishment, an artistic flagellation intended to cleanse the artist of all commercial vices, leaving him purer and better. The Dogma rules can thus be seen as a spiritual cleansing process that touches on religion, sexuality and, in the last analysis, on aesthetics.

Lars von Trier shooting *The Idiots* (© Jesper Jargil Film)

Just after the publication of the Dogma rules von Trier started shooting his next major production. *Breaking the Waves* was a peak in his career. Most other directors given the chance to make an expensive international production would desert their youthful experiments and more or less automatically adapt themselves to a standard mainstream style. Not von Trier. *Breaking the Waves* offers hand-held CinemaScope and out-of-focus shots and special rules, such as the following statement in the manuscript: 'Often Bess will, as the only person, look directly into the camera during the film' (von Trier 1996: 23).

With his Dogma films *The Idiots* and the collaborative work *D-Dag* (*D-Day*, 2000) (which besides being a Dogma film also involved special work methods such as experimenting with multiple plots, live shooting and interactive viewing), von Trier finally made his rules explicit. In that respect *The Idiots* is the ultimate Dogma work, because it not only uses but is *about* the Dogma rules. In Vinterberg's *Festen* (*The Celebration*) the Dogma technique functions primarily as a means of guaranteeing the dynamic of the actors in a flexible cinematic flow. In Kragh-Jacobsen's *Mifunes sidste sang* (*Mifune*), the Dogma technique is mostly a liberating factor, a contract that stimulates narrative pleasure and acting energy in an otherwise old-fashioned story. Only in *The Idiots* is the following of technical and aesthetic rules matched by a story about rules and the observance of rules, about the courage to pass a challenging test. Does the teacher dare to 'spass' in front of his art class? Does the returned wife dare to 'spass' in front of her family? Does von Trier dare to spass with film language? The idiot group tries to return to an original state of being and to realise an inner idiot (seemingly related to the inner child), just as von Trier is on the track of an original film art. This return to a kind of natural origin, a cinematic Rousseauianism, is anticipated in the romantic passage from the first manifesto, which accompanies *The Element of Crime*: 'We will search for and return to the time when the love between film-maker and film was young and when the joy of creation could be read in every frame' (Degn Johansen and Kimergaard 1991: 157–58). A symptomatic expression of this theme occurs when the film examines and oversteps conventional barriers of nudity and sex as a test of the overstepping of conventional bourgeois norms, which in turn is matched by the overstepping of a film-aesthetic consensus. Von Trier goes so far as to introduce a shot showing authentic penetration in the group sex scene – a device guilty of manipulation, obscured by the fact that these shots do not show the real actors but were made with porno stand ins!

Von Trier reveals that he is aware of this duality when, in the diary about the making of *The Idiots*, he complains about the 'damned Dogma rules' (von Trier 1998: 180) and at the same time enthusiastically congratulates himself: 'Man, you know how to do this shit, you sure know how to set these things free' (von Trier 1998: 184). It is also in this context that the use of a hand-held camera can be understood. Hand-held camera as a stylistic element has since the 60s traditionally expressed either a character's intense sense of self (subjective camera), or has been associated with political documentaries such as those reporting on marches, demonstrations or riots. Now, with the Dogma films, hand-held camera becomes a searching tool that never gives up, but untiringly pins down a truth that must be found in spite of all obstacles, as the Vow of the manifesto demands (*The Celebration*). Or it marks an intended relinquishing of formalist control over the picture or picture composition (framing) by pointing to the action, the acting of the characters, and the characteristics of the locations in a spontaneous manner (as in *The Idiots*). In connection with *Dancer in the Dark*, von Trier summed up his new attitude towards the camera as follows.

> Frame – here you are interested in the frames, but if you just point with the camera, then you are looking for content … When composing a picture, it is essentially control you are looking for. But you could ignore it and forget about it for a moment and then try to work yourself into the picture and find out what is in the centre and then you just point there because then it will come to you … (Schepelern 2000: 233).

For von Trier, Dogma also supports the new liberated and liberating attitude towards acting and actors that began in *The Kingdom* and triumphed in *Breaking the Waves*. In *The Idiots* he got very intense performances from a team of largely unknown young actors. But there is a certain ambiguity present here as well. Ironically, one could say that even when von Trier relinquishes control, he is still totally in command. He still makes the rules. And Jesper Jargil's documentary about the making of *The Idiots*, *De ydmygede* (*The Humiliated*, 1998), clearly demonstrates as much.

SEEMINGLY ALL IS WELL

Von Trier, in his early career, was a *provocateur*. The aggressive tone is evident in his manifestos. It was not enough to make films like *The Element of Crime*, *Epidemic* and *Europa*. Von Trier wanted them to be part of a general cultural project – *The Europe Trilogy* – an ethical and religious challenge to society. And to this end he made use of manifestos, often written in both a provoking and turgid literary style. The manifestos for the trilogy all begin with the same sentence: 'Seemingly all is well' (the sentence is also in English in the Danish texts). But as it turns out, all is not well after all. The metaphors refer to religion and eroticism. In the first manifesto (*The Element of Crime*), film, with a touch of chauvinist arrogance, is compared to a wife. The relationship between the film-maker and the film is like a marriage of convenience, where ideally, as von Trier claims, it should be more like the relationship to a mistress. Von Trier calls for a film that rivals religion and sensuality, talks about carnal desire, and proclaims himself to be a mere 'jerk-off artist of the film screen' (Degn Johansen and Kimergaard 1991: 159). He attacks bourgeois civil manners and points to sexuality and intense religious faith as suitable parallels for the real film artist.

This strategy of using the irrationality of religion as an artistic stimulation continues in *Breaking the Waves* and is also one of the forces behind the Dogma text. But we cannot totally exclude the possibility that this is an ironic provocation. The very tone of the Vow of Chastity, where film-making and celibacy converge, could be suspected of being another stunt by the 'jerk-off artist of the film screen'. Von Trier is generally evasive on the sincerity of his religiosity: 'Although the film isn't an introduction to religion, it is an expression of my religiousness, but it's also, once again, an attempt to provoke myself' (Hjort and Bondebjerg 2001: 220).

The mock-religious aspect of Dogma is reminiscent of passages in his earlier manifestos. 'We want to see religion on the screen' (Degn Johansen and Kimergaard 1991: 158), we read in the first manifesto. And in the third manifesto, about *Europa*, the film-maker humbly addresses himself to God: 'condemn me for my alchemistic attempts to create life out of celluloid. One thing is sure, life outside the cinema can never be matched for it is His creation and because of that, divine' (Degn Johansen and Kimergaard 1991: 159). His religious attitude is also implicit in the whole programme of restraint, where renunciation is used as a valid artistic principle. It is self-punishment and masochism, if not connected to that general propensity for sexual perversity that is always present in his work, then for the sake of art:

> Those of the Dogma rules that I myself have been responsible for are to a high degree
> designed with pedagogical motives in mind – a pedagogy directed against myself. They point
> to problems that I otherwise would be messing around with. The film has to be in colour, and
> if there's something I've worked with a lot, then it's the idea that the colours should be worth
> looking at. But now I've given myself a rule that says that I'm not allowed to mess with that
> (Monggaard Christensen 2000: 100).

Von Trier, who, in films such as *Europa* and *Breaking the Waves*, had his name presented in letters of a megalomaniac size, inflicted the ultimate punishment on himself when he in the last of the Dogma rules forbade all mention of the director. All the darlings of his earlier film style – the long, complex and calculated shots, the meticulous post-production process where picture and sound are polished and manipulated, the refined colours, the delicate use of music and the submersion in genres, especially in non-contemporary milieux and strange, artificial settings – all this had to be abandoned. The project was to find out how his artistic expression would find its way without its usual tools.

This aspect of von Trier's work can be seen as a development of cinematic expression through an artistic and technical liberation of method. It is comparable to his other attempts in recent years to demystify film-making and make it accessible to the general public. Besides being an egocentric individualist in contemporary Danish cinema, von Trier has also taken the role of generous leader figure. The individualistic *auteur* has become a collaborative player, an approachable member of teams and groups, as evidenced by his involvement in and enthusiasm for collective projects such as Dogma and the Film City. In the long run, his obsession with technique has not been able to obscure his more human side, and now that he is brilliantly playing with the breakdown of technique, the human being becomes unmistakably visible. His early films were virtuoso shows of an undeniable coldness and cynicism. In von Trier's later work the tone changes and his universe now has a more psychological and humanist dimension, though the warmth perhaps has a certain element of calculation and deliberate sentimentality. But rules are still his strategy in the creative process, for it is ever a matter of making rules, at times reflecting a pattern of shifting constraint and liberation, seemingly based on the assumption that whatever obstacle the artist is faced with, art will always find a way.

THE ART OF REDUCTION

Most recently *Dancer in the Dark* (2000) works with its own rules and a two-layer structure. Reality scenes are presented in a hand-held style and with subdued colors, while imagination and dream scenes (the musical sections) are presented in bright colour shots from the 100 stationary video cameras. *Dancer in the Dark* (which was accompanied by a number of Selma manifestos) is not a Dogma film. It breaks nearly all of the Dogma rules but it manages to keep two of Dogma's most effective means of expression: the intense acting and the hand-held camera.

Not surprisingly, von Trier's forthcoming film, *Dogville* (2003), has its own unique set of work methods. Everything is to be shot on a stage without sets, with only a few props to suggest the outline of the small Rocky Mountain town where the action takes place. There are connections to Brechtian *Verfremdung* and similarities with Thornton Wilder's *Our Town*. Von Trier has killed his darlings yet again, condemning himself to another reduction, another renunciation of cinematic tools. He has cancelled the use of locations and the impact of physical surroundings to see what he can do with nothing but story, actors and camera. Next time, perhaps, he will cancel the use of the camera and see what happens.

REFERENCES

Degn Johansen, T. and L. B. Kimergaard (eds), *Sekvens Filmvidenskabelig årbog 1991 – Lars von Trier* (Copenhagen: Copenhagen University, 1991).

Halliwell, L., *Halliwell's Filmgoer's and Video Viewer's Companion* (London: Paladin, 1989).

Hjort, M. and I. Bondebjerg (eds), *The Danish Directors: Dialogues on a Contemporary National Cinema* (Bristol: Intellect, 2001).

Monggaard Christensen, C., 'Danske dogmer', in P. Christensen and B. Tao Michaëlis (eds), *Film & Fin de Siècle* (Copenhagen: Gyldendal, 2000).

Schepelern, P., *Lars von Triers Film. Tvang og befrielse* (Copenhagen: Rosinante, 2000).

von Trier, L., 'The Director on Epidemic', in *Epidemic* [press book] (Lyngby: Element Film, 1987).

von Trier, L., *Breaking the Waves* (Copenhagen: Per Kofod, 1996).

von Trier, L., *Dogme 2: Idioterne, Manuskript og dagbog* (Copenhagen: Gyldendal, 1998).

4

Dogma 95 and the New Danish Cinema

Ib Bondebjerg

After 1995, the New Danish Cinema was influenced not only by the Dogma 95 concept but also by a general shift in aesthetic and generic approaches to cinematic production and style. 'New Danish Cinema' refers to a new generation of film-makers trying to get back to the basics of authenticity and a realist film technique and acting style, characteristics which are also to be found in the New Waves of the 60s. And as was the case with the first New Waves, the new generation of Danish film-makers is also developing a more relaxed attitude towards genre films, which are integrated in an international context. Genre films were officially banned by Dogma 95, which seems to indicate a difference between Dogma works and other post-95 Danish productions. Nonetheless, it is difficult to overlook the inspiration from romantic comedies in Dogma films such as Søren Kragh-Jacobsen's *Mifunes sidste sang* (*Mifune*) and Lone Scherfig's *Italiensk for begyndere* (*Italian for Beginners*), just as it can be difficult to see the difference in cinematic style between a non-Dogma film like Jonas Elmer's *Let's Get Lost* (1997) and some of the Dogma films. All in all, although a specific Dogma aesthetic is visible in the Danish Dogma films, each is also very different from the others. Furthermore, there are thematic and stylistic traits shared by Dogma films and some of the other New Danish Cinema films. The Dogma rules have refined and created a specific formal and stylistic aesthetic, but many of the other New Danish Cinema films which do not adhere to the Vow of Chastity are still part of the same trend.

The intention of this article is to situate the Danish Dogma films, and especially the more recent ones by Lone Scherfig (*Italian for Beginners*), Åke Sandgren (*Et rigtigt menneske* [*Truly Human*]) and Ole Christian Madsen (*En kærlighedshistorie* [*Kira's Reason*]), in the larger context of New Danish Cinema. The focus is on the putative specificity of the Dogma project and its relation to the general aesthetic tendencies in other New Danish Cinema films. The point will be to show that features considered specific to the Danish Dogma films are in fact shared by other films that may to a certain extent have involved similar production processes, but certainly no formal commitment to any specific set of rules. Similarities can be seen not just in acting style but also in thematic and visual approaches, for instance, between Elmer's *Let's Get Lost* and the three Dogma films just mentioned. Parallels can also be drawn between a short film like Thomas Vinterberg's *Drengen der gik baglæns* (*The Boy Who Walked Backwards*, 1994) and the magic realism of Sandgren's Dogma film *Truly Human*. The question, then, is whether the special creativity found in Dogma really is linked only to rule-following or whether it is also linked to more general tendencies within Danish film culture.

RULES OF FREEDOM

There is an apparent contradiction in the Dogma films that is clearly expressed in interviews with directors who have followed the rules, a contradiction having to do with freedom even though the rules seem to be about restrictions. This contradiction is also articulated in some of Lars von Trier's statements in which he speaks about improvisation, despite the fact that, as the manuscript for *The Idiots* clearly demonstrates, almost no significant improvisation or major deviations from the script took place. Nevertheless, the rules are described as a liberation: the restrictions are clearly experienced as freedom. In an interview with von Trier (27 September, 1999; printed in Hjort and Bondebjerg 2001) I asked him why he co-wrote the Dogma 95 manifesto and his answer was clear: 'The whole idea behind the rules is that, in setting limits to freedom, we enhance freedom within circumscribed limits' (220). Von Trier's own reflections about his Dogma film foreground the idea of 'getting rid of control', but only in the sense of getting rid of established rules and norms. He points to a similar break with established norms in the early 60s, which provided the New Wave and even 'Swinging London' and the Beatles' films with the same kind of freshness and cinematic joy that one finds in Dogma (von Trier 1998).

However, this liberation produced by restrictions is not just the result of rules. Von Trier's earlier films were also governed in many ways by self-imposed rules and technical constraints, a fact that seems to indicate that even the pre-Dogma von Trier was working in a rule-governed aesthetic and cinematic universe (see Schepelern 2000, and this volume, pages 58–69). On the other hand, von Trier characterised his major popular breakthrough, the film and TV series *Riget* and *Riget II* (*The Kingdom* and *The Kingdom II*), as a work made with his 'left hand', indicating a broader tendency towards a liberalisation of creative energy. This freedom was derived from a need to try everything, even the silliest or most melodramatic genre. Thus, the creativity and liberation that come from following rules are not just the result of Dogma, but come from a broader and more general tendency in von Trier's own work and in New Danish Cinema in general, as Danish cinema in the 90s moved away from the restrictions and traditions of Danish National Cinema.

The sense of liberation felt through the Dogma rules is also clearly expressed in interviews with Lone Scherfig, Ole Christian Madsen and Åke Sandgren. Lone Scherfig has proven in her earlier film, *Kajs fødselsdag* (*The Birthday Trip*, 1990), that she can create a special intensity between humour and tragedy. *The Birthday Trip* is a bitter-sweet story about Danish men hunting for sex and love in Poland. The film plays on intercultural clichés and portrays the gawky and silent characters of everyday life. A clear thematic line can be drawn from this romantic comedy to her romantic Dogma comedy *Italian for Beginners*, which deals with similar characters who have a kind of magical breakthrough in life and in love.

Lone Scherfig's own relationship to the Dogma rules seems relaxed. In *Berlingske Tidende* (2000) she says that she has only made films she herself wanted to make, and that she has not felt any constraint in following the Dogma vows: 'We do of course have hand-held camera, but we are very relaxed in our use of it. It is used to get close to the characters so the audience can experience and feel things as they happen' (Scherfig 2000). She also says that most shots were done in one take of long duration, which made the film very easy to edit. There also seems to have been a common experience of guided improvisation while shooting the film, though *Italian for Beginners* does follow the script rather closely. But while Scherfig navigated the actors through the script, she was also open to the actors' suggestions. This sense of 'team spirit' on Dogma shoots is shared by almost all the actors and directors interviewed. The rules seem to allow new creative powers to free themselves from the more restricted and controlled movements often resulting from a more fixed camera and studio-based setting. The reversal of power between actors and the camera seems to be the core of the unique intensity often found in Dogma films.

Thematic parallels can also be drawn between Åke Sandgren's Dogma film *Truly Human* and his earlier productions, which are dominated by magic realism and heavy symbolism. In *Johannes' hemmelighed* (*The Secret of Johannes,* 1985), Jesus appears in the shape of a girl to teach the nine-year-old Johannes the truth about life, good and evil. The film combines an intensely psychological and realist perspective in the portrait of a child, with a magical symbolic plot. *Miraklet i Valby* (*Miracle in Valby,* 1989) is of course completely out of tune with the Dogma rules since it is a modern fantasy about two boys who are sent back in time to the Middle Ages. But the film has elements of the magic realism found in almost all of Sandgren's films and in many other contemporary Danish films for children.

Among other contemporary films about or for children is Thomas Vinterberg's fine short *The Boy Who Walked Backwards*, a film evoked in *Truly Human* in the scene where the nameless boy enters reality by walking backwards. But the same tendencies towards a magic realism can also be found in Aage Rais' *Anton* (1995) and Lone Scherfig's *Når mor kommer hjem* (*On Our Own,* 1998). In both films, the imaginary world of kids replaces or compensates for the harsh reality of social problems and family conflicts. So magic realism is not an invention of the Dogma films, and Åke Sandgren's Dogma film is clearly part of a larger trend in New Danish Cinema, to which some of his earlier films also belong.

Åke Sandgren experienced the Dogma challenge as a huge release. He found that it was 'an enormous relief to get away from the cumbersome, expensive production apparatus in which there is seldom any leeway for improvisation or new ideas during shooting. On a Dogma film shoot the director enjoys more freedom to work with his cast' (Sandgren 2001a: 7). He further comments:

It was so damn joyful ... I felt like I had been forced to abandon my manners ... the circus horses were suddenly forced to change direction. You plan your days and scenes differently. I knew that the actors and the story had to be in focus, and I feel good about having to take it lying down. I really enjoy it, because I discover that I can do things that I haven't already done. It creates an intensity ... The biggest difference is that you start working right away ...

Dickie [the photographer Dirk Brüel] and I invent as we go along; we have no fixed shooting plan. We walk in and create something, use our intuition and often film whatever comes into our minds and we make up new scenes (Sandgren 2000).

But, as he clearly states, freedom is also a very tough constraint on the normal process of editing, at least editing of scenes with sounds. In Sandgren's words this means that you 'cannot rewrite the script at the editing table' by adding or changing sound and music since the second Dogma rule states that sound must be recorded on location (Sandgren 2001a: 7). On the other hand, because of the ascetic rules of Dogma 95, Sandgren felt purified from his tendency to use too heavy a symbolism and a grandiose narrative style:

Originally I planned a documentary about a mythological creature, the *vira* that lives in Norrland ... But it got too grandiose, and I had trouble making the story credible. Something was missing. Then I was asked if I'd make a Dogma film, and I knew at once that I'd found my form – my essential form – that would never allow me to make the plot pretentious. The Dogma rules generate a reportage-like atmosphere that is a productive counterpart to my fable-imbued story (Sandgren 2001a: 6).

Ole Christian Madsen broke completely away from his earlier films with *Kira's Reason*. In his short film *Sinans bryllup* (*Sinan's Wedding*, 1996), he created a story about ethnic and cultural conflicts. This was also a strong theme in *Pizza King* (1999) with its in-depth portrait of two small-time crooks in the second generation immigrant culture in the Nørrebro section of Copenhagen, filmed in the same style as many New Danish Cinema stories about desperate young men.[1] His last work before *Kira's Reason*, the intense, dramatic and violent mini-series *Edderkoppen* (*The Spider*), continued the theme of desperate young men, although it was based on a true post-war story about crime and corruption. Ole Christian Madsen clearly states in interviews that the Dogma rules helped to free him from his tendency to make mainstream genre films about marginalised male individuals. His new-found freedom was used to produce a very intense, emotional love story, 'an intimate psychological story, where you move very close to the inner feelings and relationships between humans'. When he talks about the production process we find the same strong metaphors of joy and liberation that are found in all the statements from Dogma directors, the joy to be found in rules that set your creativity free. The film becomes intensely focused on the actors and the story as it unfolds here and now, not constrained by a huge cinematic apparatus:

It has been an emotionally exhausting, but also a professionally and creatively liberating experience to make *Kira's Reason* ... In *The Spider*, there is a demand for crystal-like precision, whereas the Dogma film is an attempt to use the resources available on location and to just be curious ... It was necessary to just lean back and let the actors play out in long shots from eight to fifteen minutes ... It was about giving the actors a great deal of freedom and about looking for their physical and mental signals ... I don't think it is possible to create a Dogma film without strong emotions ... it is as if the emotions must be doubled all the time to find their right expression. It is simply necessary to make them explode, to be very expressive, because you don't have anything but the actors, the camera and this lousy picture on a video screen. The greatest challenge when editing the film is to try to maintain the improvised energy which comes naturally from shooting this way (Madsen 2001a).

PSYCHOLOGICAL INTENSITY, AUTHENTICITY AND NEW REALISM

It is clear from the Dogma 95 manifesto and the rhetoric surrounding it that Dogma films are a declaration of war against the blockbuster and the mainstream film, and an act of purification from the reliance on technological manipulation often found in the dominant cinema. In many articles about Dogma 95, a line is drawn back to at least two historic breaks with mainstream cinema: Italian neo-realism in the 50s and the European New Wave cinema of the 60s. Both of these cinematic movements are characterised by a break with mainstream genre film, by a tendency to mimic the authenticity of documentary that moves towards a contemporary realism focusing on social themes, often with an edge of social criticism and militant ideology. All these elements are present in the staging of the Dogma 95 movement and manifesto.

But these elements are also explicitly highlighted by some of the directors of the three Dogma films we are dealing with here. From this perspective, Dogma simply means a return to a new kind of realism with a social awareness and political edge that revitalises the realism of earlier cinematic trends. In the words of Åke Sandgren:

> I wouldn't call *Truly Human* a political film, but I see the Dogma Rules as a signal that the time is ripe for a resuscitation of the political cinema. We've come closer to everyday life. Since the 1970s, realism has been a dirty word but audiences have accepted the Dogma films, which are very simple and evince a commitment to their characters and the life they depict. This is very gratifying because in my opinion, films like this are closer to being art. They take a stand and explore. They seek a truth, and although in some ways that's absurd, it's also an important ambition to possess. If they're entertaining at the same time, well there's nothing wrong with that. But audiences want to see them because they mean something (Sandgren 2001a: 7).

In that sense we can see a continuation and a parallel between Dogma films and New Danish Cinema as well as a discontinuity. There are clearly two main tendencies in Danish cinema after 1995. First of all, we have a more post-modern, fast-paced action style cinema often deeply inspired by American genre films. These films are characterised by a strong use of digital colour manipulation and an aggressive use of music, camera style and editing with shock-like effects. Although the films tell contemporary stories, this type of film uses a very expressive film language focusing on extreme and often desperate characters. Nicolas Winding Refn is the main exponent of this tendency in films like *Pusher* (1996) and *Bleeder* (1999), but it is also apparent in Ole Christian Madsen's pre-Dogma films and Ole Bornedal's thriller *Nattevagten* (*The Night Watch*,

1995) which in many ways started this trend in New Danish Cinema. The female version of this style can be found in Lotte Svendsen's colourful and often absurd satiric social comedy, which she describes as a cross between Mike Leigh and Emir Kusturica with more of an emphasis on caricature than naturalistic acting (see Hjort and Bondebjerg 2001: 260). However, Lotte Svendsen's films are clearly part of a revival of a political and social cinema.

The second trend is a new realism, marked by a more impressionistic and improvised narrative and based on character-psychology where everyday life is often portrayed poetically or in a very sharp, dramatic way. The main representative of this tendency is Jonas Elmer (see Hjort and Bondebjerg 2001: 249ff.), who is not part of the Dogma movement, but whose first film *Let's Get Lost* launched a film style linked to that which we find in Dogma films by Lone Scherfig and Åke Sandgren. A more dramatic, contemporary realism is developed in both Thomas Vinterberg's and Ole Christian Madsen's Dogma films, where the life of the bourgeoisie or the upper middle class in contemporary Danish society is placed under a microscope. The Dogma films can therefore be seen as the consolidation of a new realism already present before Dogma 95, but with a much more intense psychological and social portrayal of characters and reality compared to the realism of the 70s or the early Bille August films (see Bondebjerg 1997).

A very precise description of this new realism can be found in the interview with Ole Christian Madsen quoted earlier:

> We have already made so many films about marginalised people that it is almost unbearable. Personally, I do not have more stories like that to tell, so when I was asked to make a Dogma film, I decided it had to be a real love story. An authentic, intimate, psychological drama, which should at the same time insist on both a realistic and a magical tone, without dirty underwear and other kitchen sink characteristics. But at the same time it had to be a film taken directly out of everyday reality and shaped in the form of a new realism (Madsen 2001a, my translation).

The rhetoric in the Dogma 95 manifesto recalls the 1960s attitude of the French New Wave towards mainstream cinema, but it also attacks the New Wave for failing to reach its goal because of 'auteurism'. However, in many ways, the Ten Commandments in the Vow of Chastity constitute a definition of a new realism, a realism that has, ironically, been developed very much according to previous themes and tendencies in the different Dogma directors' earlier works. But a sense of liberation combined with a search for intense emotions, authenticity and a contemporary realism unites all the Danish Dogma directors. At one point in his diary written while filming *The Idiots*, von Trier defines the inner core of the manifesto and the rules as a 'search for the genuine'(von Trier 1998: 238). In *The Idiots*, there is a search for the deeper, more personal aspects of life, recorded as a kind of X-ray of the private self and of the family, but the film is certainly also a story about contemporary society. The technical rules in the Vow of Chastity seem to have evoked this search for the genuine, the authentic, and an almost documentary sense of presence. This feeling is reinforced by the hand-held camera style and the often grainy colours which signal a mode of documentary realism. Von Trier and the three most recent Dogma directors we are dealing with here – Lone Scherfig, Åke Sandgren and Ole Christian Madsen – all recount similar impressions and experiences.

Manifestos, as Scott MacKenzie (2000) has demonstrated, are rarely very successful in actually creating a movement with a uniform and well-established aesthetic style. However, this is perhaps the strength of at least the more technical and aesthetic rules of the Vow of Chastity, which do in fact create a framework for the search for authenticity in form and expression. But the manifesto in and of itself, with its very militant rhetoric aimed at the dominant cinema and the *auteur*, is not always lived up to by the Dogma directors, since most of them also work on big-budget movies and because they themselves are certainly very different *auteurs* and not a uniform group. Nevertheless, just as the first three Dogma films were about approaching the family institutions from different perspectives, the three films we are dealing with here also focus on family and love as visual and narrative metaphors for contemporary society.

ALL YOU NEED IS LOVE: LONE SCHERFIG AND DOGMA

Lone Scherfig's Dogma film, the biggest box office success in Denmark since 1975,[2] begins in a church, introducing a mad priest and his young substitute (Andreas), who is marked by the recent death of his wife. Nonetheless, it ends on a happy note in Venice where a group of rather lonely and shy people, all longing to find love and a place in life, seem to have found what they were looking for. Just as the romantic comedy *Four Weddings and a Funeral* (UK, 1994) managed to find a balance between farcical humour, warm expressions of love and moments of despair and tragedy, this film moves between all the basic aspects of regular Danes' psychology and social lives. The film is shot in the Copenhagen suburb of Hvidovre, and in its use of locations makes every effort to stress the almost depressing routine of daily life.

The choice of Hvidovre as the main location gives the film a visual anchoring in the everyday life of a typical Danish lower-middle-class neighbourhood. All of the film's locations are completely authentic and indicate an average, joyless, modern welfare-state Denmark. Already here we see a distinct difference between *Italian for Beginners* and the other big romantic comedy success in New Danish Cinema, Susanne Bier's *Den eneste ene* (*The One and Only*). The locations in Bier's film are stereotypical, just as the characters in many ways start as stereotypes, but gradually develop, showing the depth of their personalities. However, the film's style and narrative structure never waver from the conventions of the modern screwball comedy. The aesthetic of *Italian for Beginners* is very different, because the film is forced by the Dogma rules towards non-generic character roles and a more authentic and realistic milieu and dialogue. Furthermore, the narrative structure and dramatic lines of the film are much more linked to a tragic, poetic and romantic tone, where love, death and conflict are not just functional elements in a basically romantic plot. A comparison of key Dogma films with contemporary Danish romantic comedies made without the Dogma rules suggests, then, that the Dogma aesthetic really does make a difference. Yet some of the same realist, comedic tendencies can also be found in Scherfig's pre-Dogma productions.

In Lone Scherfig's *Italiensk for begyndere* (*Italian for Beginners*), Olympia (Anette Støvelbæk) and Karen (Ann Eleonora Jørgensen) will eventually discover they are sisters, while Olympia and Andreas (Anders W. Berthelsen) are destined to find love through tragedy (Still: Lars Høgsted, courtesy of the DFI)

Unlike both von Trier's and Vinterberg's Dogma films, but much like Søren Kragh-Jacobsen's *Mifune*, *Italian for Beginners* has a very steady and calm hand-held camera style, and utilises a very slow and rather traditional, functional editing structure. The only difference between *Italian for Beginners* and a classical Hollywood editing style is a very strong tendency to minimise the use of long and establishing shots, and to keep very much to interior locations. The framing of the images thus creates an atmosphere of intense intimacy and psychological depth, although not to the degree found in *Kira's Reason* or parts of *Festen* (*The Celebration*) and *The Idiots*. There are no longer sequences using close-ups or even extreme close-ups, but medium shots and close-ups are very dominant in the film as a whole.

The balance between tragedy and romance in *Italian for Beginners* is clearly deeper and more existential in nature than it is in Søren Kragh-Jacobsen's *Mifune*, but these two films do basically share the same commitment to realism in their use of location, dialogue and character roles, which is the watermark for all Dogma films. But the same tendency can also be seen, as already indicated, in Jonas Elmer's pre-Dogma film *Let's Get Lost*, a low-budget film also characterised by a more calm hand-held camera style than the first two Danish Dogma films. Here, the poetic realism in the portrait of a group of young people trying to find their place in life and to cope with the difficulties of love reflects the same intense and seemingly improvised realism and authenticity. However, *Italian for Beginners* still stands out in comparison with all other modern, Danish romantic comedies, both when it comes to realism and psychological depth.

If one examines the narrative and dramatic structure of *Italian for Beginners* there is a very clear pattern in the way the narrative unfolds – from individual stories to connected collective stories, from loneliness to love. The first seven scenes of the film provide a pretty thorough introduction to each of the most important characters, who are all marked by loss, a lack of goals and lack of social recognition. *Scene one* (the church) introduces Andreas, the young priest chosen to replace the old priest. Both characters have lost their wives and each man has lost some direction in life through this experience. *Scene two* (Scandic Hotel) introduces the socially and erotically 'handicapped' Jørgen, who is told to fire one of his good friends, Halvfinn, from his job at the Stadion restaurant. *Scene three* (the bakery) shows us the very oppressed and clumsy Olympia, with a character quite in contrast to what her proud name might suggest. In *scene four* (Stadion restaurant) Halvfinn, Julia and Jørgen are all introduced, and potential conflicts are developed and laid out through their interaction. *Scene five* (Olympia's father's flat) shows Olympia being humiliated once more, this time by her father, who treats her like a housekeeper, allowing the theme of a generational divide to be established. *Scene six* (the hairdresser's) has the first indication of a potential romance between Karen and Halvfinn, but romance is immediately cut off by Karen's mother, who is very sick and dying – the generation gap again. And *scene seven* (the hospital) is where the death theme is clearly developed, but where the serendipitous poetry possible in everyday life is also alluded to (Karen sees a piano player in the distance).

The narrative set-up here is a series of individual story lines apparently only linked by location and a common existential problem: loneliness and a suppressed identity. Consequently the next part of the film follows a double narrative strategy. On the one hand, a resistance towards the individual situation is marked both philosophically and in the almost incidental creation of connections between the characters. On the other hand, a series of tragic family events facilitates those incidental meetings with fate. The two narrative threads thus combine optimism, resistance, mistakes, hope and coincidence – all the elements that make for good comedy. Death is of course tragic, but in the film (as in life in general) it is also the basis for new hope: things must change and die to make way for new life. This tragic–comic axis and the intensity of the portrayal of the everyday lives of the characters give the film its poetic tone and deeper meaning, thus lifting it above banal genre clichés.

It is thus in line with the film's theme that both priests have lost their wives and their firm belief in God, but only one of them has lost the will to live. The first scene in the second part of the film is a hilariously spectacular episode in which Andreas preaches to a handful of elderly people in an almost empty church, but talks about paradise on earth, where religion and God are among us. This theme of love and compassion and the possibility of change for the better is also stressed by the fact that the female verger in this scene tells her story and turns out to be a former bank robber and drug addict. Change is possible! Furthermore, the theme is underlined in a later scene where Andreas is memorising his new sermon, and talks about God as an expression of love among people. The death scenes start immediately after the church scene, with the Italian teacher's death, which is followed by Olympia's father's death. And with her mother's death, Karen (the hairdresser whose real name is Carmen!) discovers that Olympia is her sister. Death and funerals spark new life and change – comic and romantic developments follow tragic events.

After the development of various individual story lines in the first part of the film, the second part creates new patterns of interconnectedness and in the third and final part, three new couples emerge: Halvfinn and Karen (Carmen), Andreas and Olympia, and Jørgen and Julia. If 'Italian' in the film's title symbolically stands for romance and freedom, and 'beginners' for the humble and somewhat clumsy suburban welfare Danes, then the romantic connections seem to link the exotic with everyday life. That Carmen and Olympia have such romantic-mythological names shows their hidden potential, but there is also an irony in ordinary, everyday characters having such names. Yet the film in fact insists on the 'divinity' and 'romantic' forces in us all. These aspects of human nature are consequently also expressed in the final scenes of the film which take place in Venice, opening the film's location to the outside world for the first time, to the open spaces of a city with far greater symbolic value than suburban Hvidovre. This strategy could be seen as a grandiose cliché, a hyper-Hollywood ending, with not just one romance and happy ending, but three! But as Lone Scherfig herself has said:

> It is a great challenge to make a film about a group of lost loners, but at the same time my film is a genuine expression of the idea that 'you can choose to be happy' if you seize the moment and act out the positive sides we all have, when you discover that something or somebody needs you (Scherfig 2000, my translation).

The strength of this Dogma film is that the banal wisdom of everyday life, social bonding and romance is given a new intense, poetic realism through the Dogma rules and the escape from the constraints of the cinema's over-reliance on the possibility of technologically manipulating the image.

MAGIC REALISM AND MODERN REALITY: ÅKE SANDGREN AND DOGMA

The opening sequences of Åke Sandgren's Dogma film, *Truly Human*, are truly magical. We find ourselves in the company of a modern Danish upper-middle-class family, as well as in the fantasy world of Lisa, the six-year-old daughter. On the one hand, we have a perfectly realistic and believable universe while on the other, we have a completely unrealistic and imaginative world seen as an infra-red p.o.v.-shot looking at Lisa, who is talking to her dead older brother. We are later told that her mother had an abortion, that the brother was never in fact born. Lisa has created her own imaginary world and companion, symbolic of the absence of human contact and love in a welfare society focused on career, money and a materialistic culture. From a narrative point of view, this is a story about a generation of stressed and overworked Danes who have alienated themselves from their own human identity and values and their own children.

Once again, the film takes place in very humble and everyday locations around the northern suburb of Bellahøj to which the family moves, when their old flat is demolished due to urban renewal. Before they move, Lisa overhears a conversation between her father (Walther), her mother (Charlotte) and some of their friends about the abortion. Her parents say that if they could have planned things differently, they would never have had Lisa, because they don't have time for her. So their career has resulted in both a dead and a living abortion. The narrative twist at the beginning of the film has the two 'dead' children trading places. Lisa is (apparently) killed in an accident during a typical modern Danish drive-to-work-and-everyone-is-too-busy-to-pick-up-the-child situation. The destructive and forceful nature of this quintessentially modern situation somehow causes Lisa's symbolic brother, who lives inside the walls of the family's flat, to be set free and he thus walks into society as speechless and blank as Kasper Hauser. He greets the world for the first time with open innocence and without prejudice or an understanding of social norms. It is through his story that we see the modern Danish welfare state as if through new eyes and from the outside.

He is looking, among other things, for his lost father and mother, and the story does indeed bring him into direct contact with them, but also with all the official institutions that act as a substitute for the family when you are an outsider. He becomes a victim in both a direct and more symbolic sense, but also a 'saviour'. The nameless brother meets his 'dead sister' in a symbolic scene where she appears as a fairy on a television screen and where the nameless brother is surrounded by a multicultural choir of children, a choir that appears several times during the rest of the film. As such, the Kasper Hauser symbolism is also connected to religious symbolism, as the lost son is a Christ figure who carries all the sins of mankind on his shoulders and lives with the lonely and with the outcasts of society.

The inner conflict between family values and natural human rights and a hyper-stressful welfare existence becomes a global conflict between the developed countries and the underdeveloped. This metaphor is made abundantly clear when the nameless son is dumped by his 'father' (Walther) in one of the largest refugee camps in Denmark, Sandholmlejren. After having escaped his imprisonment in the wall of the flat, the nameless son spends the first day sleeping under Walther's car. The next day, when Walther – stressed as usual – drives to work, the exact same accident that occurred with Lisa at the beginning of the film is repeated with the nameless son in her stead. However, the nameless son is only hit by the windshield and slightly hurt, and is picked up by Walther, who takes him with him to work. Walther decides to drive the son to the Sandholm camp when the young man makes it impossible for him to perform properly during an important presentation.

The satirical and symbolic dimensions of the film are fully developed at this point, as it gradually becomes clear that the nameless son is actually treated with respect and as an equal by the other outcasts and refugees. Since he has no identity, he takes the name Ahmed. For the remainder of the film, Ahmed the foreigner is treated with mistrust, beaten and bullied by his employer and even put in jail following paedophilia charges, all because of his foreign identity and name. Nonetheless, his quiet goodness, complete honesty and helpful human nature bring out the best in everyone he meets and in this way expose a world void of human goodness, but one with hope. His simplicity is like an

X-ray of the stony walls of an inhuman society caught in the vicious circle of modernity.

Åke Sandgren's film style is much more reportage-like than Lone Scherfig's, a fact already made clear by the very lively hand-held camera style in Sandgren's film. In this sense it has the same raw authenticity in its visual expression as the Dogma films of Vinterberg and von Trier, but it also has the magical, poetic and romantic touch of Scherfig's films. The combination of an imaginary and a realistic world, the parallel plots in the beginning of the film, and the presence of a symbolic son trying to become human – all this creates a richly metaphorical and visual universe. This mix and balance comprise exactly the elements of which magic realism is made.

Just as in Lone Scherfig's Dogma film, reality is magically restored at the end of *Truly Human* when the beginning is repeated and Lisa reappears. Before that, the relationship between Ahmed, Charlotte and Walther is turned upside down as Ahmed becomes the wise and responsible parent and they become children, crying on his shoulder. Ahmed releases their suppressed emotions and goodness, thus preparing them for Lisa's return. But when a miracle occurs at the end of the film in the guise of Lisa's resurrection, there is also clearly a much darker and deeper symbolic dimension. The neighbours in the apartment block where Ahmed, Walther and Charlotte live persecute Ahmed even after he has been acquitted of paedophilia charges. He is abducted, beaten and left by the side of the road with the letter P painted across his back. He then disappears into the wall of a new building. The narrative comes full circle, the beginning of the story is repeated and Ahmed is resurrected in the shape of Lisa.

The religious symbolism is quite obvious, but the Dogma style and rules keep the film very much on a realistic level and even turn the magic and the symbolism into a believable and credible expression of reality. The lack of technological intervention in the creation of his magic and symbolic universe makes Sandgren's film more realistic and the intensity of the acting turns a figure like Ahmed, who could easily become a cliché, into a being with genuine humanity. The two worlds and stories thus interact realistically and with an air of authenticity.

THE MERCILESSLY INTIMATE CAMERA-EYE: OLE CHRISTIAN MADSEN AND DOGMA

The first few minutes and sequences of *Kira's Reason* really say it all. We see the main female character, Kira, played by Stine Stengade, a young and rising star in Danish film, restlessly walking back and forth in the dismal Danish summer rain in front of a psychiatric ward where she has been for quite some time. She is obviously not well, and in a display of tense emotion and nervousness, her body and facial expressions spell despair. The camera is as frenetic as Kira is and in a very fast-paced sequence the camera follows her from several angles. Having been catapulted into Kira's neurosis, we flash back to her conversations with the psychiatrist in a voice-over as the camera fixes on Kira's right eye in an extreme close-up, the eye staring directly at the viewer.

These opening sequences are quite symptomatic of this emotionally intense and psychologically intimate film, where feelings radiate from all the cracks, pouring out of faces, minds and bodies in an otherwise very neatly composed, well-organised and eco-

In Ole Christian Madsen's *En kærlighedshistorie* (*Kira's Reason*), close-ups are systematically used to align the viewer with the main character, Kira (Stine Stengade) (Still: Per Arnesen, courtesy of the DFI)

nomically secure family. We are in the same social and psychological world as in Åke Sandgren's film, but there is also a clear parallel to von Trier and Vinterberg. Furthermore, a line can be drawn back to the cinematic universe of Ingmar Bergman, to his psychological films from the late 60s and the 70s, and to Cassavetes, especially *A Woman Under the Influence* (USA, 1974). There are also parallels with TV, for instance to Bergman's famous TV serial *Scenes from a Marriage* (Sweden, 1973), or with the TV plays of Leif Panduro.[3] This film and television tradition represents a realism in which the use of close-ups and non-verbal signs for the first time is developed more systematically. These trends do not so much represent a social realism as a sharp psychological analysis of the emotional costs of a certain way of life, especially for married women in a male-dominated society.

Although the Dogma rules add new elements and expressions to this tradition of psychological films, the film continues a long European and American independent tradition, which has resurfaced in Denmark both in New Danish Cinema and in Dogma. Ole Christian Madsen's film is more intense in its psychological expression and visual language, and it is a love story which, unlike Søren Kragh-Jacobsen's or Lone Scherfig's Dogma films, is not inspired by romantic comedy. It also lacks the touch of magic realism found in Åke Sandgren's work. *Kira's Reason* represents a clean and very unromantic anatomy of marriage, and though it has a happy ending, this is paid for by large sums of tragedy and drama. As it turns out, Kira actually loves her husband and her two children, but she has lost contact with her inner self and those emotions that sparked her love for them in the first place. So she first has to find herself and then *de facto* break out of the marriage in order to re-establish her love and reclaim her life.

Ole Christian Madsen has declared that apart from being a specific study of one particular marriage, the film is also about women and men as archetypes. On the one hand, Kira is an impulsive and imaginative woman with emotions and longings that are larger than life, but socially she is very vulnerable. On the other hand, Mads is a seemingly socially strong and self-controlled male, but he is emotionally handicapped and undeveloped (Madsen 2001a). The whole film is thus an emotional tour de force, a psychological battle between a woman and a man who are really in love but who are separated by a deep social and psychological divide.

The frenetic parallel editing between the female and male universes and points of view is visually very original. In general, the film is shot in medium to extreme close-up, but with only the female universe and Kira in extreme close-up. The film's visual set-up tells us that it is *her* film, and mostly *her* point of view. But *Kira's Reason* also uses the locations in a very direct way as psychological signs. For instance, in the beginning of the film, when Kira tells her story to a psychiatrist in a flashback, the camera focuses on an extreme close-up of her face. But Madsen also inserts empty and silent pictures of Mads and Kira's house, while she tells how everything suddenly felt wrong to her, and these empty pictures of depersonalised human beings reappear throughout. The camera is hand-held and shaky pictures from empty rooms and an empty garden signify the psychological emptiness and alienation found in this wealthy and highly structured welfare family. The parallel montage of Mads sleeping with Kira's sister while she is in the psychiatric ward is dominated by intimate but not extreme close-ups: we stay within the boundaries of normality. It is in the sequences after Kira has been picked up by Mads and the children and has been driven back to the house that we become aware of the relationship between extreme close-up sequences and Kira's p.o.v. or scenes where she is directly involved.

This aesthetic is definitely a result of the Dogma rules and the hand-held camera, which is just as hectic as in *The Celebration* and *The Idiots*, where we also find the same heavy reliance on close-ups. However, the systematic and consistent use of female or female related p.o.v. shots makes *Kira's Reason* a very intimate and psychologically intense film. But *Kira's Reason* also has other moods, such as the humorous moments when Mads and Kira suddenly break out of their social roles and behave unpredictably and with a certain abandon. Or when Kira completely loses control of her emotions and creates a scene, inadvertently ending up in some total stranger's flat in Malmö, Sweden, from where she calls Mads and asks him to come and pick her up. Or the dramatic showdown in Malmö which begins in a café, continues up and down the street and ends when Mads rapes Kira in a hotel room. The dramatic and socio-satirical climax of the film, which culminates with the party Kira has arranged for Mads' business associates, has Kira breaking down, but also finally winning Mads back, and is a masterpiece of visual choreography and verbal timing. 'All I really wanted to do was go dancing,' says Kira in a moving farewell letter written to Mads but read aloud to him before they are reunited in a dance. Body language or non-verbal communication is one of the key elements of this film, as seen in this, the last scene of the film.

DOGMA – A NEW REALISM

All the Danish Dogma films are, despite obvious differences and signs of individual *auteur* styles, clearly works with a concern for intense psychological states and realist principles. The Dogma rules are no doubt key factors here, for they forced the directors to focus on contemporary social conflicts and issues and to shoot on location. More importantly, they provided the actors with a new sense of freedom and an intensity of expression. The moving camera and the use of very long takes privileged an acting style that is much closer to real life and that allows for far greater freedom to use the human body, for non-verbal communication and emotional expression.

This new and intense realist style is clear also in the last three Danish Dogma films analysed here. But the analysis of the earlier, pre-Dogma films by the same directors also shows that although the rules released new creative energies and were experienced as a liberation from old habits and traditions in all three cases, there is clear evidence of thematic and stylistic continuities. From her first film onwards, Lone Scherfig was a director with a sharp sense of the comic, romantic and tragic sides of everyday reality; the Dogma rules allowed her to refine this gift. Åke Sandgren was already adept at magic realism, and this talent was further developed in a strongly realistic and symbolic fable suitable for both children and grown-ups. Only in the case of Ole Christian Madsen was the encounter with Dogma a breakthrough to a completely new type of film, one that essentially liberated him from earlier commitments to action-paced genre films.

Just as there is a strong continuity between films by the same director before and after Dogma, there are also clear connections between Dogma and New Danish Cinema. Many of the new directors not directly linked to Dogma have made films in the same realistic style. The powerful effects of Dogma on Danish film are thus not the result of a single magical formula working to create a coherent type of film otherwise not produced in the New Danish Cinema of the 90s. But Dogma has certainly strengthened the new wave of realism and its related styles of expression by giving this pre-existing tendency a distinctive, indeed properly collective, profile.

REFERENCES

Bondebjerg, I., *Elektroniske fiktioner. TV som fortællende medie* (Copenhagen: Borgens forlag, 1993/1999).

Bondebjerg, I., ' Fra Brønshøj til Hollywood. Bille August og hans film', in I. Bondebjerg et al. (eds), *Dansk Film 1972–1997* (Copenhagen: Rosinante, 1997).

Hjort, M. and I. Bondebjerg (eds), *The Danish Directors: Dialogues on a Contemporary National Cinema* (London: Intellect Press, 2001).

Jørgensen, J. C., *Leif Panduro. En biografi* (Copenhagen: Gyldendal, 1987).

MacKenzie, S., 'Direct Dogma. Film Manifestos and the *fin de siècle*', *p.o.v.: A Danish Journal of Film Studies* no. 10, 2000, pp. 159–71.

Madsen, O. C., 'Ikke nogen almindelig film', *Information*, 16 February, 2001a. Interview by Christian Monggaard Christensen.

Madsen, O. C., 'Alt handler om kærlighed', *Weekendavisen*, 2–8 November, 2001b. Interview by Marianne Krogh Andersen.

Sandgren, Å., 'The Name of the Game', *Information*, 15 December, 2000. Interview by Christian Monggaard Christensen.

Sandgren, Å., 'A Satirical Glance at Modern-Day Life', *Film* no. 15, May–June, 2001a, pp. 6–7. Interview by Claus Christensen.

Sandgren, Å., 'Getting Under the Skin of Marriage', *Film* no. 15, May–June, 2001b, pp. 3–4. Interview by Liselotte Michelsen and Morten Piil.

Schepelern, P., *Lars von Triers film. Tvang og befrielse* (Copenhagen: Rosinante, 2000).

Schepelern, P. (ed.), *100 års dansk film* (Copenhagen: Rosinante, 2001).

Scherfig, L., 'Man kan vælge at blive lykkelig', *Berlingske Tidende*, 2 December, 2000. Interview by Dorte Myhre.

von Trier, L., *Idioterne. Manuskript og dagbog* (Copenhagen: Gyldendal, 1998).

NOTES

1. The best-known films belonging to this category are Anders Winding Refn's *Pusher* (1996) and *Bleeder* (1999) and Thomas Vinterberg's *De største helte* (*The Greatest Heroes*, 1996). But it is also worth mentioning Nils Arden Oplev's *Portland* (1996).

2. By the end of 2001 *Italian for Beginners* had been seen by 870,313 spectators and, on the top-20 list of all films shown in Denmark in 2001, the film is number two, only beaten by *Harry Potter*. In comparison with the two other Danish Dogma films mentioned in this article, it was clearly the most successful: at the time of writing, *Kira's Reason* is still playing but has only been seen by 68,438 viewers, and *Truly Human* by just 53,666 (figures given by the Danish Film Institute).

3. Leif Panduro (1923–77) is considered to be the initiator of modern psychological realism in the Danish TV-fiction tradition. His twelve TV plays between 1963 and 1977 gathered the nation around a screen that suddenly became the mirror of the Danish welfare state, acutely reflecting the psychological costs of rampant modernisation and urbanisation (Bondebjerg 1993 and John C. Jørgensen 1987).

PART TWO

5

Naked Film: Dogma and its Limits

Berys Gaut

The Dogma rules are striking both in their specificity and in their apparent arbitrariness. What is the point of these rules? One answer is that they constitute a superbly successful marketing exercise, generating immense publicity for Dogma-certified films. A second answer is that they foster creativity by constraining the options open to film-makers: 'If there is something you are not allowed to do, it activates you to think: Then we have to do things in a different way!' says Thomas Vinterberg (Rundle 1999a). Both answers are good ones. But, interestingly, neither is the answer returned by the founding Dogma documents, the manifesto and the Vow of Chastity. These motivate the rules in a surprisingly specific way, arguing that they exist in order to combat the 'film of illusion' and 'the individual film'. The project of the present paper is, first, to examine these motivations in some detail; second, to show how they have shaped the first two Dogma films, *Festen* (*The Celebration*) and *Idioterne* (*The Idiots*); and third, to critically examine them, and show that despite their merits, they are in several ways flawed.

THE FOUNDING DOCUMENTS

It is easy to dismiss the founding documents as a mere exercise in irony. Talk of chastity, rules which like the biblical ones number ten, the associated ritual of confession, an overheated rhetoric against bourgeois art and proclamations that the rules are 'indisputable' conjure up an image of a cadre of deranged Marxist monks, shredding their way through cinematic history. The temptation not to take the manifesto seriously is strengthened by the revelation that it was 'written in only 25 minutes and under continuous bursts of merry laughter' ('Frequently Asked Questions', <www.dogme95.dk>). But we are also assured by the same source that though ironical, the manifesto is also 'most serious(ly) meant'. And it should be taken seriously, for it contains an interesting diagnosis of the plight of cinema today and how Dogma strives to rescue it.

The manifesto states that the film of illusion is decadent and bourgeois, its supreme task being to 'fool the audience'. It is aided in this by new technology, which washes away the truth, and applies 'cosmetics' to it; today this type of film is dominant. Its plots are predictable and superficial, not being justified by the characters' inner lives. The result is a set of emotional illusions, of love and pathos, generating only 'sensation'. The French New Wave correctly set out to undermine the film of illusion; but it chose the wrong means to do so: the individual film. This is identified with the *auteur* film; the *auteur* concept is held to be 'false', and itself based on a bourgeois perception of art, founded on individualism and freedom; so the New Wave was doomed to fail as a way to undermine the bourgeois film of illusion. The manifesto implies that the film of illusion is now an individual film, made by 'the individual artist's free choice of trickery'. It tells us that the Vow of Chastity combats both the film of illusion and the individual film, mounting a rescue action on cinema. The way to combat the individual film is by putting films into uniform, i.e. applying an indisputable set of rules in making them. It does not explain why the rules should have the particular form that they do, nor how they combat the film of illusion.

The manifesto raises several puzzles. What is the film of illusion? What is its connection to the individual film? And how is the content of the rules supposed to combat both? Talk of the film of illusion calls to mind the Brechtian school of contemporary film theory, with its attack on realism as 'illusionism', a cinematic practice which fosters the belief that we are in the presence of real events and real characters; this practice allegedly tends to strengthen bourgeois ideology, and it should be countered by the reflexive film, which calls attention to itself as a film. (For a critical discussion of the Brechtian school, see Carroll 1988: 90–106.) Much within the manifesto and the first two Dogma films, with their jittery, swooping images, might seem to support this reading of what is to count as the film of illusion and what as its remedy. But though the documents oppose bourgeois ideology, it would be a mistake to interpret them in a fully fledged Brechtian fashion. For the manifesto does not oppose the film of illusion to reflexive film practice, but to *truth*, and nothing within the document suggests that the goal is to call attention to the film as film.[1] The Vow of Chastity seconds this emphasis on truth, stating that the director's supreme goal is to 'force the truth out of my characters and settings'. And, since it is false that even realist films tend to produce the belief that we are in the presence of real events, charity also advises against a Brechtian reading.

So the film of illusion is not one that encourages false beliefs about the presence or reality of fictional events. Rather, it is one that represents or encourages false beliefs about the world – and given the anti-bourgeois rhetoric, it seems to be false moral and political beliefs in particular that the manifesto has in mind. Further, the film of illusion aims at producing emotions which are unjustified and sentimental, in that they rest on such false beliefs. Dogma films, in contrast, aim to show the audience how the world *really* is, and to evoke the emotions appropriately grounded on that understanding. Thus the manifesto does not oppose the realist film, as does the Brechtian view: on the contrary, in aiming to show us how the world really is, it itself endorses a kind of realism.

This way of understanding the manifesto's aim also explains why several of the rules have the content that they do. Firstly, Dogma's concern is to show how the world really looks and sounds. Hence manipulation of how things look and sound by the use of cinematic technique is discouraged: no optical work or filters are allowed (rule 5); no special lighting is permitted to transform the way things look, and the use of colour is required (rule 4); sound and images must not be separated, so the possibility of sonic manipulation is countered (rule 2); and even shooting on 35mm film (rule 9) was originally required because film was thought to be less susceptible to manipulation than video, as Lars von Trier remarks (Rundle 1999b).[2] Moreover, if one wants to show how the world really is, one will be concerned to counter misleading appearances generated not just by manipulation of cinematic techniques, but also by too great an interference with the pro-filmic setting. This thought can be seen as grounding the requirement to shoot on location and not to bring in props (rule 1): for if the director can construct whatever sets he or she wants, or transform locations as desired, then space is allowed for the full play of his or her fantasy, and the film is no longer recording how the world really is. Even the requirement to employ a hand-held camera (rule 3) has the effect that actors are given more freedom to improvise their characters, rather than having to keep to their predetermined blocked-out movement, and so again directorial manipulation of what is in front of the camera is countered. (As the rule explains, 'The film must not take place where the camera is standing; shooting must take place where the film takes place.' – i.e. where the actors are.) Rule 7 requires films to be set in the here and now; and this means that audiences are in a good position to spot deviations from how things really are – unlike, say, historical dramas, where specialist historical knowledge may be required to see this.

Secondly, as part of its aim to show how the world really is, Dogma is concerned to show not just how the world looks and sounds, but also to show the *kind* of events that can occur in the world. As already noted, the manifesto criticises the film of illusion as involving superficial action, i.e. plots which are not justified by the characters' inner lives (a very Aristotelian criticism). But in reality, people's actions are in part explained by their inner lives, their thoughts, feelings and characters. The film of illusion thus does not reveal actions as grounded in what they are really grounded in: psychological states. Two Dogma rules counter this tendency: most directly, superficial action is banned (rule 6); and so are genre movies (rule 8). Genre movies are likely to have predictable plots, being driven by generic patterns, rather than their plots being motivated by the characters' inner lives.

Turning now to the individual film, the manifesto takes such a film as having its paradigm in the practice of the New Wave, and identifies the individual film with the *auteur* film. The *auteur* concept is said to be rooted in the bourgeois perception of art and to be thereby false. If the *auteur* theory is understood as holding that a film involving several actors as well as a director can nevertheless be the product of a single artist (usually the director), just as a painting or novel can be the product of a single artist, then, as I have argued elsewhere, the theory is indeed false; all such films have to be understood as instances of collaborative authorship (Gaut 1997). However, *auteur* films so construed do not exist, and the New Wave could not be criticised for producing them. So the *auteur* film will be understood here as a film in which the director is the *dominant collaborator*, having significant input into all aspects of the film, typically (co-)writing the script, and enjoying final cut. In this sense, such films have existed. But what connection do they have with the film of illusion?

The answer lies in the Vow of Chastity: the directors swear to pursue truth as their supreme goal, and to do so by any means necessary – in particular, not allowing personal taste, good taste, the creation of an artwork or aesthetic considerations to stand in the way of this goal. They say they are no longer artists. From this, it is clear that they think of the director's attempt to fashion a film according to his or her own aesthetic sensibility as a threat to the pursuit of truth. The *auteur* film which gives the director a central role is precisely the type of film which most threatens the representation of truth. The individual film is prone to impose a director's potentially distorted vision on the world, rather than record an accurate picture of it. So construed, the main point of the rules is to combat the film of illusion, and avoidance of the individual film is the means to promote this end, being thus a subordinate goal.

Many of the rules have the role of constraining the directorial threat to truth. This is symbolically represented by the ban on crediting the director (rule 10). But it is more practically implemented by several of the other rules: as noted, manipulation of the representation of reality by cinematic techniques of sound editing, special lighting, use of filters and the use of the video camera for overt manipulation are ruled out (rules 2, 4, 5 and 9). The requirements for location shooting and the hand-held camera (rules 1 and 3) also restrict directorial control, making it more difficult for the director to force a possibly idiosyncratic vision onto reality. And the manifesto claims that the requirement to follow the discipline of rules will combat the individual film. As von Trier puts it, 'Many of the rules are, after all, designed to rob the director of his power over these things (lighting, colour, etc.), to make him concentrate on other things. To get something from the surroundings instead of forcing it out of them' (Rundle 1999b).

There may seem to be a pressing objection to all this: Dogma's style is similar to *cinéma-vérité*; is it really coherent to import a documentary form and assumptions into fiction films? In particular, does it make sense to try to restrain directorial control by the Dogma rules, given that the films are fictional? For the director must have exercised extensive control in order to create the fictional world in the first place, choosing and directing the actors, perhaps writing the story, and so on. Related objections have led one commentator to hold that 'contradictions haunt the [Dogma] project' (Christensen 2000b: 118). But it is not incoherent to take as one's goal the revealing of the truth about one's characters and situations, even though one has created them oneself. For this is in effect a commitment to follow out, according to rules of probability that obtain in the real world, what would happen if some scenario were enacted; this is to be contrasted with following out the implications of these scenarios by some other rules, such as the needs of entertainment, generic plots, etc. The director asks him or herself 'what if …' and rigorously follows out the implications – what we might call the discipline of truth. Nor is it incoherent to give up control over aspects of the fiction film-making procedure, simply because one is making a fiction film and therefore to some extent a created construct. It is not incoherent, for example, to decide to limit oneself to location shooting, just because the location is to serve as a fictional setting. Indeed, as we noted, since the director is not constructing a studio set, his or her fictions are constrained by the reality of a particular location, and this should help to enhance the discipline of truth.

I have argued so far that the manifesto and Vow of Chastity, despite their playful and ironic imagery of religious solemnity coupled with revolutionary fervour, offer an interesting account of what is wrong with mainstream cinema today, and how to combat it.

Cinema has become the purveyor of fantasy and illusion, aided and abetted by genuflection to the individual director's artistic dominance; the solution is to make the pursuit of truth supreme, and to restrict directorial control by a set of rules. That is, according to the founding documents, the point of the rules, whatever other functions they may serve. The cosmetics of film must be wiped away – and the naked truth of how the world really is should be revealed.

THE FIRST TWO DOGMA FILMS

Vinterberg and von Trier were the main authors of the founding documents, and their films were conceived with the rules and the programme in mind. Unsurprisingly, their 'confessions' of transgressions of the rules record fairly minor violations. Their films employ a hand-held camera (whose movements are conspicuous), are shot on location, optical work is not employed, and they do not credit the director. Their plots are not at least overtly generic, are rooted in the here and now, and are character-driven, i.e. the action is not superficial.

The main point of the rules is also respected: both films 'force the truth out' of their characters and settings. In *The Celebration*, the revelation is of Christian and his sister's sexual abuse by their father; in *The Idiots*, of Karen's loss of her son, and how this has affected her. The emotions grounded on these plots are not sentimental: indeed, the works both produce and justify the classical tragic emotions of fear and pity, and *The Idiots* is also at times very funny. Though as we shall see, the restraint on directorial control is far more problematic, there are some respects in which such control is restricted: the films at least appear to be ensemble pieces, with much focus on the acting. Some degree of control was ceded to the actors: for instance, von Trier asked his cast to bring to the location what they thought their characters would bring to an empty house, and so devolved this decision-making power to them (Rundle 1999b). And some scenes, such as the visit of Josephine's father, involved a high degree of improvisation (Jensen and Nielsen 2000: 20).

So the films for the most part conform to the rules, and aim to force the truth out of their situations. But not only are the films instances of the rules and accord with their (main) point, I will argue that they are also *about* the rules and their point. In *The Idiots*, the group's members are clearly intelligent, Ped, the group's diarist, being highlighted as prominently so. Yet their project is 'spassing': pretending to be idiots. They are spectacularly good at this; they are never rumbled as frauds, and we can see why, since they are extremely accomplished at acting. But the question that their behaviour prominently raises is this: what is the point of spassing? An answer is given by Stoffer (the group's leader) to Karen (the new recruit): he tells her that spassing is a search for one's inner idiot and that idiots are the people of the future. These reasons, with their pop-psychological, sub-Nietzschean resonances, are singularly unconvincing, and correspond to nothing in the characters' behaviour. Rather, it becomes clear that the characters have different reasons for spassing (also noted by Christensen 2000a: 38). For Stoffer, the point seems to be in part to maintain leadership of the group – spassing is his idea – and in part to vent his anger at authority figures (memorably displayed in his naked charge down the road, screaming 'Søllerød fascists' at the retreating man from the council). For Axel (an advertising man) and Henrik (an art teacher) spassing seems to serve as a summer escape from their dreary jobs. For Katrine, it is a way to rejoin the group so that she can try to win Axel away from his wife, and then to embarrass him at work when he refuses to comply with her wishes. Karen's motivation is different. She alone is prepared to spass in front of her family, allowing cake to dribble down her mouth at their but-toned-up gathering. Having lost her young son, and having been too distraught to attend his funeral, she returns to her family to show them what she thinks of their callousness, their repression, their cold, bourgeois cruelty. By spassing, she forces the truth out of the situation, revealing her grief and anger, and their inability to confront their loss; and she thereby morally condemns them. It is this closing scene which gives the film much of its extraordinary power, and yields the answer to the point of spassing. For the other char-acters, it is ultimately a kind of self-indulgence: for Karen, it is a way of revealing the truth about her and their situation, expressed in a morally and emotionally charged way.

Now consider von Trier's direction of the film. Following Walton, we can call the *apparent artist*, the artist who appears on the basis of inspecting the artwork to have made it (Walton 1976). So, for instance, the artist who apparently wrote Mozart's *A Musical Joke* is musically incompetent, even though Mozart himself was highly competent, which is the point of the joke. What is the apparent director of von Trier's film like? He allows a cameraman and a sound boom to appear in some shots; many shots are out of focus, clumsily framed and sometimes mismatched; he seems not to have heard of standard shot/counter-shot techniques of filming; in conversations, the camera pans from one speaker to another, often without reaching the person who is speaking in time; the axis of action is crossed; the image often wobbles unsteadily; the editing is abrupt and badly handled; shots are composed with no apparent consideration as to their colour balance or formal qualities; and so on. The apparent director of this film is spectacularly incom-petent and deeply ignorant of film-making. He is in fact an idiot. But von Trier is one of the most accomplished film-makers of his generation. Spassing is the activity of an intel-ligent person pretending to be an idiot; so the conclusion is inescapable: von Trier is spassing. And he is spassing by employing the Dogma rules, which, given their eschewal of several basic cinematic techniques and practices, can easily be employed so as to appear incompetent.

Since the film raises the question of the point of spassing, and von Trier is spassing by means of the Dogma rules, this renders salient the question as to what is the point of those rules. And given the centrality and prominence of the final scene, the answer returned by the film can only be the answer that Karen's behaviour provides about spass-ing – to reveal the truth about her situation, attacking the bourgeois conventions that surround her, and to produce the emotionally powerful effect of a revealed truth. But that of course is pretty much what the founding documents identify as the point of the Dogma rules. So von Trier's film is not only about the Dogma rules, it also returns the same answer about their point as do the founding documents. Indeed, von Trier acknowledged the parallels between spassing and the use of the Dogma rules in an inter-view. Asked about the moral of the film, he replied, 'The moral is that you can practise the technique – the Dogme technique or the idiot technique – from now to kingdom come without anything coming out of it unless you have a profound, passionate desire and need to do so' (Knudsen n.d.).

This interpretation makes the film in part about the conditions of its own making, a kind of documentary of its own genesis. The thought is strengthened by the documentary feel to much of the shooting; the inclusion of the interview scenes with the characters or possibly the actors themselves (the interviews are conducted by von Trier behind the camera), which take the idea of 'forcing the truth out' of his characters almost literally; and the fact that the characters spend much of their time being actors, as they act as idiots. And it is tempting to take Stoffer as symbolic of the director – the project is his idea, he directs the characters acting as spassers, and he is the authority figure within the group. His downfall also seems to re-enact the Dogma programme – he suffers a kind of nervous breakdown in the latter half of the film, his authority lessens, the group gradually disintegrates, and it is Susanne and Karen who emerge as central figures, commanding a moral sensitivity and insight that Stoffer never did. Even the pervasive use of nakedness in the film suggests the central trope of Dogma – stripping film of its cosmetics.

The Celebration is also in part about the Dogma rules and their point, though perhaps less overtly so than is *The Idiots*. Certainly there is no adoption of an idiot persona by use of the Dogma rules in *The Celebration*. On the contrary, the cinematography (Anthony Dod Mantle) and the editing (Valdis Oskarsdóttir) are almost breathtakingly bravura. But the focus is on rules of behaviour and their replacement by a different set of rules, a transition that offers a natural analogue to the rules of decadent cinema, and their replacement by Dogma rules.

The celebrations planned for the sixtieth birthday party of Helge are to be highly rule-governed. There will be a set order of speeches in his praise over dinner, beginning with his eldest son, Christian, followed by his wife, Elsie, and so on; there will be the re-enactment of family traditions, such as a march around the house; there will be a break-fast the next day; and all the rituals will be overseen by a toastmaster. The rules are those of an overtly bourgeois family, rules designed to keep in place the appearance of a happy, extended family. Christian's project, carried out at times despite his own panicked shying away from it, is to bend those rules to his own aims, to disinter the buried truth. His is not an anarchic, rule-less revolt: rather, he employs each occasion for the following of a family rule to substitute in effect his own rule, aimed at forcing the truth out of the situation. As the eldest son, his is the first speech over dinner, and he uses it to drop almost casually the revelation of his father's sexual abuse of him and his sister, Linda, as children. A stunned reaction follows. Having overcome his panic, and fortified by the support of his childhood friend, the cook, Kim, he then proposes a toast to his father as his sister's murderer. Again, this is not an anarchic revolt: rules are followed, but bent to his purpose of revealing the truth. His mother, Elsie, later makes a speech, and asks him to reply, offering an apology. Again, he follows a rule, the rule of reply – and accuses her of having known about the sexual abuse, and wilfully ignored it. Having been thrown out of the house, he bursts back in to finish his speech, but has time only to hurl abuse at his mother before being turfed out again. His next intervention too bends the rules to his own purpose – he hands Linda's suicide note to his sister, Helene, as she wends her way in the traditional march around the house; and he then leaves a note with the toastmaster, asking him to request Helene to read out a letter – the suicide letter. It is from this point that others start using the rules to reveal truth. Helene reads out Linda's letter, Christian is finally vindicated, and Helge's patriarchal authority is broken. During the breakfast held the next day, Helge uses his speech to admit the truth of what he has done, and Michael, Helge's other son, makes another speech ushering him out.

It should be clear that the story of old rules hiding the truth, and new versions of rules forcing the truth from the situation exactly matches Dogma's announced programme, and can plausibly be seen as symbolising it. In fact, the symbolism is even tighter than this. The manifesto is a call to overturn bourgeois cinema; the family in *The Celebration* is overtly bourgeois. Helge's mansion is substantial enough to be a hotel, with a large number of servants, and the guests, decked out in dinner suits or evening gowns, are clearly very affluent. The majority of the guests and family are also racist, singing racist songs at Michael's instigation, and the women are firmly subordinate to the men, as witnessed by Elsie's relation to Helge and by Michael's brutal beating of his one-time mistress, Michelle. The bourgeois family parallels the bourgeois cinema. And what results? Revolution: a class revolt by the servants, who help Christian at each turn; a revolt by the women – Linda reads out the suicide letter, the female servants, Pia and Michelle, hide the guests' keys to force them to stay and hear Christian speak the truth. And a racial revolt occurs too: Helene, it is clear, will marry Gbatokai, her black boyfriend, despite the racism of the family. So the rule of truth here is also an anti-bourgeois rule.

Christian (Ulrich Thomsen) is forcefully removed from the celebration when he claims to be the victim of his father's incestuous desires in Thomas Vinterberg's *The Celebration* (© Lars Høgsted)

And just as the manifesto attacks the individual film, thus demoting the director from his autocratic position, so does *The Celebration* topple Helge from his autocratic command of the family, and exile him. The new order is not an autocracy, but rather a collective and equal society: Elsie does not exit with Helge, but stays with the family, her first sign of independence from her husband; Helene is liberated to marry Gbatokai; by implication Michael has found a new stability in his life; and Pia will leave her servant's existence, to live with Christian in Paris. The collective replaces the individual autocrat both in the manifesto and in the film.[3]

THE LIMITS OF DOGMA

I have sketched a sympathetic reconstruction of Dogma's programme, rendering it as coherent and plausible as I can, and have shown how the first two Dogma films do not just to a large degree implement the programme, but also are in part about it. The question remains as to how we should critically judge the programme.

Dogma film practice, at least in the first two films, is, as we have seen, generally in accord with the programme. However, there are two significant respects in which the films stray from it. First, as Vinterberg remarks, 'we are trying to step back from the product, trying to be as un-auteur-like as possible. Funnily enough, the result is some pretty auteur-like films' (Jensen n.d.). This is particularly true of *The Idiots*. Though in some respects von Trier ceded control to his cast, he nevertheless in many ways hoarded control for himself. There were three cameramen, of which von Trier was one, employed in shooting the film; but in the final cut, 80 to 90 per cent of the footage was shot by von Trier himself (Knudsen n.d.). Though he did encourage the cast to improvise, he usually selected one of the earlier takes, which were closely modelled on the script (which he wrote), rather than later takes, which were more improvisational; and the most important scene, Karen's spassing in front of her family, was not improvised, being very closely modelled on the script, and was accorded more time to shoot than any other scene (Jensen and Nielsen 2000: 13–14). Where it mattered most, von Trier kept control. Indeed, he even inserts himself into his film, conducting interviews with his cast from behind the camera in the interview scenes – just as Vinterberg inserts himself into his film, appearing in a cameo role as a taxi driver. Any Freudian would be heartened to see such clear examples of the return of the repressed.

Some will see such *auteur*-like behaviour as a clear sign that the anti-*auteurist* stance of the programme is theoretically flawed: even its originators seem incapable of keeping to it in this respect. But this would be a mistake: it clearly is possible for a director to cede more control to his or her collaborators than the two Dogma directors were wont to do. Nor should we suppose that a more collectivist film is necessarily a worse film: there are instances where films have benefited artistically from the conflicting intentions of their multiple collaborators (Gaut 1997). The *auteur* aspects of *The Idiots* are to be traced not to any flaw in the anti-*auteurist* stance, but more plausibly as Jens Albinus (Stoffer) remarks, to the fact that von Trier is 'a control freak who constantly tries to sabotage his own control measures' (Jensen and Nielsen 2000: 18).

There is a respect, though, in which film practice does highlight a flaw in the pro-

gramme. The manifesto wants to put films 'into uniform', holding up a disciplined application of rules as an antidote to the individual film. Yet *The Idiots* and *The Celebration*
are, it is clear, massively different in style and tone, despite their overall adherence to the
rules. This diversity is even more striking when one views later films, such as Dogme #3:
Mifunes sidste sang (*Mifune*), which manages to employ a hand-held camera (operated by
Anthony Dod Mantle again) with a steadiness, and an editing style with a conservatism,
that suggest that the film could have been a product of Hollywood International. (The
film also manages to be generic – a romantic comedy; sub-genre – whore with a heart.)
The fact that individual style and tone manage to flourish despite the films' appearing in
uniform is not to be traced entirely to the brethren's guilty indulgence in individualism.
The problem goes much deeper: *any* set of rules must fail to cover all aspects of every
action, simply because there is an infinite number of properties that any action may possess; moreover, any rule is subject to interpretation, and thus can be complied with in any
number of ways. And do not suppose that if one could agree on the rule's interpretation,
all would be settled – any interpretation is itself a rule, which can itself be interpreted in
different ways. (For the classic discussion of rule-following and its puzzles, see
Wittgenstein 1953: proposition 143f.) The brethren discovered the latitude for interpretation themselves when they differed about how to interpret rule 9, eventually deciding
that it covered only the distribution format. And the move to allow would-be Dogma
directors to self-certify, rather than for the films to be certified by the original Dogma
brethren, seems in part to have been prompted by controversies over how to understand
the rules and whether films were following them correctly. Had the brethren read
Wittgenstein, they might have saved themselves a lot of trouble.

There are further problems. Dogma is often thought to be a kind of realism, and I
have so interpreted it in the first section. But closer analysis reveals problems within the
programme. Distinguish *content* realism from *perceptual* realism. Content realism obtains
to the degree that the content of a film (its scenario – its setting, characters and plot) is
like the real world (the locations, people and events that occur) in salient respects.
Perceptual (or formal) realism obtains to the degree that perceiving a cinematic representation of some thing or event is like perceiving that thing or event in salient
respects.[4] These two kinds of realism are independent of each other. One could shoot a
very naturalistic film (high content realism) in a way that is not very perceptually realist
– for instance, it might be shot in high-contrast black and white through anamorphic
lenses, with jump-cutting. Conversely, a film can be reasonably perceptually realist (e.g.
shot in colour, employing normal lenses and unobtrusive editing) but to a large degree
be content unrealistic – it might be, for instance, a film of a Terry Pratchett Discworld
novel. Many of the Dogma rules help promote content realism: the ban on superficial
actions and genre movies, and the requirement to shoot on location, for instance. Others
help promote perceptual realism: the use of colour, for example. But there are limits on
how well the rules secure realism. Regarding content realism, though the rules restrict the
possibility of directorial deviation from naturalism in various ways, they do not and
cannot remove it entirely. Directors can still, for instance, create extremely odd characters and situations that depart far from their real world counterparts, even if the plot

follows out strictly what would then happen according to the rules of probability. Regarding perceptual realism, the Dogma rules have a striking anomaly: why does not Dogma have a rule requiring unobtrusive editing and very long takes (which are more like our normal way of seeing)? The exuberant use of complex montage in *The Celebration* is flag-rantly in tension with perceptual realism, since we don't see the world via jump-cuts; and *The Idiots* also makes its editing salient. Contrast this with, say, neo-realist films, or Frederick Wiseman's early Direct Cinema films, which do consistently pursue perceptual realism (as well as content realism). So, in respect of the motivation for these rules, construed in terms of a broad notion of realism, Dogma's adoption of some rules while eschewing others seems at times arbitrary. And Dogma's account of the relation of cinematic technology to cosmetics is also untenable. It regards technology as problematic, since it has led to cosmetics, i.e. anti-realistic practices. But while technology can be employed this way (both to create fantastic content and also to create perceptually unrealistic films), technology can be and has been used to create naturalistic and perceptually realistic films. The overheated rhetoric of the manifesto signally occludes this simple point.

Finally, and perhaps most importantly, the Dogma programme rests on too crude an account of the relations among individual vision, art and truth. The programme criticises the *auteur* theory for granting supreme power to the individual director, whose pursuit of an artistic vision threatens the presentation of truth. The remedies are to curtail directorial power, hence by implication moving towards a more collaborative form of film-making, and to avoid making films that are artworks. Yet while a director may pursue a path that occludes truth (Leni Riefenstahl, rather notably), it is also true that a group of more evenly matched collaborators may also have a biased vision of the world; and, conversely, a director may employ his or her power to give a powerful and accurate presentation of how the world is. Moreover, the programme's announced rationale for avoiding making an artwork is misguided, for it assumes that art is opposed to truth – that producing an artwork somehow threatens truth. Yet the pursuit of truth has been a central aim of many great artists (Dostoevsky and Dickens, for instance), and indeed it is a commonly recognised virtue of artworks that they give insight into the world, or are profound (i.e. reveal something true and important about the world). Dogma's implicit oppositions of individual vision to truth, and of art to truth, are simply too crude. And the manifesto's apparent equation of truth with an anti-bourgeois vision is also too simple, even by the light of Dogma's own film practice; after all, one of the revelations of *The Idiots* is that Stoffer's own anti-bourgeois position is as authoritarian as that of the conventional authority figures whom he despises.

The manifesto's announced motivation of the rules is to combat the film of illusion and the individual film. Though we saw in the first section that the rules do to a degree combat the film of illusion, in the present section we have also seen the limits to which this is subject, perhaps most strikingly in respect of editing. Nor does technology have the simple tendency to support the film of illusion that the manifesto claims. Concerning the individual film, we have seen that there is no invariant connection between it and the film of illusion, since directorial power may be used to pursue truth as well as to occlude it; the following of rules provides no sure resistance to the individual film; and it is a mistake to oppose art and truth in the way that the manifesto assumes. (Indeed, the first two Dogma films are, luckily for us, violations of these assumptions, being considerable artworks about important truths and to a large degree *auteur* projects.) Hence there are serious flaws in the theoretical stance of the manifesto.

The manifesto's own motivation for the rules, then, though well-grounded in some respects, also has several salient flaws. As we noted, however, the rules have other merits – they have created a powerful brand, and have plausibly stimulated creativity; and, not least, they have been the inspiration for two excellent films. But these facts should not be allowed to occlude the defects of the announced programme. And what may be the most enduring legacy of Dogma is not even stated in the programme. Dogma films are by Hollywood standards low-budget, and the reception of Dogma has generally been in terms of the merits and possibilities of low-budget film-making. The most cost-effective medium for shooting low-budget movies is video, a technology which ironically it was the initial intention of rule 9 to ban; yet both *The Idiots* and *The Celebration* were shot on video for economic reasons. Dogma announces the democratisation of cinema through new technology, and it has helped to advance that tendency. But the technical means for doing so involved the very technology that Dogma had initially sought to ban. In that respect, at least, Dogma has been a success despite itself.

REFERENCES

Carroll, N., *Mystifying Movies: Fads and Fallacies in Contemporary Film Theory* (New York: Columbia University Press, 1988).

Christensen, O., 'Spastic Aesthetics – *The Idiots*', *p.o.v.: A Danish Journal of Film Studies* no. 10, 2000a, pp. 35–60.

Christensen, O., 'Authentic Illusions – The Aesthetics of Dogma 95', *p.o.v.: A Danish Journal of Film Studies* no. 10, 2000b, pp. 111–22.

Gaut, B., 'Film Authorship and Collaboration', in R. Allen and M. Smith (eds), *Film Theory and Philosophy* (Oxford: Oxford University Press, 1997).

Jensen, B., 'Interview with Thomas Vinterberg', <www.dogme95.dk> (n.d.).

Jensen, J. and J. Nielsen, 'The Ultimate Dogma Film. An Interview with Jens Albinus and Anne Louise Hassing on Dogma 2 – *The Idiots*', *p.o.v.: A Danish Journal of Film Studies* no. 10, 2000, pp. 11–33.

Knudsen, P., 'The Man Who Would Give up Control', <www.dogme95.dk> (n.d.).

Rundle, P., 'It's Too Late: Interview with Thomas Vinterberg', <www.dogme95.dk> (1999a).

Rundle, P., 'We Are All Sinners: Interview with Lars von Trier', <www.dogme95.dk> (1999b).

Walton, K., 'Points of View in Narrative and Depictive Representation', *Noûs* no. 10, 1976, pp. 49–61.

Wittgenstein, L., *Philosophical Investigations*, trans. G. Anscombe (Oxford: Basil Blackwell, 1953).

NOTES

1. Though, as we will see, there are important elements of reflexivity within the first two Dogma films.

2. When the rule was reinterpreted to be about the distribution format, and not the shooting format, it was agreed that video could be used for shooting, but that the controls had to be set where possible to automatic, so that manipulation of lighting, colour, etc. were not possible (Rundle 1999b).

3. It is interesting to compare *The Celebration* to *The Rules of the Game* (France, 1939), to which it seems to allude at several points. Both films are set in a large mansion, with a bourgeois family presiding over a gathering of friends and family; the order is revealed as corrupt, and its rule is denounced. But, though in form a comedy, *The Rules of the Game* has an ultimately tragic vision: the truth of André Jurieu's killing is smoothed over, and we know that the corrupt order will fall to a German invasion. Though not in form a comedy, *The Celebration* in contrast has an optimistic vision: the old order is overturned, and a better one replaces it. Dogma is essentially an optimistic programme.

4. There are complex philosophical issues concerning what would be the criteria of salience on these definitions, but I'll ignore these complexities here for the sake of ease of exposition.

6

Artistic Self-Reflexivity in *The King is Alive* and *Strass*

Paisley Livingston

A salient feature of the Dogma 95 movement has been a critical reflection on the art of cinema – beginning with the manifesto's contentions about the evils of mainstream cinema and the decline of *la nouvelle vague* as a viable alternative. Such critical reflections have been developed in contrasting ways in subsequent Dogma-inspired films, one of these reflections being the representation of artists, art-making and works of art. An elucidation of aspects of this artistic self-reflexivity is the task of this chapter. A first step is a brief examination of what the manifesto or Vow of Chastity can tell us on this score. Focusing on the explicit attack on cinematic illusion, I explore different ways of understanding this theme and conjecture that a central object of the Dogma critique – charitably construed and extended – is the cinema of fantasy. My discussion of the difference between fantasy and fiction sets the stage for an analysis of the forms and functions of artistic self-reflexivity in Dogme #4: *The King is Alive* and Dogme #20: *Strass*. As the other papers in this book amply demonstrate, it is unlikely that a single, coherent interpretation can line up all of the ducks of Dogma in a tidy row. Thus I undertake no systematic survey of Dogma in this chapter, aiming instead to single out what I take to be significant aspects of the two films under discussion.

FROM PROGNOSTIC TO DIAGNOSTIC: ON THE MANIFESTO'S CRITIQUE OF ILLUSION

The manifesto has been lucidly analysed elsewhere (see, in particular, Berys Gaut in this volume, pages 89–93), but a few points need to be made in this context concerning some additional implications of the 'nested' aesthetics in the two films to be discussed in this chapter. On the brethren's account, the oppressive *'cinéma de papa'* from which *la nouvelle vague* ultimately failed to free itself is a globally dominant system of production, marketing and distribution in which large-scale money, machines and propaganda are harnessed to the service of 'illusion'. As this core evil remains undefined in the manifesto, readers must draw their own inferences as to which specific features of 'mainstream cinema' are under indictment – an obvious danger being the temptation simply to fill in the blanks with one's own preferred complaints about 'McMovie'. Our inferences on this score can be guided in part by our interpretation of the rules themselves, on the mildly risky assumption that the manifesto's prognostic cogently responds to its own understated diagnostic. The prognostic does, in any case, rather unambiguously redirect film-makers' attention away from scenographic construction and technically elaborate use of the means of audiovisual depiction (as indicated in the injunctions against sets, props, optical work, filters, etc.). Attention is instead directed towards the articulation of story and perform-ance by means of a pared-down approach to such specifically cinematic crafts as editing, camerawork and sound-image relations.

Yet how, one may well wonder, is this general strategy supposed to achieve a break with illusion? It clearly cannot do so if we rely upon that *'pensée '68'* article of faith which was that the real source of the illusion is cinematic representation *per se* (as in *'effets idéologiques de l'appareil de base'*). Nor is the Dogma critique of illusion plausibly inter-preted along Brechtian lines, as Gaut usefully points out in his essay. Nor do the Dogma rules promise to free anyone from illusion if the latter is thought of in terms of *fiction*. Although the manifesto does call for a cinema made in the service of truth ('My supreme goal is to force the truth out of my characters and settings'), such an exhortation is per-fectly compatible with the emphasis on fictional storytelling that runs throughout the Dogma corpus and manifesto (characters and settings are, after all, elements of fiction). Whatever else it may be, Dogma is not a non-fiction movement: even *Strass*, with its extended, *mise en abyme* documentary, is a work of fiction.

If neither cinematic representation nor fiction is illusion, then what is? The word 'illusion' can, of course, be used in many ways, and what is needed is a more charitable and theoretically developed manner of reading the manifesto's mobilisation of this term. My proposal in this regard is that the primary target be understood as the dominant cinema's reduction of imaginative fiction to certain forms of fantasy. That not all fiction is 'illusion' in the sense of fantasy is what saves the Dogma storytellers from the sheer incoherence of condemning cinematic illusion and then going on to make engaging works of fiction.[1]

The needed distinction between fiction and illusion *qua* fantasy may be sketched along the following lines: while fiction is a discourse the primary design of which is make-believe of various sorts, fantasy is a species of imagining (and fiction) which occasions pleasurable experience in a particular way. Although many fictions are like fantasy in that their imaginative contents involve radical departures from actuality, fantasy is unlike fic-tion in that it must in addition hinge upon a hedonically rewarding orientation towards events which are deemed by the fantasiser to be 'out of reach'. This latter clause pertains not to what we take to be the case in the real world, but to what the fantasiser believes or is disposed to believe. Suppose, for example, that a talented athlete looks forward with pleasure to a victory which he considers likely (but by no means certain). Such a person is not indulging in fantasy, and we would say instead that he or she is engaged in pleasant, hopeful thoughts about a possible achievement. Yet an amateur who enjoys watching a fiction film about a great athlete's victory could very well be fantasising, pro-vided, that is, that this spectator deems it highly unlikely or impossible to accomplish such a thing himself. Whether the spectator deems the events possible or likely is not always decisive, however, and the 'out of reach' clause is intended to express a broader condition. Sometimes the events fantasised about are not out of reach in the sense of being thought impossible or even unlikely; instead, they are out of reach in the sense of being deemed transgressive of some moral or ethical norm of which the fantasiser is cognisant. Such actions are in some sense illicit or taboo, yet the fantasiser derives pleasure from imagining what it would be like to engage in them.

One could devise a distinction between two sub-species of fantasy along these lines, namely, transgressive ones focusing primarily on illicit events, and others targeting situations held remote from the real. Psychoanalytical theories of fantasy tend to focus exclusively on the latter sort. I see no reason to take on board this or other, risky psychoanalytical assumptions about fantasy, such as the Kleinian idea that 'unconscious fantasy accompanies all experiences of reality' (Hinshelwood 1989: 37). Freudians of various stripes tend to characterise fantasy as a species of 'wish-fulfilment', yet it remains quite unclear in what sense the wishes or desires 'expressed' and 'concealed' in fantasies are and are not 'fulfilled'.[2] The one wish that fantasising can, of course, fulfil in a literal sense is the wish to indulge in fantasy, but the fantasiser need not have such a wish.

Fantasy, then, is a species of imagining defined in terms of its contents and hedonic pay-offs. Another, related contrast is between works of fiction in general and that subset thereof that may be defined as works of fantasy, i.e. fictions designed to promote hedonically rewarding imaginings about events the fantasisers deem 'out of reach' in the specified, disjunctive sense. Given such a conception, one can go on to say that cinematic fantasies are films in which the medium's representational techniques – its 'illusionistic' devices – are employed to guide, stimulate and enable the spectator's pleasurable imaginings. The pleasures that are the allure of such representations, we know, need not always be saccharine, as demons and dangers, as well as their violent overcoming, can be part of fantasy's picture.

Yet how can this account of fantasy serve to fill in the Dogma manifesto's attack on 'illusion'? Illusion is linked to fantasy in the relevant sense because in fantasy, the 'how' – that is, the rhetorical or technical devices – are subordinated to, and effaced in the service of the 'what' – that is, the 'out of reach' events that it is pleasurable to imagine. And it is this sort of hedonically motivated exploitation of cinematic artistry and rhetoric that is constitutive of the illusion or 'cosmetics' overtly denounced in the Dogma 95 manifesto: the make-up is not meant to be seen by the fantasiser, who is thereby allowed to enjoy the hedonically rewarding appearances unobstructed by thoughts about their contrived nature. Such a critique of cinematic fantasy is expressed in the Vow of Chastity's very title, and is fully consonant with the document's condemnation of the 'illusion' of pathos and love, 'the deadly embrace of sensation', and the communication of emotion through 'trickery' and 'cosmetics'.

Once the cinema of fantasy is taken as a primary target of Dogma's attack, many of the manifesto's other elements fall into place. The emphasis on contemporaneity of story and the requirement that films be shot on location fit well in this context, because they jointly bolster the constraints of verisimilitude and fact which fantasy loosens. The ban on 'genre', which has befuddled and scandalised some commentators, also makes better sense when understood as part of an anti-fantasmatic project. 'Genre', then, should not be construed abstractly as 'type', 'kind' or 'category' of film (for even a unique film is 'one of a kind'). 'Genre' should instead be grasped as referring to the mainstream cinema's system of stereotyped species of dramatic types, for in its most common usage in that context, a film's generic designation serves to inform producers and consumers alike of the sorts of story events, and associated pleasures, central to a product's design.

What reasons motivate an attack on the cinema of fantasy? The quasi-Marxist, quasi-religious rhetoric of the manifesto is not especially clear on this score. Its misleading, anti-aesthetic phrases shift attention away from one plausible line of response, which is that the production of props serving to stimulate a broad audience's fantasies tends to be a repetitive and artistically stagnant affair. The manifesto's most explicit ground for the rejection of 'illusion' is epistemic, as the brethren speak in the service of 'truth', implicitly promoting some form of realism. Socio-political aims of various sorts may also motivate the idea that indulgence in transgressive and otherworldly imaginings is not to be preferred over a range of more sober and constructive pursuits, but here again the manifesto is not forthcoming. One can, in any case, plausibly inscribe the Dogmatic critique of fantasy within the more general, cognate tendency of artistic modernism, aptly characterised by Herbert Read as 'an immense effort to rid the mind of the corruption which, whether it has taken the form of fantasy-building or repression, sentimentality or dogmatism, constitutes a false witness to sensation or experience' (1968: 290).

My hypothesis is, in any case, that a critique of cinematic fantasy and a search for effective alternatives to it are significant aspects of the Dogma project. It remains to be seen whether any of the films associated with the movement mesh with such an orientation to any significant degree and, as indicated above, it is not my contention that all of the Dogma films and utterances form a coherent system in any case. In what follows I shall explore the critique of fantasy in Dogma by referring to some significant moments of artistic self-reflexivity in *The King is Alive* and *Strass*.

THE KING IS ALIVE

A central element of this film's story is an attempt at a rather unusual staging of Shakespeare's *The Tragedy of King Lear*. Although this play-within-the-film never gets performed in full, parts of it are rehearsed and 'delivered' in a process that takes on great significance for both the characters and spectators. And it is the film's depiction of this process that develops a critique of, and an alternative to, the cinema of fantasy.

An elaboration of this point will require some retelling of aspects of the story – which retelling, however, cannot stand in for attentive viewing and reviewing of the film itself. Stranded at an abandoned mining camp in the Namibian desert (filmed on location at a place called Kolmanskap), frightened passengers and their driver seek to distract themselves as they wait for someone to discover them. The lengthy parenthesis which this crisis opens is soon filled with tense interaction and anguished self-reflection. Most of this conflict is conjugal, though there is also rivalry between the two youngest women, Catherine, who is French, and Gina, an American. When Henry, the intellectual in the group, proposes that they attempt a staging of *Lear* – based on roles he has written out from memory, the initial reaction is divided, some wanting to participate, others thinking it an absurd thing to do. Offered the part of Cordelia, Catherine refuses, but she becomes increasingly jealous when Gina accepts the part and grows closer to Henry. In a strange embedded narration, Catherine responds to Gina's request that she tell her something in French, a language Gina cannot understand but finds charming. Breaking into French as requested, Catherine viciously recounts their situation, vulgarly highlighting the American woman's stupidity and concupiscence. Then she shifts back into English, sweetly commenting that her incomprehensible utterance was 'a fairy tale'. This bilingual narrative is an illusion in the strictest sense, a lie that offers the hearer something she finds pleasant, but that masks the expression of a curse.

Preparations for the performance of *Lear* proceed slowly. Only Henry, an experienced actor, is comfortable with Shakespearean idiom and the mechanics of performance. The others are awkward and uncomprehending, for they cannot see how these old-fashioned sentences could apply to anyone real. Henry patiently encourages them to keep trying. In between the rehearsals the multiple conflicts between members of the group intensify, and then the rehearsals provide further occasions for renewed conflict. Angry at her husband, one of the women flirts with the bus driver and leads him off to have sex with her, but when she tells him her motives, adding that her husband will be especially bothered that she has chosen a black man, the driver refuses to play along and humiliates her. Yet she uses a rehearsal of the scene in which Goneril kisses Edmund (4.2. 12–24) to pursue her plan of torturing her husband with jealousy. Feigning dissatisfaction with her performance of Goneril's part, she asks to rehearse the scene three times, each time kissing the driver more passionately, until her husband wanders off into the desert in jealous anger. Another member of the party assaults the driver for what he wrongly characterises as the black man's transgressive affair with a married white woman. This man's aggressive, racist behaviour disgusts his passive and defeated-looking wife, who is incited to let him know what she really thinks of him, and declares their relationship finished. The jealous husband eventually returns to inform the others that he has found the corpse of the member of their party who earlier had marched off to find help.

In what is no doubt the story's most ugly and sordid business, Gina agrees to have sex with Charles if he will consent to play the part of Gloucester. He has previously expressed great disdain for the amateur theatrics, preferring to practice sand-wedge shots in the desert's capacious bunker. Yet when it becomes apparent to him that the young woman wants something from him, he is quick to propose a lewd *quid pro quo*. The ensuing fornication turns out to have been the culmination of years of longing and physical training, as the conceited man reveals in a gush of post-coital pride. Gina's body is but a prop in the 'realisation' of his imaginary theatre of sexual prowess, for he is oblivious to the girl's actual feelings while misrepresenting them along the lines of his desires. He pays for this later when Gina, having been poisoned by Catherine, is deathly ill. She viciously tells Charles off, expressing her disgust for his lechery and smugness. Devastated to have his erotic fantasies so violently negated by her, he urinates in her face, suffocating her, before he hangs himself.

The survivors gather in shock around a fire. Until this moment, their Shakespeare recitals have provided a diversion and, at times, an incentive and prop for their rivalry. Now they in turn recite lines which have a clear and direct application to their present anxieties, these 'performances' culminating in Henry's moving recitation of a suitably shortened version of the 'Howl' speech, spoken not only of the lost Cordelia of fiction, but of Gina:

> Howl, howl, howl! O you are men of stones.
> Had I your tongues and eyes, I'd use them so
> That heaven's vault should crack. She's gone for ever.
> I know when one is dead and when one lives.
> She's dead as earth (5.3. 231–35)[3]

To which Ray, no longer merely fumbling at playing Kent, responds: 'Is this the promised end?'

As if in keeping with Dogma 95 strictures, the players in the desert do not create a work of art, nor do they even bring off a complete staging or performance of a theatrical piece. Yet their fragmentary artistic efforts in the end achieve a purpose of playing which epitomises the Dogma 95 desideratum, which is to 'force the truth' out of characters and settings – including a bleak, unpleasant truth, the truth of anxiety that awakens in fantasy's pause. As the rehearsal scenes underscore, these players perform well only when they understand how the words could be spoken truly as the direct expression of thought and feeling. Such an understanding is finally reached through their critical encounter with the work and each other, the play ceasing, at the critical moment, to be a mystifying or irrelevant cultural monument – ceasing, in fact, to be a play at all.

STRASS

In its self-reflexive depiction of artistic activities, Dogme #4, I have suggested, contrasts the austere and courageous virtues of a poetics of authenticity to the delusions and fantasies that allow people to avoid the anxiety that accompanies the recognition of unpleasant truths. Dogme #20: *Strass* similarly employs embedded depictions of artists and their activities, the primary difference being that the Belgian film, in the manner of a Gidean *sotie* or farce, comically exhibits its values *via negativa*, that is, by vividly showing us where they have not been realised.

Strass is a work of fiction consisting entirely of a nested documentary or non-fiction film about a state-supported theatre conservatory in Brussels: with the exception of the final credits and the 'this film is a work of fiction' disclaimer with which the film opens, all that we see and hear is presented as the documentarists' work.[4] The embedded documentary includes depictions of its own making and reception, over-the-camera interactions between the documentary crew and theatre school people, and even a glimpse of the televisual broadcast of some of the footage taken at the theatre school. The director of *Strass*, Vincent Lannoo, plays the part of the documentarist, and we may well imagine that the word 'Strass' scrawled on a board, a shot of which is shown after an introductory sequence, serves the dual function of indicating the title of both the nested and nesting works (again, in the Gidean manner of both *Paludes* and *Les Faux-Monnayeurs*). This satire's primary target is neither the documentarist himself nor the style of audiovisual discourse he and his co-workers create, though questions about their intrusive and exploitative presence are raised at several points. Instead, the main subject is provided by the antics of the theatre school's teachers and students, especially those of the central figure, Pierre Radowsky (brilliantly portrayed by Pierre Lekeux), an extraordinarily offensive individual who tells us that he is famous for having developed something called 'open pedagogy'. As the conservatory's director informs us in an interview towards the beginning of the film, the gist of Radowsky's 'method' is supposed to be the abolition of all forms of power and hierarchy in the classroom – in short, some kind of generic avant-gardist fantasy of total emancipation. What the documentarists capture 'on the hoof', however, is Radowsky's unbelievably dictatorial and abusive manner with his students, the violent conflicts that arise when some of them rebel, and the tyrant's eventual dethroning and group humiliation.

A detailed account of these conflicts is unnecessary here, but a selective evocation of some key moments can serve to highlight the sharp contrast between the stated ideals of the school and its grotesque realities. Early in the film the documentarists surprise Radowsky quarrelling with a young woman who angrily declares that she is breaking up with him because she has found out about his sexual involvement with yet another female student. It soon becomes apparent that finding a replacement for this lover moves to the top of the teacher's agenda. Finding no prospects in his class, he cynically demands that the school's director break the rules and agree to admit some new female students. Radowsky bargains for three new prospects, but the director holds him down to one. At the ensuing auditions, it is obvious that Radowsky's erotic preferences will provide the decisive criteria. As soon as Radowsky has the desirable new student in the classroom, he demands that she strip naked in the presence of the other acting students and the documentary crew and cameras. When she refuses, he drops his trousers and assaults her. The others in the room put a stop to this, and the footage ends up in the news.

In short, Radowsky is an over-the-top 'sleaze', but he is one with an artistic rationale. The thrust of his experimental 'method' seems to be that good performances require spontaneous outbursts of emotion. One of the theatre instructor's most outrageous pronouncements on this score is that Shakespeare's theatre, like all good drama, is 'trance', and he seems to assume that the creation of worthwhile theatre necessitates the abolition

Pierre Lekeux as the abusive theatre teacher, Pierre Radowsky, in Vincent Lannoo's *Strass* (courtesy of Radowsky Film)

of any and all rules or conventions. He is at his most abusive in attacking a rival teacher whom he accuses of being 'conventional', and he assails students who ask for help with technique or guidance in understanding a scene. Promising to make one of the students a star, he encourages her to be 'an emotional machine'. To help get her passions stirred up, he ignores her protests and tries to fondle her breasts while she rehearses the part of Donna Elvire.

While Dogma 95 is an application of the doctrine that artistic creativity requires constraints, Monsieur Radowsky's entire approach can be seen as the living 'reductio' of any doubts one may have about that idea. In the vacuum left by the abolition of artistic norms and guidelines, what occupies centre stage is the wasteful display of performers' base impulses. Radowsky and his hapless students have the goal of staging a performance of Molière's *Dom Juan*, but it is far from clear how such a goal can be realised by the teacher's subjecting his students to his boastful and abusive tirades. The abortive rehearsals we glimpse suggest that the targeted acting style is but a species of shouting. The play, in any case, does not go on: when the theatrical troupe reaches Villiers-la-Ville, the 'sacred' festival site where they are to perform, they learn that they have no audience. This *échec de scandale* is the turning point in the school's relation to Radowsky: the conservatory's director, who has again and again supported the man, finally tells him off and informs him that he is fired; following his lead, the students take turns cursing and striking Radowsky, who falls to his knees, defeated.

Radowsky's Artaud-derived ideas about performance were somehow supposed to lead to a more genuine and valuable form of theatrical art, but the movie's final scene of crude, collective humiliation plausibly serves to illustrate the more likely outcome of any sustained quest for raw, unconstrained emotion and the abolition of artistic norms and constraints. As a 'guilty scapegoat', Radowsky is a symbol of decades of half-baked artistic programmes about theatre and violence, so many masks for self-indulgence and egotism. Finally, the avant-garde 'working' methods illustrated by Radowsky, who spends more time talking about himself than the play being staged, may be usefully contrasted to the process involved in the making of *Strass*. Weeks of improvisation and rehearsal led to the refinement of character, scene and story ideas, which were then further articulated in the filming of the partly improvisational performances. As production costs were kept to a minimum in keeping with the technical austerity of Dogma 95, multiple retakes were possible, allowing the performers collectively to come up with some truly genial moments.

Pierre Radowsky orchestrates a scene of domination in *Strass* (courtesy of Radowsky Film)

In sum, part of what is valuable in the two innovative Dogma films I have discussed can be elucidated in terms of a critique of fantasy and a corresponding search for a significant alternative to the arts of fantasy and 'illusion', be they those of the mainstream cinema or of the avant-garde. In both works the film-makers' search for that alternative is thematised fictionally through the depiction of the characters' relations to art. In *Strass*, the path is the *via negativa*, as not even the documentarists' veridical exposé of Radowsky et al. is presented as the needed alternative. Nor does the sorrowful, Shakespearean epiphany of *The King is Alive* stand as a positive model for the making of art, as it requires the sincere and assertive utterance of theatrical dialogue. The aesthetic norms implicitly underscored in these critiques of fantasy involve the values of authenticity, sincerity and clarity, precisely the opposite of muddled entertainment and distraction, the sexual propaganda of advertisement discourses, or the eroticised and predatory thinking that distorts the characters' interactions and leads to hatred and violence. The positive artistic values exemplified in these films are to be located, finally, in the brilliant dramatic and cinematic artistry of the performers and film-makers, in part brought within reach by the rules of Dogma.

REFERENCES

Hinshelwood, R. D., *A Dictionary of Kleinian Thought* (London: Free Association Books, 1989).

Hopkins, J., 'Introduction: Philosophy and Psychoanalysis', in Richard Wollheim and James Hopkins (eds), *Philosophical Essays on Freud* (Cambridge: Cambridge University Press, 1982).

Livingston, P., 'Nested Art', *Journal of Aesthetics and Art Criticism* (forthcoming).

Read, H., *A Concise History of Painting*, revised edn (London: Thames and Hudson, 1968).

NOTES

1. It is not my contention here that the emphasis on a critique of fantasy saves Dogma 95 from all incoherence. For example, I agree with Berys Gaut's claim in this volume with regard to the incoherence of the anti-*auteur* and anti-art themes.

2. See, for example, the equivocation around wish-fulfilment as 'imagined belief in, or experience of the gratification of desire' in Hopkins (1982: xxi–xxviii).

3. What Henry skips is Lear's request for a looking-glass to determine whether Cordelia is still breathing, a line which, if it may have some sense in Lear's context, has none in Henry's. The roles Henry has written out from memory are not, in any case, perfect reproductions of the relevant parts of the text of either version of *Lear*.

4. For definitions and a more general discussion of the phenomenon, see my 'Nested Art' (forthcoming).

7

Lars von Trier: Sentimental Surrealist

Murray Smith

Dada is working with all its forces toward the establishment of the idiot everywhere.
Tristan Tzara[1]

The Idiots is one of those films that has provoked strong emotions and high dudgeon, and seems to have been calculated to do so. (This should not surprise us, coming as it does from the director of *Breaking the Waves*.) But it is not a straightforward film in these terms; whether we deem it a success or failure or something in between, it is certainly an object of some complexity. As a film about a group of avant-gardist pranksters encountering a woman grieving over a lost child, shot in a part-scripted, part-improvised fashion and directly linked with a self-declared 'radical' movement in film-making, it is a film that traverses an enormous range of styles and modes of film-making. But in particular, *The Idiots* is very much a character- and actor-driven film.[2] So let us take a careful look at the emotional and moral landscape inhabited by the film's characters, the kind of response it wants from us, and consider what this suggests regarding the film's and its makers' stance towards the avant-gardism that is evoked both by the film's narrative and by the Dogma manifesto which inspired the film, and which the film aims to observe and exemplify.

The film begins and ends with scenes of emotional directness, but in between these two points most of our assumptions regarding the authenticity of the characters and their states of being are thrown into the air. What, then, happens at the beginning, and how do our initial assumptions begin to unravel? We are introduced to a rather plain, slightly dowdy woman (who we will come to know as Karen), first as she takes a horse-and-carriage ride around Copenhagen, then as she awaits service in a restaurant. Virtually penniless, she asks only for a glass of water, and is treated with barely concealed contempt by the waiter. Into the social gulf between Karen and the waiter flow our emotions – of compassion for Karen, and complementary anger at the waiter for the needless and petty spite of his actions. Then the focus of the action shifts, as a group of mentally retarded customers in the restaurant begin to 'act out', shouting and bothering diners at adjacent tables. The waiter tries to contain the situation, imploring the woman apparently responsible for the mentally retarded group to discipline them or remove them from the restaurant. Karen comes to the assistance of one of the disabled, trying to

The Idiots: 'spassing'

connect with him on his own terms and calm him down. Already victimised by the waiter, our sympathy for Karen is consolidated by her tenderness towards these victims of the waiter's desire to enforce social propriety (Karen is the only bourgeois figure, across the entire film, who responds with genuine and sustained sympathy to the retarded). Not five minutes into the film and Karen is already shaping up as a great sacrificial heroine, not so distant from the maternal figures at the centre of the Hollywood woman's picture.

Helping to escort the disabled folk out to a taxi, Karen goes with them (confirming our growing sense that she is troubled, drifting and unfocused). A little way into the cab ride and, quite abruptly, the rug is pulled from under our feet: the two purportedly retarded men burst into laughter, Stoffer collapsing onto Henrik with mirth, while their 'guardian' – Susanne – rebukes them but without any real force (indeed, she's enjoying the joke as she scolds the two men). Where does this leave us? Loosely speaking, with Karen. Like Karen and the other diners, we have been misled by the fake retarded – the 'spassers' – leaving us to wonder whether we have anything to gain from having been so duped. Or, more strictly speaking, while Karen has been fooled (and victimised again) by the spassers, *we* have been taken for a ride by the film.

All of this recalls a discussion of the nature of emotional response to fiction in a famous essay by Colin Radford and Michael Weston (1975). Radford[3] asks us to imagine being told by someone about a tragic death in the family. We are moved to pity for this person, only then to be told that the story was a fabrication. Naturally, our pity evaporates. And so it does with the spassers. But these are not really parallel situations: in Radford's scenario, someone lies to you; in the case of *The Idiots*, a fiction has been created, and the storyteller has simply withheld an important part of the fiction up to this point – surely a legitimate exercise of dramatic licence. The opening

The Idiots: cracking up

The Idiots: Karen's reaction

of the film is more like a 60s 'happening' – a piece of street theatre bursting unannounced and 'unframed' onto an accidental audience of bystanders – than it is a simple deception.

Now, you might dispute the idea that *The Idiots* presents itself to us as straightforward fiction. The style of the film evokes the direct cinema documentary tradition, most obviously through its use of hand-held camerawork and dependence on available light, bestowing on the film a pervasive rough-hewness. Moreover, the film eschews the most obvious, explicit markers that would characterise it clearly as either fiction or non-fiction – namely, credits. All of this conforms with the letter and spirit of the Dogma manifesto, which at one point proclaims: 'To DOGME 95 the movie is not illusion!' If it is not an illusion, then presumably it is – in some sense of this notoriously flexible word – real.

The problem is that the roughness is thoroughly contrived (and thus not 'real', in the sense of 'spontaneous'). Although clearly inspired by documentary practice, the hand-held shooting style was established as an option for fiction film-makers some forty years ago, through the work of the *nouvelle vague* and the New American Cinema directors like John Cassavetes and Shirley Clarke.[4] Film-makers who adopt this approach do not, obviously, plan out each halting camera movement, but they do knowingly shoot in a way that will result in a jittery, uneven visual texture; and to that extent they are adopting a style. I am not denying that this style allows for – indeed actively creates – a space for improvisation and unpredictability as the camera rolls, and in that sense we could say that *The Idiots* captures certain 'real' (unplanned, uncontrived) events as they unfold. And more generally, there are certainly moments in *The Idiots* where the impression of authenticity is so great that we wonder if certain figures on screen knew that the camera was shooting footage for a fiction film, rather than footage of a group of actually retarded people (I'm thinking of the patient, but bemused and increasingly perplexed, foreman at the Rockwool factory). This raises the possibility of another set of dupes created by the film: not only the audience (for the first few minutes) and certain characters (like Karen, and others later on, many of whom never get to know that the spassers are just play-acting), but also certain performers in the film.

But none of this overrides our underlying sense that this *is* a fiction film. Taken as a whole, the film does not try to fool us into taking it for a documentary, in the manner of *David Holzman's Diary* (Jim McBride, USA, 1968) or *Daughter Rite* (Michelle Citron, USA, 1979); the interpolated 'documentary interview' sequences, in which members of the group are interviewed for what we imagine will be a documentary about them, only *add* to the sense of fictional contrivance rather than undermining it. (I think this is so because these sequences compound the self-consciousness of the film's narration, foregrounding its ability to move between different modes of address, and stressing the different conventions of the documentary interview on the one hand, and the improvised dramatic feature film on the other.) That is why it would be a mistake to equate the withholding of the (fictional) truth about the spassers at the beginning of the film with a lie. There is a world of difference between believing that the foreman (whether he really is a foreman, or an actor) was not fully in the picture as the shooting occurred, and believing that we are watching a documentary about a real (existent, non-fictional) group of surrealist pranksters who visit a factory. This is the difference between *realism*, a feature of fictional representations, and the literal reality of the events represented, a feature of documentary or historical representations. It is as fundamental an epistemological difference as that between the fragments of newspaper embedded in certain Cubist paintings by Picasso, Braque and Gris, and the events reported in the newspapers themselves.

Nevertheless, we can say that in each situation – Radford's and that created by *The Idiots* – we have been *misled*, and the legitimacy of this tactic in *The Idiots* will hinge on what the film does with this opening manoeuvre. How does it use the annoyance, the offence, or even outrage, we might feel for Karen, for ourselves, and for the disabled whose predicament has been taken in vain – made the mere vehicle of a dramatic stunt, a means to an aesthetic end?[5]

We can begin to answer this question by continuing to track Karen's place in the film and, along with this, by considering the goals and motivation of the spassers. After the opening scenes, Karen slips from centre stage, as the film turns its attention to the spassers as a group. At moments she even becomes a secondary figure, eclipsed by the antics of the spassers and their (increasingly bitter) infighting. It is her peripheral status within the group, however, that allows her to shed light on various members of it at different points. In this sense, Karen constitutes a vital, binding emotional thread that runs through the film, even as she becomes obscured from time to time.

Karen makes no appearance, for example, in the interview sequences. And yet she is immediately marked out in the first interview sequence – through comments made by Axel and Katrine – as exceptional, not just another member of the group. Karen stumbles into the group and joins them out of emotional necessity, while the rest of them are engaged in a game of play-acting – literally 'acting the idiot' – motivated by the desire to 'poke fun' and 'take the piss out of' bourgeois proprieties. The legitimacy of this goal – or at least, the reality of its target – seems to be established by the mean behaviour of the waiter in the restaurant; but as the film continues, both the goal itself and its centrality to the group's activities come into question.

The question as to whether 'poking fun' is the sole or main motivation becomes explicit in those sequences in which the spassers lack an audience or foil other than themselves – consider, for example, the various scenes in which they spass within the house, such as the occasion when they have group sex. Without a bourgeois target – Stoffer's uncle, who owns the house in which the spassers have made their camp; a potential house-buyer; a representative of the local council – the satirical aggression of the group can only be directed inwards. This is what seems to happen in those scenes in which Stoffer questions the commitment of other members of the group to the project, and criticises the quality of their 'performances' (Jeppe in particular comes in for some harsh comments and treatment). The tendency reaches its apex towards the end of the film, when Stoffer challenges the other members of the group to take their spassing into their homes and workplaces. Here we can discern two other possible motivations for the group's spassing: a desire to experience the world differently and, in particular, more innocently, in which the group performs a therapeutic rather than satirical function (more on this later); and, in direct contrast to this, a will-to-power on the part of Stoffer, a desire to control and master the group for its own sake. The film poses the question: does Stoffer want to know what ('liberated', 'innocent', 'uninhibited') retarded sex feels like – or does he just want to fuck his friends, literally and thus metaphorically? If the spassers can be thought of as reviving a project of wilful Surrealist dementia, Stoffer is their André Breton.

The romantic relationship between Katrine and Axel opens up another front on which the purity of the notional (satirical) motivation of the group is challenged. Axel has a wife and child, and works for an advertising agency. As with the other members of the group, he appears to be on some sort of leave, which enables him to live with Stoffer and company and participate in the spassing game. But the two spheres of his existence – his ordinary life and the holiday world of spassing – begin to encroach upon one another. Axel is obliged to step out of holiday mode in order to take care of some urgent business at his office. Katrine, meanwhile, resents her place as the 'other woman', and seems determined not to allow her relationship with Axel to be confined by the boundaries of the holiday. The two conflicting desires collide at Axel's office, where Katrine shows up, representing herself as an important client at a meeting involving Axel and a senior colleague, throwing in some spassing really to complicate things for Axel. His job and career under real threat, Axel is blackmailed by Katrine into surrendering his credit card to her, as a condition of her ending the potentially ruinous stunt at the ad agency. Plastic cash in hand, Katrine then goes on a shopping spree, loading a shopping cart with luxury food items. The integrity of the group is thus compromised by their dependence on 'bourgeois' money: initially in the form of Stoffer's rich uncle's house, which provides the 'play space' necessary for the spassers, and here in the form of income derived from the ordinary working lives of some members of the group.

The purity of the project comes under threat in a quite different way in the last third of the film. One day a man from Søllerød (the residential district in which the house is situated) council arrives with an offer of a grant to help Stoffer relocate his 'home for the mentally retarded' to another district. (The offer is unsolicited, and we can only conclude that complaints have reached the council from nearby residents, who don't want such a

The Idiots: authentic hysteria

home in *their* backyard.) Acting interested for a while, Stoffer eventually launches himself into a tirade against the man and all he represents, chasing him off the property. This is one of many scenes – like the opening one in the restaurant – that suggest the legitimacy of the group's invective. So even as the film undercuts the idea that Stoffer and company act *simply* out of a sense of high moral purpose, it insists that the stuffy, intolerant attitudes they want to expose and mock are real enough. But Stoffer's anger in this scene is different in kind to anything we've seen before. He chases the man from the council away from the house and up a nearby residential road, cursing and shouting abuse ('Fucking fascists! Cocksuckers! Council bastards! Søllerød fascists! Shithead! Søllerød fascist! Fucking Søllerød fascists!'), gradually stripping himself and entering a demented, 'spassed out' plane of being. Eventually caught and restrained by his comrades, he is dragged back to the house and physically tied to a bed until his mania subsides.

This is the first of several episodes in which fake spassing is displaced by authentic hysteria. (Or at least, these episodes undermine our ability to distinguish authentic and fake derangement.) In the wake of the 'spass orgy', Josephine leaves for her room and is followed by Jeppe (the two have been shown to have an as yet unconsummated sexual interest in each other). They appear to sustain, mutually, the spassing act, as they embrace each other and make love; but as with Stoffer's outburst, Josephine's state of being slips imperceptibly into what now seems an authentic state of nervous breakdown. (We have glimpsed Josephine in a similar state earlier in the film; in this way, Josephine comes to parallel Karen, as a truly disturbed person in the midst of the fakers.) The next morning Josephine's father arrives – an event with momentous consequences for the group. Unlike the other visitors to the house – Stoffer's indulgent uncle, the house

The Idiots: authentic hysteria

buyers, the man from the council – Josephine's father offers a real (that word again, this time meaning something like 'staunch') challenge to the (already fraying) unity and certainty of the group. Refusing to engage with the group's games, he is at first civil, but as his patience wears thin with what he (and we, increasingly) regard as the self-serving and clichéd radical rhetoric of the group, he becomes contemptuous. It emerges that Josephine suffers from some sort of personality disorder (depression?) for which she is medicated; her father believes that she has ceased to take her pills, and is a danger to herself. Our intuition that she is genuinely ill, and not merely 'spassing', is thus corroborated. Having gradually prised Josephine free of the group, Josephine's father is about to drive his daughter away when Jeppe – her newly anointed love – launches himself at Josephine in a fit of *amour fou*, clinging desperately to the father's car and at one point lying intransigently on its bonnet. This constitutes the third instance of authentic (or, once again, not obviously or straightforwardly fake) madness. Howling and screaming, Jeppe is pulled away and restrained by several members of the group, enabling Josephine and her father finally to drive away.

Enraged by this act of capitulation, Stoffer ups the ante, challenging everyone in the group to extend the spassing beyond the holiday space and into their ordinary lives. In other words, Stoffer proposes removing the 'game' frame from their activities. In emulation of Russian roulette, a bottle is spun in the middle of the group; whoever the bottle points to must take up the challenge first. Axel is the first to be picked out – and he immediately withdraws from the venture and the group, a development adumbrated by the earlier action concerning Katrine, his wife and his work. The bottle then points to Henrik, who accepts the dare. But in the subsequent scene, Henrik simply finds himself unable to be so contemptuous of the elderly, middle-class ladies who populate his art classes, and who are so appreciative of his return. Henrik does not possess the burning hatred of the malcontent Stoffer, and his failure of nerve – if that is what it is – signals the end of the group.

It is at this point that Karen resurfaces dramatically and, as at the beginning of the film, becomes the focus of the action. As the members of the group gather their belongings to leave the house, she intervenes with a heart-rending speech of thanks to the group, which overrides the acrimony into which it has fallen. Just at the point when we are ready to write off the group – to varying degrees with each member – as more or less corrupted by hypocrisy, bad faith, naiveté or arrogance – so Karen's speech redeems them (again, in different ways and to different degrees). Karen's actions and reactions have throughout held up a critical mirror to the group, as they do in this climactic scene. From early on, she is bemused and disconcerted by the group, voicing some of *our* concerns: Why do you do this? Do *all* of these people deserve such ridicule? What about people who are truly disabled? How can you gorge yourself on caviar when there are people out there starving? As Karen gradually becomes bound into the group, her reactions nevertheless continue to differ from those of the rest of the group: after the scene at the ski-jump practice slope – the most innocent episode in which the group engages in uncompromised, 'idiotic' fun which harms no-one else – Karen says she feels guilty at feeling such happiness. Later, a visit by a group of actual mentally retarded people to the house accentuates the fault line between Stoffer and the others. The visit also takes the wind out of the spassing sails of the group – but it seems to liberate Karen, who begins to spass actively (as opposed to merely accompanying the group on their missions) in the immediate wake of the visit. And finally, as the rest of the group ultimately succumbs to Stoffer's desire for a 'spass gang bang', Karen quietly withdraws.

The central conceit of the group, and perhaps the film itself – that 'idiocy' is not to be condemned or pitied, but celebrated, especially as a tool of mockery directed at bourgeois hypocrisy, oppressive self-consciousness and other failings – can be traced back through the history of the avant-garde to the Dada movement, and still further, if more loosely, to Romantic art and philosophy, with its stress on the innocent and pre-socialised. We might note here also the prevalence of *idiots savants* in other von Trier works – Bess in *Breaking the Waves*, Björk in *Dancer in the Dark* – and in other Dogma films, like Julien in Harmony Korine's *Julien Donkey-Boy*. What's more, the central desire expressed in the Dogma manifesto – to strip away the 'decadent', corrupting and obscuring layers of advanced technology-for-its-own-sake, professional technique, generic convention, the pretension and mannerism into which a 'personal style' may lapse – is profoundly Romantic, even if it is partly expressed in the language of Lutheran renunciation. In this respect, the manifesto resonates with both the style and subject matter of *The Idiots*. Thus, while the Dogma manifesto castigates the new waves of the 60s for 'bourgeois romanticism' in their obsession with the *auteur* as creative individual, *The Idiots* is itself marked by a commitment to romanticism, albeit an anti-bourgeois variety.

But Romantic advocation of simplicity is clearly not the whole story, given the overtly ironic aspects of the characters, the film and the manifesto. Compare, for example, the seriousness of the 'First Statement of the New American Cinema Group' with the pseudo-religious buffoonery of the Dogma manifesto, with its proliferation of exclamation marks, vows of chastity, confessions and, not least, the self-ironising name of the group (von Trier, on the question of observing the Dogma rules: 'That's where I am very dogmatic. It's not interesting if you don't do it seriously – why do a Dogma film? It's a little game. Why play football if you don't want to put the ball in the goal?' [quoted in Kelly 2000]).[6] Or think of the scene in *The Idiots* in which Stoffer explains the creed of 'idiocy' to Karen in an idyllic forest space, while Nana is simultaneously shown to care about nothing but tanning her tits. Where, then, does *The Idiots* – and the Dogma manifesto – leave us in terms of the Romantic appeal to the simple and the authentic? Is it annihilated by irony – or does some shred of it remain?

The Idiots walks a fine line between cynicism and nostalgia. On the one hand, Stoffer's spassers become as much the objects as the vehicles of satire in the film, their pretensions skewered as mercilessly as those of the chic terrorists in Fassbinder's *The Third Generation* (West Germany, 1979). On the other hand, von Trier is not quite ready to give up entirely on the anti-bourgeois ideals, rhetoric and tactics of the avant-garde. Not only does the Dogma manifesto take the characteristically avant-garde form of a hectoring rant, it boldly states that 'the more accessible the [film] medium becomes, the more

The Idiots: Karen and Susanne

important the avant-garde', and goes on to elaborate the military etymology of the phrase by proposing that 'we must put our films into uniform'. Meanwhile, *The Idiots* provides plentiful evidence of the insular and self-centred character of the bourgeoisie. Notably, those characters who prove to be most tolerant and able to adapt to the needs of the mentally handicapped are not straightforwardly middle class – the foreman at the factory; the bikers in the café; and, of course, Karen, who has walked away in distress and disgust from her lower-middle-class husband and family. It is no accident that Karen is advanced, in the closing scenes of the film, as the redeeming angel of the group, for she comes to connect the group (represented by Susanne in the final scene) with the truly damaged outcasts and misfits of ordinary middle-class life. In this way, *The Idiots* supports the traditional rhetorical alliance between the avant-garde and the socially marginal.

REFERENCES

Carroll, N., *'Entr'acte*, Paris and Dada', in *Interpreting the Moving Image* (Cambridge: Cambridge University Press, 1998).

Kant, I., *Groundwork for the Metaphysics of Morals* in *Practical Philosophy,* trans. and ed. M. J. Gregor (Cambridge: Cambridge University Press, 1996).

Kelly, R., *The Name of this Film is Dogme95* (London: Faber and Faber, 2000).

Radford, C. and M. Weston, 'How Can We Be Moved by the Fate of Anna Karenina?', *Proceedings of the Aristotelian Society* no. 49, 1975, pp. 67–93.

Schlosser, E., 'Dogme/Dogma, or Live Cinema', <www.brightlightsfilm.com/28/dogme1.html> (2000).

Stevenson, J., *Lars von Trier* (London: BFI, 2002).

Tilden, L., Press package, *Reunion* (2001).

NOTES

1. Quoted in Carroll (1998): 26.

2. As Eric Schlosser (2000) has noted, 'While most of the interest in the Danish-based film movement Dogme has focused on its bare-bones technique, the heart of its appeal lies in the celebration of character – and actor … The essence of the Dogme technique is to provide favourable conditions for actors to find or create characters, favourable conditions to capture human movement, "happening" characters'.

3. I am concerned here only with Radford's argument, not Weston's response, so I will refer henceforth only to 'Radford'.

4. Leif Tilden, director of Dogme #17: *Reunion*, has remarked that 'many directors such as indie legend John Cassavetes have been making Dogma-style films for years' (press package, *Reunion*), a remark wryly echoed by Paul Morrissey: 'I was already making Dogma films thirty years ago [as the director of various 'Andy Warhol' films in the late 1960s and early 1970s] … Back then they were called something else, and were 'dogma' out of pure necessity. But I am probably thus far the only director who has adhered to the manifesto's point 10: that the director must never be credited.' Quoted in Stevenson (2002): 135.

5. *The Idiots* thus plays fast and loose with the moral notion most famously articulated by Kant, as the Categorical Imperative in the form of the 'Formula of Humanity': 'So act that you use your humanity, whether in your own person or in the person of any other, always at the same time as an end, never merely as a means.' Kant (1996): 79–80.

6. It would be easy to misread the tenor of von Trier's remark here, since he is, on the face of it, insisting on the seriousness with which he takes the Dogma rules. The point, however, is that the whole thing is conceived as 'a little game', which one should take seriously to the extent that one chooses to play it. All of this is in marked contrast to the earnest militancy of the New American Cinema statement.

8

Dogma in Paris: Jean-Marc Barr's *Lovers*

Ginette Vincendeau

Released across continental Europe in December 1999 as Dogme #5, *Lovers* was the first film as director and cinematographer for actor Jean-Marc Barr, star of Luc Besson's cult movie *Le Grand bleu* (France, 1988). Barr acted in several of Lars von Trier's films, including *Europa/Zentropa* and *Breaking the Waves*, forging a professional and personal friendship with von Trier which led to the *Lovers* project, the first Dogma film to be made by a non-Danish film-maker. *Lovers* charts the passionate but doomed relationship between two young lovers crossed by international politics: Jeanne, a Parisian bookseller (Elodie Bouchez), and Dragan (Sergeï Trifunovic),[1] a painter from the former Yugoslavia. Jeanne and Dragan meet in the bookshop where she works and they fall in love. She encounters a few of his Yugoslav friends, especially Zlatan (Dragan Nicolic), who lives in the same artists' studio compound as Dragan. A routine police check reveals to Jeanne and the spectator that Dragan is an illegal immigrant. He hides by moving into her flat but, at the end of the film, he is repatriated to Belgrade by the French police.

With its gentle romantic tale set in the iconic city of Paris, *Lovers* marked a departure from both the confrontational contents and the more anonymous surroundings of earlier Dogma films such as *Festen* (*The Celebration*) and *Idioterne* (*The Idiots*) and, while conforming to the requirements of Dogma, it clearly moved into the territory of the New Wave. This chapter will examine *Lovers* as a film that attempts a hybrid between the techniques of Dogma and the aesthetics and themes of the New Wave.

BETWEEN DOGMA AND NEW WAVE

Like all Dogma films, *Lovers* was much discussed on its release in relation to the ten Dogma 95 'rules'. Strictly speaking, it did not conform to the letter of the Vow of Chastity. Among its 'sins' (to use Dogma jargon) are the make-over of a Parisian apartment to serve as Jeanne's flat and the use of additional lighting both indoors and outdoors (Kelly 2000: 41). Presumably too, designer Mimi Lempicka's complex plotting of clothes for the two leads and a lengthy search for key props, such as the antique screen Dragan gives Jeanne, also contradict rule no. 1, which states that props 'must not be brought in' (many details of the shooting can be found in Françoise de Maulde's entertaining behind-the-scenes reportage, *Lovers*, *chroniques de tournage*). In other ways, though, *Lovers* certainly obeys the spirit of Dogma 95. The film's budget was very modest – 4.7 million francs ($400,000). By comparison, in 1999 the average French film budget was between 15 and 25 million francs.[2] The *Lovers*' crew was reduced to seven core members, including Pascal Arnold, Barr's co-scriptwriter and co-producer. Barr has repeatedly stressed the speed with which the whole project was completed from writing the script (with Arnold) in July/August 1998 to the completion of the shoot before the end of December of the same year, a speed he attributes to the Dogma method. Barr's film was shot entirely on location in Paris with a small hand-held digital Sony 900 camera (with the tape later blown up to 35mm film) and the film's visuals bear witness to this method: long, mobile and sometimes wobbly takes abound. The music is all diegetically justified. Characters are seen putting the radio or CDs on, or playing music; when we hear a nostalgic French song over Dragan walking in the street near the beginning, the camera tracks down to reveal it emanating from a nearby car in which a woman (Barr's mother as it happens) is sitting.

Lovers elicited a certain amount of critical interest because of the combination of Barr's name and the Dogma label. It was shown at the 1999 Cannes festival, the day after obtaining its Dogma certification (Roman 2001: 70). However, upon the film's release in December 1999, French critics were underwhelmed – in contrast to the enthusiasm and prizes previously lavished on *The Celebration* and *The Idiots*. Although a few reviewers showed indulgence towards the film's 'charm' and 'spontaneity' (Frodon 1999 and Péron 1999), many found it 'naïve' and 'banal', while others condemned its 'ugly' digital video image. In some cases, the film was judged a proof of the limitations of the whole Dogma project which, four years after its inception, was beginning to be seen as a 'commercial gimmick, a PR stunt' (Geuens 2001: 191). While Barr was candid about the fact that the credibility of Dogma enabled him to make the film cheaply (Roman 2001: 68), he may not have helped his own cause with statements such as 'I held the camera on the shoot without any experience as cinematographer. I felt like I was back at the beginning of the history of cinema' (Guéret 2000). Nevertheless, despite tepid reviews and poor attendances, the film recuperated its costs. According to Barr, 'When we went to Cannes with the film, we sold it to twenty countries and made back our money with the pre-sales to fourteen countries' (Roman 2001: 70). This enabled him to shoot two further films – *Too Much Flesh* (France, 2000) and *Being Light* (France, 2001) – which make up his self-styled 'free trilogy', although the latter two are not Dogma films.

By definition, as Jonathan Romney notes,[3] Dogma films demand to be judged according to special criteria, since they advertise themselves as 'different' and create expectations – in particular of originality and authenticity, of pushing at the boundaries of representation. After all, for its supporters, Dogma is 'nothing less than re-making the cinema' (Geuens 2001: 201). Consequently, though, the films are almost bound to disappoint. This was clearly the case with *Lovers*. It does, however, seem harsh to suggest, as *Positif* did, that Barr simply 'used' Dogma to disguise his lack of experience, as a 'pretext to film with a small crew without having to bother with correct lighting' (PhR 1999: 59).

The accusation of technical incompetence interestingly replays similar arguments from the time of the New Wave – especially coming from *Positif*, a journal historically hostile to the movement, and for which in the late 50s and early 60s, spontaneity and rule-breaking were similarly recast as 'amateurism'. Barr, of course, claimed the legacy of the New Wave in much more positive tones:

> It felt like the *nouvelle vague*, when the shoulder-mounted 16-mm cameras came along and put production in the hands of the directors themselves. I think Lars [von Trier], by using this digital technology, put himself in that same position and with *Lovers*, we wanted to try the same: to do what we want, and not just follow the same rules and marketing systems that have defined the cinema for the last twenty or thirty years (Kelly 2000: 37).

By conflating technology and mode of production with *mise-en-scène*, Barr exhibits a familiar misunderstanding of the New Wave – a confusion maintained at the time by *Positif* (and in many ways by the film-makers themselves), for polemical reasons. For if prominent early New Wave films were made by novice film-makers like Godard, Truffaut and Chabrol, the same films were shot by eminently professional directors of photography such as Henri Decae and Raoul Coutard.[4] In other words the impression of spontaneity and rule-breaking was underpinned by solid technique, not the result of improvisation. The novelty of the New Wave *mise-en-scène* was to film on location (as opposed to the studio sets of the Tradition of Quality) and to create a new topography – the real apartments, streets and cafés of Paris. This 'revolution' endured and since then, despite a return to studios in the *cinéma du look* and heritage cinema, location shooting has become part of the orthodoxy of French film-making, certainly for *auteur* productions. Thus, if Barr's small budget and crew replay the historic 'back to basics' of the late 50s, his filming in real Parisian locations does not constitute aesthetic innovation per se.

Beyond technique, topic and performances also explicitly place *Lovers* within the New Wave orbit. Barr's project is to explore the intimacy of a couple in the day-to-day unfolding of their romantic entanglement. On the surface the Dogma commitment to realism – its 'Neo-Bazinian' aesthetic (Conrich and Tincknell 2000: 173), as seen in the deployment of long takes – should make Dogma perfect for such a story. Yet, as Conrich and Tincknell also argue, 'Dogma films can only inadequately represent psychological interiority, desire, dreams and fantasy because of a commitment to the empirical' (Conrich and Tincknell 2000: 178). On the other hand, although many New Wave films appear to concentrate on romantic couples in the city, a closer look shows that their romantic tales are informed by a documentary realism but at the same time underpinned by genre plots (the gangster film in *À bout de souffle*, France, 1960, and *Vivre sa vie*, France, 1962), theatrical entanglements (*Paris nous appartient*, France, 1960), the musical (*Une Femme est une femme*, France, 1961), dramatic suspense (*Cléo de 5 à 7*, France, 1962) or large-scale historical events (*Jules et Jim*, France, 1962) … all of which are 'forbidden' under Dogma rules. And although *Lovers* claims to mix its love story with immigration from the Balkans, the latter remains a mere background; the device of the repatriation hardly sustains the plot. Even potentially explosive situations, such as encounters with the police or Dragan's drunkenness, are diffused into low-key realism or humour. Thus we are far from both Dogma's dysfunctional families (MacKenzie 2000: 168) and the New Wave's canny mixture of genre, documentary and romance.

What most clearly evokes the New Wave in *Lovers* is the performance style of the two central actors – Bouchez especially – which fits into the New Wave quotidian realist mode. Noted for her portrayal of sensitive but sensible young women in *Les Roseaux sauvages* (France, 1994) and *La Vie privée des anges* (France, 1998), Bouchez (whom Barr calls a 'Godardian heroine') here skilfully combines youthful charm, spontaneity and humour. And while Trifunovic came with a reputation as a volatile, highly strung actor from the Belgrade stage (a reputation apparently confirmed by his off-screen behaviour during the shoot) (Maulde 2000: 58), his performance in *Lovers* has a nonchalant charm that recalls the young Brialy and Belmondo. But in another, important way, *Lovers* differs from both the early Dogma films and the New Wave. Both aimed to put on international screens a new type of national cinema: French in the case of the New Wave, Danish for Dogma. *Lovers* by contrast inhabits an international media space that problematises this very category. It is now time to turn to the film in more detail.

A EUROPEAN FILM

From its title left in English in the original, *Lovers* advertises itself as an international production, and Barr was adamant that he had made 'a European film, not a French film' (*Queer View*, 1999b). Barr's biography is not irrelevant here. Born in Germany of an American father and French mother, the Franco-American actor/film-maker has spent his career so far moving between northern Europe, France and America, where he shot *Too Much Flesh*. The fact that he is married to a woman from the former Yugoslavia was stressed in interviews at the time of the release of *Lovers*, suggesting a close personal knowledge of Dragan's culture as well as of the dynamics of international coupledom. In addition, Barr's wife, Irina Decermic, plays a small part in the film, that of Maria, a young woman who insists on driving to the Seine after the 'Slav party' attended by Jeanne and Dragan. Decermic (a concert pianist) also plays the piano pieces overheard in Jeanne's building.

The central couple of *Lovers* embodies the increasing globalisation of Western Europe by virtue of their respective national identities (French and 'Yugoslav').[5] This enables the film to contrast two cultures and two habitats within Paris, moving from Jeanne's bookshop and flat in a central Paris *quartier* (the Bastille environs), to Dragan's studio in a more impoverished area – La Forge, an artist's squat in Belleville, seen by Barr as a 'totally "Dogme" kind of place in its spirit: a small haven of freedom and enthusiasm' (Barr, *Première* 1999a). Jeanne's discovery half-way through the film that Dragan's status is illegal provides a mini-climax in the unfolding of their otherwise unexceptional tale, and from then on a modest amount of suspense builds up (will the police catch up with him?), until his arrest and impending extradition at the end of the film.

Reciprocal language incomprehension within the couple is mobilised, as it was by Godard in *À bout de souffle*, for both comic and erotic purposes rather than tragic ones (this is not a tale of alienation between lovers) – when, for instance, Dragan teaches

Jeanne the correct stress on his nickname 'Gaga' and later tells her that 'you are so beautiful when you speak Yugoslav'. But mostly Jeanne and Dragan use English as a *lingua
franca*, in line with the film's title. For Barr, the young lovers are typical of the 'new generation' of those who belong to Europe rather than their country of origin: 'people,
especially Elodie's and Sergei's generation, speak English – or 'American', let's say –
much better than our generation' (Kelly 2000: 39). This is true, however, only of the
chosen milieu of the film. Jeanne and Dragan's English is that of the educated middle
classes (Dragan, as an artist, is only 'poor' in a Bohemian sense), a distant manifestation
of the French and German aristocrats in Jean Renoir's *La Grande illusion* (France, 1937)
who crossed national barriers by conversing in English, whereas the French and German
working-class characters did so by gestures. Similarly, poor Balkan immigrants to the
Paris suburbs today rarely converse with their French neighbours in English.

From her first appearance in the film, Jeanne is surrounded by books and thus associated with the 'culture-rich' city of Paris. The bookshop is a small independent one and
undoubtedly a different effect would have been achieved had she been a cashier at the
bookshop chain FNAC. High culture is the terrain on which the lovers meet: in the
opening scene Dragan walks into Jeanne's bookshop asking for a book about the painter
Rossetti. Dragan's paintings – those of the late Yugoslav painter Dusan Gerzic who
inspired the character of Dragan and to whom the film is dedicated (Maulde 2000: 73)
– are only briefly glimpsed in the background but they provide a key aspect of his characterisation. National forms survive as folklore: an old French *chanson* heard on the radio,
warm Yugoslav accordion music and songs. But Dragan and Jeanne commune through
international music: classical, jazz and rap. The lovers' cultural world is represented as
varied but consensual rather than conflictual. Thus *Lovers* represents national difference
through cultural variety rather than economic inequality (as opposed to, for instance,
Michael Haneke's *Code inconnu* (France/Germany, 2000), and puts forward a vision of
a young, mobile and bourgeois Europe steeped in Euro-American culture.
Unsurprisingly, the French Communist newspaper *L'Humanité* picked up on this point:
'The first French film with the Danish Dogme label is in English. This tells us a lot about
the commercial target of this trendy youth product' (Ostria 1999).

Lovers thus inhabits an uneasy transitional space in respect of its national identity,
which may in part explain why this 'trendy youth product', as *L'Humanité* put it, only met
with limited success. In its topic and setting, *Lovers* departs from earlier Dogma films,
but in its adherence to Dogma and its use of English, it distinguishes itself from French
auteur cinema. In the spirit of Dogma 95, it aims to challenge mainstream genre cinema,
including successful transnational blockbusters such as those of Luc Besson in which
Barr started his acting career, which better fit the 'trendy youth product' label. On the
other hand its celebration of a chic mixture of European high culture and Anglo-
American language and culture, coupled with the absence of any real attention to the
politics of exile (indeed to politics in general), puts it outside the realm of the post-col-
onial 'accented cinema' defined by Hamid Naficy (2001). *Lovers* is thus too French for
Dogma but too foreign for French *auteur* cinema, too small-scale for international youth
audiences but too trendy for inclusion in the category of 'exilic' world cinema.

LOVERS IN THE CITY

One much-discussed aspect of Dogma has been the ruling out of 'genre' film-making, or at the very least the 'rupturing [of] existing genre expectations' (Blincoe and Thorne 2000). But this rule is clear only if 'genre' is thought of within the classic Hollywood paradigm, as in for instance the Western. The notion becomes more problematic and slippery if genre is understood in a wider sense, since most films fall within a genre, if only that of 'European art cinema'. In this respect, *Lovers* falls squarely within the narrative of lovers in the city, which, especially if the city is Paris, has a long history in French cinema that can be linked to two distinct, though related, 'sub-genres'. One is 30s Poetic Realism, in which a young couple, through 'pure' love, transcends the constraints and corruptions of the social world, figured by antagonistic older figures and representatives of the law (as in *Hôtel du Nord*, France, 1938, *Le Quai des brumes*, France, 1938 and *Le Jour se lève*, France, 1939). The other is the early 60s New Wave, in which young couples roam the city of Paris, transformed thereby into a playground (*Les Cousins*, France, 1959, *À bout de souffle*, *Paris vu par*, France, 1965, etc.). Both traditions have continued to inform French films through the post-New Wave decades and have seen a forceful comeback in the 90s in such films as Chantal Akerman's *Nuit et jour* (France, 1991), Leos Carax's *Les Amants du Pont Neuf* (France, 1992) and Eric Rochant's *Un Monde sans pitié* (France, 1992). Besides the differences with New Wave films outlined earlier, *Lovers* partakes of this tradition in two major ways: the use of the city and the figuration of the lovers as 'children'.

In contrast to Dogma 95's aim to 'abandon aesthetics and good taste', *Lovers*, remarkably in view of its limited technical means, presents a view of Paris which is often beautiful (contra the critical accusations of 'ugly' digital images). In the opening shot, a blurred silhouette moves towards the spectator. The silhouette soon comes into focus: it is Dragan outside a shop, with classic Haussmann-like buildings in the background. Inside the bookshop, the warm glow of lights reflected on books, artifacts and literary posters connotes both Jeanne's warmth and comfortable Parisian high culture. Though not excessively glamorous, Jeanne's flat continues this scheme, with its elegantly eclectic décor of ethnic rugs, antique fireplace, theatrical masks and tall windows through which more old Parisian buildings can be glimpsed. When Dragan sells a painting, his impulse is aesthetic: he buys a beautiful antique screen for Jeanne in a nearby shop. His own surroundings in the first part of the film are more spartan, yet they belong to the aesthetics of Bohemian Paris rather than that of poor immigrants. In contrast to the confined spaces of exiled characters discussed by Naficy (2001), there is a sense of space around Dragan which enables him to 'express himself' as an artist – there are many paintings propped against the walls of the studio.

Outdoor scenes make excellent use of the beauty of the city at night, with walks through picturesque streets, the lovers kissing against the backdrop of the Louvre and two separate scenes on the Pont des Arts (a much-photographed pedestrian bridge), with glowing lights and historic buildings reflected in the water. The closing scene, in which Jeanne, sobbing, slowly ascends the stairs to her flat after the police have taken Dragan away, gives us ample time to look at the pretty old staircase and the courtyard through the windows. Thus both the monumental and the intimate city are a romantic backdrop to, and a participant in, the lovers' story. Significantly, their first brush with the police takes place on the street while they are kissing. The policewoman's gentle admonition to 'watch out, *les amoureux*, it's dangerous to kiss in the middle of the road' furthers the notion that in Paris, even the police are sympathetic to lovers. Alice, Jeanne's neighbour (and the only friend of hers we see), seems to exist only to comment on the state of Jeanne's love life, her parting words being that 'the important thing is to be together'. She is played by Geneviève Page, the 'Madame' in Buñuel's *Belle de jour*, the mature but chic and sexy actress providing another association with an erotic vision of the city.[6]

In keeping with the French 'genre' of lovers in Paris, Jeanne and Dragan are presented through the prism of youth and innocence. Jeanne's clothes emphasise a girlish appearance: a 'fun' fake leopard skin coat, child-like red woollen hats and scarves, sweaters and tights and even a bra in bright, pastel greens, oranges, purples and reds. Her short hair echoes Dragan's and at times their clothes too contribute to making them alike – for instance both wear similar red scarves. A scene pointedly shows them watching children on a merry-go-round in a park, which ends in them having a slightly tense discussion about Dragan not wanting children. Here, their physical proximity to the children, their own clothes and their dialogue emphasise their child-like nature. In Jeanne's flat and in Dragan's studio, the lovers 'play' at homemaking, drinking coffee, playing music, creating a regressive space in which only a fairy godmother (Alice) and a fairy godfather (Dragan's friend Zlatan) ever intrude, and even so minimally. Significantly, love-making remains off screen, this putting the accent on romantic love rather than sex, in sharp contrast to *The Celebration* and *The Idiots*.[7]

This fairy-tale childish universe enhances the marginalisation of the social world. Dragan constantly tries to get Jeanne to skive off work. Though she doesn't always oblige and is generally portrayed as more responsible, her work remains off screen after the opening scene. In a traditional (not to say misogynist) vision of gender, and notwithstanding the fact that she initiates the relationship, the film presents Jeanne as concerned with domestic details, while Dragan embodies the cliché of the *enfant terrible*, whose getting drunk, squandering money and running up huge electricity and telephone bills after he has moved into her flat are somehow 'justified' by his artistic nature. When things threaten to turn nasty, the situation is defused through music and dancing. In this respect Dragan's purchase of the antique screen also acts as a transfer of a potential social issue on to art (we briefly glimpse his agent but never see him at the 'business' of either painting or selling his pictures).

Granted, Barr declared in several interviews that he wanted to put the accent on the 'emotional intimacy' of the couple. But there is a jarring mismatch between the romanticised, regressive view of the characters' actions and relationship and the 'authenticity' of the Dogma-style *mise-en-scène*. The use of available light is signalled by jolting jumps in colour – between rooms in Jeanne's flat, between indoor and outdoor scenes. The hand-held camerawork is discreetly wobbly, the movements within the long takes entail frequent focus readjustments. However, these features rarely equate with narrative exigency. Only occasionally does *mise-en-scène* significantly contribute to constructing characters' feelings – for instance, the astute use of the cold weather location shooting to symbolise the 'hostility' of the world towards the lovers, the long takes and the dynamic, prowling camera at the 'Slav party'. Most spectacular in this respect is the very long single take (more than six minutes) which follows Jeanne back into her flat after Dragan has been taken away at the end of the film, where her slow ascent makes her growing pain more tangible. More often, though, the *mise-en-scène* creates expectations of urgency which are almost comically disappointed: for instance, when the camera 'spies' on the lovers like a prowler through the dirty window of a café but with no obvious follow-up, or when Dragan picks up Jeanne at her bookshop and forces her to run along the streets, camera breathlessly in tow, only to show her a painted screen in an antique shop. Barr's quasi-documentary *mise-en-scène*, magnified by the blown-up image, in the end serves to draw attention to its own marginalisation of social issues. What are we to make, then, of the *deus-ex-machina* intervention of the police at the end? As Dragan says 'the dream is over', is this the return of the real? The fact is that in realistic terms, both in the extra-cinematic world and within the diegesis, the lovers' separation is not inevitable. As other characters in the film point out, Jeanne and Dragan could avoid the separation in a number of ways (getting married, Dragan legalising his situation and coming back later, Jeanne following him to Belgrade). Yet their parting is treated as final and tragic. This poetic licence of course serves to inscribe the film within a romantic concept of love, according to which love gains in power by being doomed. But it also allegorises the difficulties in conceptualising the 'new Europe' which the film means to celebrate, underlining, unwittingly perhaps, the gulf between countries of uneven means that romantic love alone cannot bridge, but also the gap between the film's aesthetic project and its narrative content.

REFERENCES

Barr, J.-M., 'Pour *Lovers*, son premier film comme réalisateur, Jean-Marc Barr s'est installé dans les rails du dogme', *Première* no. 262, February, 1999a.

Barr, J.-M., 'Interview with Jean-Marc Barr', *Queer View*,
    <www.queer-view.com/01300er/1337lovers/interview1337barr-ef.html> (November 1999b).

Blincoe, N. and M. Thorne (eds), *All Hail the New Puritans* (London: Fourth Estate, 2000).

Borde, R., F. Buache and R. Curtelin, *Nouvelle vague* (Lyon: Serdoc, 1962).

Conrich, I. and E. Tincknell, 'Film Purity, the Neo-Bazinian Ideal, and Humanism in Dogma 95', *p.o.v.: A Danish Journal of Film Studies* no. 10, 2000, pp. 171–90.

Frodon, J.-M., 'Jean-Marc Barr, Dogma sans dogmatisme', *Le Monde*, 8 December, 1999.

Geuens, J-P., 'Dogma 95: A Manifesto for Our Times', *Quarterly Review of Film and Video* no. 18, 2001, pp. 191–203.

Guéret, O., 'Jean-Marc Barr: Réalisateur du renouveau', *Cinopsis*, <www.cinopsis.com>
    (31 December, 2000).

Kelly, R., *The Name of this Book is Dogme95* (London: Faber and Faber, 2000).

MacKenzie, S., 'Direct Dogma: Film Manifestos and the *fin de siècle*', *p.o.v.: A Danish Journal of Film Studies* no. 10, 2000, pp. 150–70.

Maulde, F. de, *Lovers, Chroniques de tournage* (Paris: La Table ronde, 2000).

Naficy, H., *An Accented Cinema, Exilic and Diasporic Filmmaking* (Princeton, NJ: Princeton
    University Press, 2001).

Ostria, V., '*Lovers* de Jean-Marc Barr', *L'Humanité*, 8 December, 1999.

Péron, D., 'Pascal Arnold, producteur de *Lovers* défend un nouveau cinéma: "L'Alternative
    numérique" ', *Libération*, 8 December, 1999.

PhR, '*Lovers*', *Positif* no. 464, December, 1999.

Roman, S., *Digital Babylon, Hollywood, Indiewood & Dogma 95* (Los Angeles: IFILM [Lanham,
    MD], 2001).

<www.cnc.fr/d_stat/fr_d.htm>.

NOTES

1. Also spelt 'Sergej'.
2. Source: Centre National de la Cinématographie Statistics at <www.cnc.fr/d_stat/fr_d.htm>.
3. Cited in the documentary entitled *The Name of this Film is Dogme95*, 26 March, 2000,
   FilmFour cable channel.
4. For the most systematically hostile account of the New Wave, see Borde, Buache and
   Curtelin (1962).
5. When asked by Jeanne whether he is 'Serb' or 'Croat', Dragan replies 'Yugoslav'.
6. Though Barr cites his desire to have her in the film as linked to his admiration of her in Billy
   Wilder (Page starred in *The Private Life of Sherlock Holmes*).
7. Sex is also explicitly the subject of Barr's later *Too Much Flesh*.

PART THREE

9

The Globalisation of Dogma: The Dynamics of Metaculture and Counter-Publicity

Mette Hjort

In his magisterial study entitled *Creative Industries: Contracts between Art and Commerce*, Richard Caves (2000) points out that the marketing of artistic products is best viewed, not as a unique feature of certain historical contexts, but rather as a crucial activity that artists have been engaged in since the very emergence of concepts and practices of art-making. In this view, creating audiences for one's work is simply part of what it in effect means to be a successful artist. At the same time, it is important to note that this particular task can be taken up in strikingly diverse ways. Some artists emphasise publicity and the creation of publics far more than others do. Indeed, some artists keep their eyes fixed, not on actual audiences, but on ideal audiences imagined only in the mind's eye. In the highly specialised world of big-budget, mainstream film-making, it is not uncommon for directors to be freed entirely from the task of actually promoting their works, which task is left instead to a marketing department.

What interests me here is the fact that the creation of audiences for audiovisual works seems to be far more difficult in some cultural contexts than others. I have in mind, for example, the indifference with which European cinemas for the most part are met, not only by the relevant national audiences, but also by European and international audiences, as compared, for example, to the global reach that Hollywood products enjoy. Even within Europe, there are key differences, for the problem of indifference weighs more heavily on the minor cinemas produced by small nations than it does on the major cinemas produced by large nations. In a small nation such as Denmark, the population is too small to sustain a vibrant cinema on the basis of indigenous audience appeal; linguistic barriers, combined with the asymmetries of import and export arrangements between large and small nations, make access to international and especially North American media spaces particularly difficult; and, finally, saturation of the domestic media space by foreign, and especially Hollywood products has the effect of generating problems of access and indifference within the home context.

There have been a number of attempts in Denmark to deal with the audience problem described above, the most obvious examples being pan-Nordic heritage film production and Nordic co-operation aimed at constituting an expanded, transnational audience. More interesting, however, is the emergence in recent times of a number of approaches that emphasise metaculture rather than shared or common culture. There are, of course, many different kinds of metaculture. Reviews of, or advertisements for, a given film qualify as cultural expressions that are *about* other cultural expressions. Yet, while reviews and advertisements may propound and even persuade potential viewers of the interest of a certain film, they do not typically become integrally connected with the work, to the point of actually constituting a key element in any appeal that the film might have. A more restricted sense of 'metaculture' pinpoints practices that make discourses about, or reflections on the cinematic work for which an audience is sought, an integral part of the product's appeal. Dogma 95 – the now globalised cinematic movement that von Trier and Vinterberg initiated by means of a manifesto requiring prospective Dogma film-makers to submit to ten apparently arbitrary rules of cinematic production – is a particularly interesting instance of film-makers mobilising this kind of metaculture for the purposes of publicity and audience appeal. The manifesto, which is separate from and about the films, is also essential to the films' very production and classification, and indeed to their public, and ultimately global, effect.

The formal framework that Dogma 95 provides as a result of its ten rules of film-making has, it is true, helped to generate a number of noteworthy films. If the Dogma concept warrants close scrutiny, however, the reason is not simply to be sought in its causal link to a film such as Thomas Vinterberg's *Festen* (*The Celebration*), but in the particularly effective dynamics of flow and circulation that it encourages and that have allowed it to constitute and sustain a still evolving and significant cinematic movement. An important part of the genius of Dogma 95 has to do with the way in which the manifesto helps to generate, in what is a characteristically performative manner, the very publics towards which it gestures in anticipation of a cumulative effect that somehow warrants the designation 'movement'.[1] Each and every Dogma film is at once an instantiation of the programme and an interpretation of its vision and specific dicta, an interpretation that in some cases involves elements of self-conscious deviation and transgression. As such, these works necessarily prompt a series of metacultural moments that have the effect not only of intensifying public interest in the films, both individually and as a corpus, but of staging the significance of an appealingly adaptable Dogma concept.

The highly publicised manifesto and rules are necessarily embedded within all Dogma films as a basic concept and as a principle of, and rationale for, production, the result being that these works provide their own initial framework of interpretation and assessment. Inscribed, then, within these cinematic works is an invitation to audiences to adopt a meta-cinematic stance that makes a seemingly straightforward phenomenon of rule-following the basis for more momentous and substantive reflections on the history of cinema, including some of its false starts and current problems. Audiences are, of course, meant to engage in the kind of first-order process of meaning-making that allows them to make sense of the unfolding plot and to be moved by the characters with whom they are encouraged to align themselves. But by virtue of the Dogma frame, they are also expected to entertain second-order considerations having to do, for example, with the pervasiveness, origin and legitimacy of certain cinematic norms. The efficacies of the manifesto form go a long way towards explaining the Dogma concept's remarkable ability to travel along a trajectory that takes it from one artistic context to another, from artistic to non-artistic contexts, and from Denmark to Hong Kong via, among other places, the US, France and Belgium, with occasional moments of repatriation or an apparent return to national origins along the way. Yet, what is returned or thus brought home is in crucial ways different from what von Trier and Vinterberg first launched, for the very concept being appropriated and circulated is itself transformed by the diverse and partially overlapping processes and pathways of its circulation.[2]

In an incisive comparative study entitled *Metaculture: How Culture Moves through the World*, the anthropologist Greg Urban foregrounds the centrality of metaculture in modern western social imaginaries and convincingly argues that its salience has to do with the way in which 'it imparts an accelerative force to culture': 'It aids culture in its motion through space and time. It gives a boost to the culture that it is about, helping to propel it on its journey' (Urban 2001: 4). If the performative and metacultural dimensions of Dogma 95 intensify the circulation of the Dogma concept, the circulations themselves effectively weave together, more or less loosely, a series of counter-publics centred on some notion of oppositionality. Each instance of appropriation brings with it a new audience, just as each extension relies on the cumulative publicity effects of prior commitments to the Dogma programme and its various adaptations. Dogma 95, in short, is very much about the creation of publics, about the forging of a social space where a given cultural expression can simply become visible in the first instance, and perhaps ultimately resonate with genuine significance. Whereas one standard approach to audience-building in the area of film focuses on the need to develop cinematic narratives that reflect (at the level of story content, iconography or setting) viewers' prior cultural investments and attachments, Dogma 95 foregrounds metaculture in the form of talk about and reflection on film-making. In von Trier and Vinterberg's vision of things, metaculture provides a more effective, more interesting and less ideologically suspect means of generating and consolidating public interest than does shared culture or what Urban calls 'inertial culture' (2001: 15–33). Dogma 95, for example, sets aside the stereotyped images of national culture that a heritage model of cinematic production construes national and even international audiences as wishing to see, in favour of a form of rule-governed production that is nationally inflected only in the sense of guaranteeing members of the originating small nation a point of access to a world of film-making. The Dogma rules, it is true, do aim to make room for, and to tell stories with, a thorough-going contemporaneity and hence putative relevance for audiences. But the point is that there is no attempt here to use a prior investment in the cumulative accretions of some *deeply* shared culture as the leveraging device for boosting the interest of a given film. Public interest, rather, is initially mobilised through an ingenious metacultural project and subsequently validated or thwarted by the actual qualities of the viewing experience. Compared to the 'thick descriptions' of the heritage model, Dogma 95 emphasises procedure over substance, formal rules over specific and collectively validated cultural articulations. This is not to suggest that Dogma 95 is an entirely neutral cultural initiative, for the very procedures arise out of, and indeed reflect a deep commitment to norms such as equality and inclusion which are by no means universally accepted. At the same time, the emphasis on metaculture rather than shared culture, on rules rather than specific results, effectively loosens the Dogma concept's connection to the specific cultural context of its emergence, thereby allowing it to make its way around the globe.

Dogma 95 represents a small nation's response to globalisation, understood as a vehicle for processes of monoculturalisation driven by the dynamics of global capital. Yet, it is important to note that Dogma 95 has itself been globalised since 1995 when the blueprint was first made public, Vinterberg's success at Cannes in 1998 having done much to imbue the concept with a kind of accelerative force. Indeed, one might go so far as to claim that Dogma 95 is an instance of a quite different and far more positive kind of globalisation than that associated with corporate finance. Relevant in this respect is Arjun Appadurai's contrast between what he calls 'grassroots globalization' and the kinds of globalisations that are prompting various intense anxieties about the decline of nation-state autonomy, among other things:

> a series of social forms has emerged to contest, interrogate, and reverse these developments and to create forms of knowledge transfer and social mobilization that proceed independently of the actions of corporate capital and the nation-state system (and its international affiliates and guarantors). These social forms rely on strategies, visions, and horizons for globalization on behalf of the poor that can be characterized as 'grassroots globalization' or, put in a slightly different way, as 'globalization from below' (2001: 3).

Dogma 95 emerges in the context of a small nation, is motivated by problems of access, and has been appropriated by agents with limited financial resources. It is worth noting, for example, that Shu Kei's essay 'Save those Bad Movies' (1999) and Ou Ning's 'In the Name of the Indies' (1999) both foreground the potentially inclusionary implications of Dogma 95's legitimation of digital video technology for aspiring film-makers in mainland China where financial constraints are severe. Inasmuch as Dogma 95's global reach has been driven by opposition to runaway capital as well as by commitments to equality and inclusion, it is by no means far-fetched to think of it in terms of Appadurai's notion of 'grassroots globalization'. It is precisely to the role played by 'the imagination in social life' that we must look, claims Appadurai, if our aim is to find evidence of 'an emancipatory politics of globalization' (2001: 6). Inasmuch as Dogma 95 represents an attempt both to stimulate creativity through constraint and to reflect on some of the social and political implications of dominant institutional arrangements in the world of cinema, the movement emerges as centrally concerned with fuelling a cinematic imagination as a goal in and of itself, but also as a means of generalising access and of replacing indifference with recognition, a form of muted expression with something resembling a genuine voice. What we have here are various elements allowing Dogma 95 to qualify as a form of positive globalisation with a potentially emancipatory thrust.

To claim that the significance of the Dogma 95 phenomenon has to do in part with the movement's successful globalisation is to invite questions about how the notion of success is to be understood in this instance. Ulrich Beck's (2000) general proposal is suggestive in this regard: 'the *extent* of successful globalization as well as of its *limits* may be posed anew in relation to three parameters: (a) extension in *space*; (b) stability over *time*; and (c) social *density* of the transnational networks, relationships and image-flows' (2000: 12). Dogma 95 is to a significant extent a festival phenomenon, with occasional cross-over effects, as in the case of Vinterberg's *The Celebration*. That is, it is a matter of drawing on an existing network that has a global reach and high degree of stability. Festival data on the Danish Dogma films alone clearly point to the kind of spatial extension, persistence over time and effective presence that help to distinguish the genuine globalisation of a concept and programme from isolated cases of global fame. As of September 2002, the number of festival appearances recorded by the Danish Film Institute for the Danish titles was as follows:

> *Festen* (*The Celebration*, 1998, dir. Thomas Vinterberg): 70
>
> *Idioterne* (*The Idiots*, 1998, dir. Lars von Trier): 42
>
> *Mifune* (*Mifunes sidste sang*, 1999, dir. Søren Kragh-Jacobsen): 38
>
> *The King is Alive* (2000, dir. Kristian Levring): 20
>
> *Italiensk for begyndere* (*Italian for Beginners*, 2000, dir. Lone Scherfig): 39
>
> *Et rigtigt menneske* (*Truly Human*, 2001, dir. Åke Sandgren): 35
>
> *En kærlighedshistorie* (*Kira's Reason*, 2001, dir. Ole Christian Madsen): 26
>
> *Elsker dig for evigt* (*Open Hearts*, 2002, dir. Susanne Bier): 7

Closer analysis of the data reveals Dogma's well-known presence at some of the most prestigious festivals – at Cannes and Berlin – but also its genuinely global reach through less recognised venues, through subsidy-driven promotional events involving either the Danish Film Institute or the European Union, and as an element in a particular programme of remembrance or celebration. While the intensity of *The Celebration*'s circulation by far exceeds that of the other Danish Dogma films, the reach and modes of its circulation are characteristic of those of the other titles. The following *selected* examples of *The Celebration*'s circulation can thus be considered highly representative. *The Celebration* was included in the following *standing festival* programmes: Melbourne International Film Festival (1998), Montreal World Film Festival (1998), Rio de Janeiro Film Festival (1998), Hamburg Film Festival (1998), Pusan International Film Festival, Korea (1998), New York Film Festival (1998), International Film Festival of India (1999), Istanbul International Film Festival (1999), Cape Town Film Festival (2001) and Ankara International Film Festival (2001). Relevant *subsidy-driven promotional* events featuring Vinterberg's Dogma work include: Warsaw Nordic Film Week (1998), New York Danish Wave (1999), St Petersburg E.U. Film Festival (2000), Singapore Danish Film Festival (2001), Paris Danish Film Week (2002), Algier E.U. Film Festival (2000), Bucharest E.U. Film Festival (2000), Bangkok E.U. Film Festival (2000), Harare E.U. Film Festival (2000), Manila E.U. Film Festival (2000) and Beirut E.U. Film Festival (2000). Finally, Dogme #1 featured in the programme for the Benin Constitution Day Celebration in 2000, an example of inclusion in *commemorative events* that can, but need not, involve film.

Initial reactions to Susanne Bier's *Open Hearts*, the most recent of the Danish Dogma films, clearly point to Dogma's continued festival presence over the next few years. First shown at Cannes in May 2002, the film's realised or projected network of festival circulation only four months later included the Haugesund Norwegian International Film Festival, the International Film Festivals held in San Sebastian, Toronto and Rio de Janeiro, and the London Film Festival.

The festival circuit, we know, constitutes a privileged source of inspiration and learning for aspiring as well as established film-makers. As a network of sites devoted, not only to viewing, but also to talk of all kinds, this circuit promotes creative assimilations as well as more or less subtle forms of imitation. There is evidence to suggest that Dogma's festival presence in the future will be a matter of informal appropriations of the Dogma concept as well as of certified works involving a fully blown adherence to the initial programme articulated in 1995. A brief discussion of the production history of *Leaving in Sorrow*, the first feature film by the Hong Kong independent film-maker Vincent Chui (a founding member of the Ying E Chi organisation that aims to promote independent Hong Kong film), helps to highlight the role played by film festivals in mediating cinematic concepts as well as the emergence of Dogma as a vision permitting informal appropriation and no doubt adaptation to local circumstances. During a Summer Institute session devoted to Hong Kong cinema and the Dogma movement at the University of Hong Kong (6 June, 2002), Chui described his relationship to Dogma as having evolved through stages of scepticism, conversion, trepidation and finally confirmed conviction. Chui indicated that his scepticism had to do primarily with the contempt that he, as a film-school graduate, initially had for the use of digital video, an attitude that the independent film-maker Shu Kei regards as widespread in Hong Kong film milieux: 'A lot of people still have a prejudice against DV or DV into film. In HK, this is still pretty much the case' (Shu Kei, interviewed by Hjort, 3 September, 2002). Chui, it turns out, first learnt of Dogma through Shu Kei, who had reported on the movement to local Hong Kong film-makers following a viewing of *The Celebration* at the London Film Festival in 1998. Chui described his encounter with *The Idiots* during the Hong Kong Film Festival in 1999 as something of a revelation, but identifies a viewing of *The Celebration* two months later as the moment of persuasion. The experience of making *Leaving in Sorrow* following some (but by no means all) of the Dogma dicta, Chui claimed, was disconcerting on account of the emphasis on continuous shooting rather than an analytic breakdown of shots. The turning point in the process, he remarked, came with the shooting of the Starbuck's café scene in Beijing. With only two hours to shoot the scene in Beijing, Chui was left with little or no time for preparation, and the result, he argued, was an exhilarating sense of 'capturing what was happening rather than making a film', a point that echoes a theme developed by the Danish Film School teacher and 'Dogma doctor', Mogens Rukov, in Jesper Jargil's documentary, *De lutrede* (*The Purified*).

Chui, it turns out, has no intention of seeking Dogma certification for *Leaving in Sorrow*, being content to associate his film loosely with the movement. Here we have an informal and even selective appropriation of the Dogma framework, an approach that the established Hong Kong film-maker, Ann Hui (*The Secret*, 1979, *Boat People,* 1982, *Song of the Exile*, 1990, *Summer Snow*, 1995), identified as appealing during the panel discussion described above. While Hui claimed to be deeply moved by the 'democratic' and 'egalitarian' vision of Dogma 95, she indicated that in her case an informal appropriation of insight was much to be preferred over the rituals of vow-taking, confessions and certification. The spirit of Dogma, it would appear, is increasingly seen as separable from the vow that defines the movement's identity, at least in its early phases.

If the festival circuit provides a stable, global network for the continued circulation of Dogma films as formal instantiations and informal appropriations of a concept or vision, the internet, not surprisingly, permits a far more anarchic mode of dissemination. The internet has, from the outset, been one of the salient ways in which Dogma's metacultural extensions have gained visibility in the form, for example, of spin-off manifestos. That these new deviations from the original do not compete with, but rather bolster the authority of the master text is evidenced by the inclusion, in the official Dogma website run by the Dogma secretariat, of links to some of the documents in question. As a complementary, but radically different mode of circulation from that of the festival circuit, the internet no doubt helps to explain the globalisation of Dogma 95 as a no longer purely cinematic phenomenon. The globalisation of Dogma 95, it would appear, is a story of how institutionalised paths of cultural dissemination, combined with the immediacy and global reach of internet communication, allow for the continued circulation of rule-governed films, informal appropriations and spin-off initiatives, all of which serve to revive and sustain a movement that has been scathingly pronounced dead on more than one occasion.

THE EFFECTIVE HISTORY OF THE DOGMA CONCEPT

Dogma 95 was framed from the very outset as a provocative gesture designed to elicit questions, passionate discussion and general polemics, in short, *talk* of all kinds. In this respect Dogma 95 is truly the brainchild of Lars von Trier, a director who has long practised the techniques of provocative self-staging. For example, during his years at the National Film School of Denmark, the middle-class Lars Trier dubbed himself with an aristocratic 'von' that he had toyed with as early as 1975 (Björkman 2000: 11). In the context of modern Danish mentalities committed, among other things, to notions of radical egalitarianism, this politically incorrect gesture was bound to attract attention, as was his sympathetic depiction of a Nazi soldier in his diploma film, *Befrielsesbilleder* (*Images of a Relief*). In more recent times, von Trier himself has remarked on the highly choreographed nature of the projected image of the dynamic Zentropa duo, which stages the film-maker as the sensitive and highly phobic artist/intellectual, and his partner, Peter Aalbæk Jensen, as the crass, cigar-smoking producer. And von Trier's laconic remarks and transgressive behaviour on highly mediatised public occasions are, of course, famous. Readers will recall von Trier's gesture of publicly discarding the ribboned roll that had just been handed over with such ceremony when *Europa* was awarded the Prix Technique at Cannes. If anyone understands how to generate 'talk', it is the film-maker Lars von Trier (Hjort 2002).

The Dogma brethren, we may assume, then, were intensely aware of the fact that the success of their proposed movement depended on the manifesto's discursive circulation. Caricatures, ironic cartoons and parodic counter-manifestos have played an important role in Dogma's discursive elaboration, but so have serious attempts to extend the concept to other areas. Of equal, if not greater significance, however, is the fact that certain Dogma films, such as von Trier's *The Idiots* and Gyorski's *Resin*, have had the effect of prompting serious public debate about issues of general concern. Dogma 95 has, in short, served as a fascinating vehicle for precisely the kind of public criticism that theorists of democracy consider central to vibrant and effective' civil societies. Dogma 95's contribution resides to a significant extent in this civic dimension, in the capacity to generate meaningful discussion of topics that are divisive, yet absolutely fundamental, including, among other things, the realities of access and voice in the world of film.

THE PARODIES

1995, the year in which Dogma 95 was first announced, witnessed the publication of a number of parodic counter-manifestos, a genre that was revived in 1999 following the release and success of the first two Dogma films in 1998. The initial emphasis on parody is a clear reflection of the general scepticism that surrounded the Dogma project in 1995. Images of the panel's response to von Trier in Paris, where Dogma was first announced, provide clear evidence of boredom, irritation, mild hostility and certainly nothing resembling enthusiasm or conviction. While Jytte Hilden and the Danish Ministry of Culture may have been persuaded by the proposal, the tendency in many quarters, both nationally and internationally, was to think of it as a self-promoting hoax, one that was likely to backfire and become a bit of a joke. An example of the parodic discourse that emerged around Dogma during the early phases of its reception is the manifesto published in March 1995 by the three set designers, Henning Bahs, Jette Lehman and Sven Wichmann. Their ten rules range from what might in another context have been a rule motivated by serious intentions – '1. Location shooting is forbidden; we'll construct everything from *Damernes Magasin* [a store in Lemvig, Jutland] to Carlsberg' – to the flamboyantly ironic: '3. Actors may not be so tall or so fat as to obstruct the view of our designs' (woj 1995).

The parodies that followed in the wake of Dogma's success at Cannes in 1998 had a slightly different flavour. At this point the focus was on professional hierarchies and on the performative self-contradictions involved in promoting the self by subscribing to a politics of self-effacement. The focus, in other words, was on success, Dogma's success *qua* programme and the film-makers' success *qua* Dogma film-makers. In May 1998 a collective of scriptwriters (identified as Mikael Colville-Andersen, Anton Carey Bidstrup, Rasmus Heisterberg and Jonas Meyer Petersen) published their so-called 'Lazy-98 manifesto' (the Danish word for lazy, *dovne*, sounds, of course like *dogme*). In this parody, the humour hinges on an implicit contrast between scriptwriters and film directors. Dogma 95 here becomes an occasion for targeting the hierarchies of power and prestige that are operative in the film industry. Indeed, Dogma 95 is indirectly characterised as a *director*'s manifesto, as a rather clever mobilisation of an anti-*auteurist* rhetoric aimed at enhancing certain directors' economic and cultural capital.

1. We refuse to write and will only use a dictaphone.
2. We want more money and more respect.
3. We want taxi receipts.
4. We want to receive telephone calls from sexy producers and directors who understand us.
5. We want research money so that we can work in peace and quiet in Latin America.
6. We only want to hand in one draft.
7. We want cigarettes and whiskey ad libido.
8. We want to be persuaded to tell our stories.
9. We want extra pay for happy endings.
10. We want hard love – anytime, anywhere (Dovne 98 1998).

Interestingly, the game of *auteurist* distinction is explicitly identified in my third example of parodic elaboration, which concerns the behaviour of viewers of Dogma films:

1. Dogma films must always be seen in the Dagmar cinema.
2. The audience has to remain standing during the entire screening.
3. Pop-corn must be hand-held and may not be popped.
4. All sounds made by the audience must be natural.
5. The curtain must be drawn.
6. Nobody in the room may mention the director's name, but he can be referred to as 'that person whose name has been all over the press during the last month and who won the Special Prize at Cannes'! (Anon 1998).

What is gently mocked here is the way in which the putatively anti-*auteurist* Dogma platform propelled the young Vinterberg into the stratosphere of cinematic fame.

INTER-ARTISTIC EXTENSIONS

Once Dogma 95 began to attract positive attention – prizes and distinctions, funding and praise – attempts were made to extend the concept to other areas, not by the brethren themselves, but by various professionals for whom the discourse of oppositionality, combined with the prospect of a genuine impact, had a deep appeal. What emerged was a still growing wave of appropriations in literature, dance, theatre, game design and, more recently, business, urban planning and politics. An early *inter-artistic* extension was the attempt on the part of a number of theatre directors to explore the implications of restraint and simplification for small, provincial theatres. Interestingly, their proposal essentially called for a certain critical distance from the practices and expectations associated with the Royal Danish Theatre, just as it foregrounded the need on the part of touring productions to work creatively with the conditions available in provincial theatres (Grove 1998). Much as in the original conception, simplicity and restraint are here part of an oppositional discourse that aims to unsettle existing relations between centre and periphery.

Whereas the parodic elaboration of Dogma 95 was confined for the most part to Denmark, many of the inter-artistic extensions of the concept involve a transnational dimension that highlights its discursive circulation within an international avant-garde art world. The Dogma Dance movement, for example, was initiated in October 2000 by Litza Bixler, Deveril and Katrina McPherson, three British dance film-makers who see rules as a means of counteracting certain undesirable tendencies within the world of dance film production. In conversation with the American philosopher, Noël Carroll, the founders of the movement construed their manifesto's rules as a response to the following problem: 'perhaps in an attempt to be taken seriously in the world of television and film, dance films are losing the connection to dance. We see many dance films in which the focus is the design, the lighting or the telling of a story through the conventions of narrative film, with the dance content becoming an afterthought' (cited in Banes and Carroll, this volume, page 176). The aim, in short, is to foster the conditions under which dance films can emerge as a genuinely hybrid art form, as opposed to a specific mode- and content-based genre of film-making. What is envisaged is 'a new genre' that properly combines 'both disciplines' by, for example, making the camera 'part of the choreography' (cited in Banes and Carroll, this volume, page 180). The Dogma Dance manifesto lists twelve rules, compared with the brethren's original ten. Although some of the rules involve an almost verbatim appropriation of elements from the Vow of Chastity – '6. The camera must be hand-held. Any movement or immobility attainable in the hand is permitted' – the concern with the specificities of dance is apparent throughout. Thus, for example, 'a moving camera' is suggestively characterised as a 'dancing camera'. Interestingly, the Dogma Dance manifesto picks up on what critics have identified as the main strength of the original Dogma 95 proposal, the fact that the prescribed use of hand-held cameras effectively liberates actors from the constraints of technology. Thus, Dogma Dance rule number 8 specifies that 'The camera, location or any other extraneous equipment should not impede the dancers' movement'. What is more, this rule becomes the basis for an entirely different criterion for certification, a criterion that reflects the problem of media asymmetry to which the manifesto is a response: 'In order for a film to be a certified Dogma Dance film, the performing dancers should sign a written confirmation that they have felt this rule [number 8] has been adhered to' (<www.dogma-dance.org>).

Dogma 95 is an attempt to reconfigure the landscape of cinematic production, to film from the margins and thereby challenge the sedimented norms of a dominant centre or core. In a parallel gesture, Dogma Dance adopts what would normally be a relatively disempowered point of view – that of the dancer – to dispute the legitimacy of some of the accepted hierarchies of commercial film-making, with particular emphasis on the way they impinge on the hybrid genre of dance film. Dogma Dance thus becomes an opportunity, for example, to thematise critically the tendency to value expensive equipment more than dancers – to the point of neglecting the latter's physical safety – or to give priority to the views of predominantly male film-makers over those of primarily female dancers (Banes and Carroll, this volume).

Of equal, if not more interest, is the reworking in 2001 of the Dogma dicta in the context of computer game design. 'Dogma 2001: A Challenge to Game Designers' is a
fascinating attempt to chart a certain creative course for the new digital media. Unlike
established art forms, such as cinema and dance, the emerging digital arts face a far more
open-ended future, with the specific uses of the relevant and still emerging new technologies yet to be determined.[3] Thus, for example, Carol Gigliotti (1999) points to the
need for careful reflection on the ethical implications of the choices we make in connection with a range of diverging digital aesthetics that might be emphasised or developed.
And in her influential *Life on the Screen: Identity in the Age of the Internet*, Sherry Turkle
(1997) similarly highlights the deeper cultural and political significance of the quite different aesthetics that early IBM- and Macintosh-based interfaces support. There is a sense
in 'Dogma 2001: A Challenge to Game Designers' of being at a crossroads, of needing to
intervene before certain undesirable practices come to assume the kind of aura of generalised self-evidence that will rule out alternative digital futures. In this case, the critique is
directed, not at Hollywood or the mainstream film-making industry, but at a number of
like-minded corporate players in the game of global capital: EA, Sony and Blizzard. The
Dogma 2001 Vow (see Appendix I pages 209–11) that is part of the Dogma formula is followed by a second-order commentary that provides the rationale for the manifesto as a
whole and clearly identifies a corporate vision of digital culture as the motivating concern:

> 'Finally, I acknowledge that innovative gameplay is not merely a desirable attribute but a
> moral imperative. All other considerations are secondary. Thus I make my solemn vow.'
>   Now I realize that, as with Hollywood and Dogme 95, nobody at EA or Sony or Blizzard is
> going to pay the slightest attention to Dogma 2001. This isn't a formula for commercial
> success, it's a challenge to think outside the box – in our case, the standardized boxes that are
> on the store shelves right now. But the rules are actually far less draconian than the Dogme 95
> rules for filmmakers, and it wouldn't be that hard to follow them. I think it could do both us,
> and our customers, a lot of good.

Although the precise sense in which this term 'good' is being used here has to be largely
inferred from the rules, the manifesto's opening sentence does provide certain pointers:
'As a game designer I promise for the good of my game, my industry, and my own creative soul to design according to the following Dogma 2001 rules'. The aim, it would
appear, is to combine a number of economic and artistic desiderata, to pursue market
viability while fostering genuine creativity through a resistance to certain forms of convergence and standardisation. Each of the rules is followed by a helpful 'justification'
which makes the manifesto as a whole less of a cryptic insiders' document than some of
the other manifestos on offer. Rules 4, 6, 7 and 8 are particularly thought-provoking
injunctions to diverge from certain content-based regularities and to think of game
design as a distinct rather than derivative form of expression. Let us start with 4, 7 and
8, which are concerned with the characters or agents of digital narratives, the mode in
which violence is represented and the basic organising structure of digital narratives:

4. There shall be no knights, elves, dwarves or dragons. Nor shall there be any wizards, wenches, bards, bartenders, golems, giants, clerics, necromancers, thieves, gods, angels, demons, sorceresses, undead bodies or body parts (mummified or decaying), Nazis, Russians, spies, mercenaries, space marines, stormtroopers, star pilots, humanoid robots, evil geniuses, mad scientists, or carnivorous aliens. And no freakin' vampires.

Justification: Self-evident. If you find that doing without all of the foregoing makes it impossible to build your game, you are not creative enough to call yourself a game designer. As proof, note that it does not exclude any of the following: queens, leprechauns, Masai warriors, ghosts, succubi, Huns, mandarins, wisewomen, grizzly bears, hamsters, sea monsters, vegetarian aliens, terrorists, firefighters, generals, gangsters, detectives, magicians, spirit mediums, shamans, whores, and lacrosse players. One of the games that made it to the finals of the first Independent Games Festival was about birds called blue-footed boobies, so forget you ever heard of George Lucas and J.R.R. Tolkien and get to work …

7. Violence is strictly limited to the disappearance or immobilization of destroyed units. Units which are damaged or destroyed shall be so indicated by symbolic, not representational, means. There shall be no blood, explosions, or injury or death animations.

Justification: Although conflict is a central principle of most games, the current 'arms race' towards ever-more graphic violence is harmful and distracting …

8. There may be victory or defeat, and my side and their side, but there may not be Good and Evil.

Justification: Good versus Evil is the most hackneyed, overused excuse imaginable for having two sides in a fight. With the exception of a small number of homicidal maniacs, no human being regards him- or herself as evil. As a Dogma designer, you are required to create a real explanation for why two sides are opposed – or to do without one entirely, as in chess.

If the above rules are an attempt to populate the digital universe in more diverse ways and to favour a more subtle, less intrusive aesthetics as well as a more nuanced logic of explanation, rule number 6 aims very directly at the self-understandings of game designers:

6. All cinematics, cut-scenes, and other non-interactive movies are forbidden …

Justification: The secret desire of game designers to be film directors is deleterious to their games and to the industry generally. This desire must be stamped out.

Game design is not, then, to be cinema by other means, but rather an independent art form that makes full use of the unique narrative potential of digital technologies.

PUBLIC CRITICISM

Now, it is the *extension* of the Dogma concept to *other artistic frameworks and other national contexts* that guarantees the term's transformation into a fully blown vehicle of public criticism in Denmark. Indeed, the Danish press's deep commitment to highlighting all instances of *international recognition* for anything Danish ensures the salience of the Dogma concept in Danish mediascapes. At this stage in the appropriative process,

Dogma 95 functions in Denmark, not so much as a concrete *programme* requiring *translation* into a different idiom, but rather as an *ethos*. And it is this transformation of the concept from programme to ethos that in turn explains the characteristic assumption in the following examples that Dogma 95 is self-evidently relevant in contexts that are not only *not* cinematic, but non-artistic. Dogma's pertinence to all areas of human existence can be taken for granted, it would appear, and no longer requires the kind of proof that a creative translation into a parallel manifesto with fully articulated rules arguably provides. Indeed, in Jargil's documentary about Dogma 95, *The Purified*, the brethren are shown discussing the mutations of the term's meanings. They reflect rather ironically on the fact that 'Dogma' has acquired a nationalist dimension. If reference were made to 'Dogma radishes', Lars von Trier remarks, the implicit suggestion would be that these were *Danish* instantiations of the vegetable in question – and therefore good. The idea that 'Dogma' is a term that can be used to qualify furniture and cakes is mocked by the brethren who clearly feel ambivalent about the nationalist ways in which their initial project is being used to leverage products that have little to do with film and even less to do with the original spirit of Dogma 95. It is important, however, to note that the brethren's take on the wider mobilisation of 'Dogma' as so many examples of crass, nationalistic marketing tactics tends to overlook the deeper and more interesting reasons for the term's broad appeal: the fact that it has been associated from the start with a notion of oppositionality, with the thematisation of crucial issues of shared concern.

Clear evidence of the extension of the term 'Dogma' is provided by the article, 'Dogma Politics against Human Indifference' ('Dogmepolitik imod menneskelig ligegyldighed'). Written by the journalist Carl Maria Bech, the piece appeared in *Politiken* (Bech 2001), a newspaper that sees itself as appealing to the more progressive and intellectual of Danish readers. Bech's intention is to debate nothing less than the very foundations of the Danish welfare state, focusing on the perverse effects to which a particular article of the Danish law – article 94 – has given rise. The Dogma reference picks out a number of negative phenomena that are implicitly understood to have been targeted by the film-makers, including excessive expense and a kind of conventionalised thinking that amounts to a form of non-thought. The claim, in short, is that the administration of social benefits in Denmark has been on 'automatic pilot' for some time and that the effects of this situation – the infantilisation and dependency of recipients – call into question the legitimacy of the relevant costs. The term 'Dogma' is here used to take issue with a dehumanising systems rationality that has been shielded from public scrutiny on account of the status of article 94 as something of a foundational text, as the taken-for-granted basis of the Danish welfare state. No reference is made to rules. No mention is made of vows of chastity. What matters is the 'rediscovery, without exorbitant expense, of warmth and feeling between people' ('varmen og følelserne mellem mennesker for små penge').

The 'Opinions' ('Meninger') or, more standardly in English, 'Letters from Readers' section of *Morgenavisen Jyllands-Posten* provides further evidence of Dogma's new discursive functions. Written by Nikolaj Feldbech Rasmussen (2001), the letter entitled 'Political Dogma Rules' ('Politiske dogmeregler') evokes the need for Dogmatic thinking in Danish politics, which, it is claimed, is currently election-driven rather than issues-

driven. Interestingly, the larger context for the reader's intervention is an article published one week earlier which thematised the problems encountered by grassroots
organisations when they attempted to win a hearing for their views in the Danish parliament, referred to as 'Christiansborg', the name of the former castle where members
officially meet. Reference to Dogma in this instance is implicitly held to be culturally
grammatical on account of the movement's oppositionality and debate with *auteurist* policies. Politicians should set aside their dominant concern with circulating the kinds of
public images that will promote re-election and a prolonged term in public office, in
much the same way that Dogma film-makers have renounced *auteurist* creditations in
order to focus on what is essential and true. The elements of irony and mock seriousness
that accompanied the movement's emergence as well as its parodic reworking or inter-
artistic extension have been discarded in these last two examples in favour of an
interpretation of Dogma as a wholly serious defence of basic human values. Unlike Carl
Maria Bech, Feldbech Rasmussen does gesture towards some possible rules: 1.
Politicians should listen to people whether or not they are potential voters; 2. Politicians
should do what is necessary rather than what is politically expedient; 3. Politicians should
be honest. The concern, however, is not ultimately with specific rules but rather with a
more general humanistic vision centred around notions of authenticity and truth. Such
are the workings of public discourse that Lars von Trier, the very film-maker who pointedly vilified humanistic film-makers in earlier manifestos, becomes the spokesperson for
a sincere and wholly serious humanism.

An article entitled 'Copenhagen is Environmental-Dogma-Town' ('København er miljø-
dogme-by') by Niels Ditlev (2001) points to yet another case in which Dogma is used to
draw attention to traditionally neglected issues of public concern. Ditlev begins by evok-
ing the many ways in which the Danish film-makers' initiative has proven inspirational in
other contexts and goes on to discuss Dogma's new role as a means of articulating a co-
ordinated environmental plan of action at the level of local government. It is a matter, it
turns out, of four Danish towns (Albertslund, Ballerup, Herning and Copenhagen) voluntarily embracing a certain environmentalist vision. To earn the honorific qualifier
'Dogma' these towns must commit to three very general guiding principles. 1. Citizens'
impact on the environment is to be measured; 2. Each of the local governments is to articulate a plan of action oriented towards improvement of the environment; 3. The private
sector is to contribute to the cost of improving the environment.

To chart the role played by the Dogma concept in various oppositional discourses is in
effect to take issue with a recurrent objection to Dogma, one that was humorously
expressed in the *Berlingske Tidende*'s 'memorable citations' section, where the following
words accompanied a caricature of Bille August: 'I made my Dogma film in 1971 when
I was in film school' (12 November, 1998). The suggestion, clearly, is that Dogma is a
matter of reinventing the wheel or of making what is ultimately routine seem deeply significant. The metacultural fanfare, the reasoning seems to be, makes viewers and critics
find novelty and innovation where in fact there is none. The idea that Dogma 95 is essentially a publicity stunt even seems to find support in statements made by Dogma
directors, a noteworthy example being Leif Tilden's remark about *Reunion*: 'We thought

CITATER

J eg lavede min dogmefilm, da jeg gik på film-
skolen i 1971

BILLE AUGUST

Filminstruktør. I Ekstra Bladet

'I made my Dogma film in
1971 when I was in film
school' (*Berlingske Tidende*,
12 November, 1998)

that doing the film as a dogme film would be a challenge and would give the film more publicity.' It is important, however, to note that the dismissal of Dogma on these grounds hinges on a purely negative conception of what the term 'publicity' entails. Yet, as anyone familiar with the history of the 18th century and its legacy knows, 'publicity' was not always linked to crass marketing devices, but was once a term associated with the emergence of a democratic public capable of articulating views at odds with official state doctrine. My point is that Dogma 95 is indeed a matter of publicity, but not only in the limited sense of vile marketing.[4] If the manifesto involves a kind of stunt, it is because of its performative effects, because it effectively, in the first instance, draws on diverse cinematic publics – the audiences for art films, film festivals, various national cinemas and independent film – to constitute a network of counter-publics centred around alternative art regards and, arguably, alternative identities. The fact that parts of the film festival circuit on which Dogma's circulation to a significant extent depends function as stable institutions driven partly by market interests by no means undermines the idea of meaningful and productive differences that can be made salient as a means of collective mobilisation. Indeed, the wider circulation or globalisation of the Dogma concept is fuelled by the elements of oppositionality and public criticism that are perceived to be an important part of the original manifesto's metacultural thrust and appeal.

While Jürgen Habermas' seminal study, entitled *The Structural Transformation of the Public Sphere* (1989; first published in German in 1962), laid the groundwork for all subsequent discussions of publicity, it is the critical response to this work by Oskar Negt and the German film-maker, Alexander Kluge, that has proven particularly helpful in the context of film studies. Whereas Habermas focused on the origins, specificity and decline of the bourgeois public sphere, Negt and Kluge were concerned, in *Public Sphere and Experience* (1993), with a proletarian public sphere. The English translation of this work, many years after its publication in German, sparked considerable interest among North American film scholars in the concept of counter-publicity. Miriam Hansen's insightful introduction to the translation played a key role in this respect, as did her groundbreaking study on spectatorship in American silent film, *Babel and Babylon* (1991), which is a rejection in many ways of psychoanalytic approaches to film scholarship in favour of the kind of conceptual models that the public sphere discussions afford.

Counter-publics, as the philosopher Nancy Fraser points out, function as sites of regroupment and identity construction in the face of demands exerted by an official public sphere.[5] A key difference between the bourgeois public sphere as theorised by Habermas and the various historical counter-publics to which Negt and Kluge drew attention is that whereas the former presupposes universal human interests, the latter find a basis in specific identity formations with diverging interests and needs. It is important to note, however, that although counter-publics emphasise specific identities, they are by no means expressions of a fundamentally separatist intent. The idea, in brief, is to achieve a certain clarity about a given group's needs within the limited public that this group constitutes before thematising the relevant concerns and demands within a larger public sphere. In this sense there is an ongoing exchange between official publics and counter-publics, between publicity and counter-publicity. In many cases, this interactive process results in growing public recognition of the *general* significance of issues that once were construed as having only restricted human relevance. Michael Warner's (2002) critique of Fraser's conception of counter-publics foregrounds the performative, world-making effects of the personal and impersonal dimensions of public speech, the result being a revised understanding of counter-publicity as a phenomenon that may, but need not, involve a strong, reflexive, identity-based group awareness. Indeed, following Warner, a given group may not exist as a distinct entity with a well-defined identity prior to the performative effects of public discourse and its specific modes of address and circulation. There seems to be evidence, in the Dogma case, of at least two types of counter-publicity, the one projecting and consolidating a specific group identity (linked, for example, to small-nation status), the other emerging from a series of loose connections motivated by a pragmatic interest in the publicity effects of the Dogma concept, rather than by converging or shared identities.

I have been suggesting throughout that the systematic linking of Dogma with issues of general and current concern, rather than being a new development, has been a feature of Dogma 95 from the outset. Recent examples include the way in which Vladimir Gyorski's *Resin* has helped to generate opposition to California's notorious 'three strikes' anti-drug legislation, which allows courts to give three-time felony offenders a life sentence. Mention should also be made here of Jean-Marc Barr's *Lovers*, which is not only framed as a Dogma film, but as part of a 'freetrilogy' with its own manifesto, the central point of which is to fight for a certain kind of freedom: 'the Freedom for every individual in Europe to love whom they want, where they want, whatever their nationality.' Metacultural strategies serve to insert *Lovers* into that discursive space where the nature of citizenship in an increasingly diverse Europe is being heatedly debated. That the Dogma concept and label lend themselves to public criticism is, however, a point most clearly suggested by the history of the reception of one of the earliest Dogma films, Lars von Trier's *The Idiots*.

The Idiots tells a story about an unusual form of societal rebellion: provoking others, and arguably one's conventional self, by pretending to be retarded.[6] This 'spassing' is practised by a group of young people, centred around a leader figure called Stoffer (Jens Albinus), who have moved into a villa in the affluent Copenhagen suburb of Søllerød (where von Trier grew up and now lives). When queried about the initial motivation for his film, von Trier remarked that his mother, a civil servant, had been responsible for setting up institutions for the disabled, and that Søllerød had categorically refused to co-operate. *The Idiots*, then, allegedly finds its starting point in a very specific set of prejudices against disability (*Playing the Fool*, Channel 4). The intensity, however, of the psychological drama is generated not only by the discomfort that the characters' spassing provokes among the able-bodied and mostly affluent citizens with whom they come into contact, but also by the power dynamics within the group. Stoffer, who is driven by a desire for control, gradually instigates a kind of runaway process of one-upmanship requiring, for example, the characters to spass in contexts where the risks to them personally are the greatest. While those who initially supported the idea of finding an inner authenticity through spassing gradually become disaffected with Stoffer's vision, the value of the project is confirmed in the concluding moments of the film by the conversion to the project of idiocy of the sceptic in their midst, the young woman called Karen (Bodil Jørgensen). Karen, who accidentally joins the group when Stoffer grabs her hand in a restaurant and refuses to let go, returns to her home, where she spasses in front of horrified family members. She is accompanied by fellow commune member, Susanne (Anne Louise Hassing), who, much like the viewer, learns that Karen abandoned her family in a traumatised condition following the death of her infant. Her husband's explosive anger at her spassing (which takes the form of imitating a disabled person's inability to eat cake with propriety) is fuelled, in part, by the deep breach that her unexplained absence from her child's funeral constitutes in his mind.

If the very idea of able-bodied individuals voluntarily mimicking the involuntary behaviours of the disabled is intentionally distasteful and provocative in and of itself, it becomes all the more so as a result of von Trier's decision to emphasise nudity and, more importantly, sexuality. Jeppe (Nikolaj Lie Kaas) and Josephine (Louise Mieritz), for example, are shown tenderly enacting a scene of imagined spastic love. In an earlier moment in the film, Stoffer, ever intent on escalation, transforms a diffuse sense of group sensuality into a focused gang-bang. Von Trier opted to include shots of full penetration in this scene and professionals from the sex industry were brought in for this purpose.

Interestingly, two quite different interpretations of the relevant shots emerge from key commentaries on the film, von Trier's own diary (which he describes as a 'kind of authorial therapy', 1998: 159) and Jargil's fascinating documentary about the Dogma brethren's project, *The Purified*. Von Trier highlights the contrast between the professionals' full acceptance of their role and the actors' difficulties in playing their parts with real copulation occurring in the room. His comments on the situation emphasise the importance of the penetration shots:

> it was odd that this resistance arose, that [the situation] was so unpleasant. They struggled with it, Anne Louise had to struggle with herself to remain, everyone was struggling. It was important and difficult, but they did it, and it's good that they did, for I now see that the images are essential to the scene. They give the scene a certain sense of danger, which makes it impossible to take distance from it. It is dangerous. There are people there pretending to be retarded while really fucking. This provides exactly the kind of transgression of limits that this scene and the film as a whole need (von Trier 1998: 249–50; my translation).

In Jargil's documentary, on the other hand, these images are singled out as the 'one moment of inauthenticity' in the film. The phrase is used by Mogens Rukov whose intense involvement with the Dogma brethren's projects has earnt him the unofficial title of 'Dogma doctor'. Rukov's rather poetic and virtually Heideggerian comments on the Dogma films foreground the ideas of truth and authenticity and locate the significance of Dogma in its attempt to capture the fleeting moment when the truth of a given situation is disclosed. And his claim seems to be that the viewer somehow senses the rote or mechanical nature of the copulation, which, although real, paradoxically comes to stand in stark contrast with the authenticity of a certain kind of pretence or performance.

What is interesting for present purposes is the way in which *The Idiots* provoked passionate and socially significant discussion of key issues having to do with the realities and perceptions of disability. Of equal significance is the film's role as a catalyst for change or vehement debate in the area of censorship law. I shall focus here on the film's reception in Britain, although brief mention will be made of its impact in Norway. In addition to its theatrical release in Britain, *The Idiots* was shown on Channel 4, where it was explicitly linked to two documentary programmes that were framed as more or less direct comments on the issues raised by the film. *Forbidden Pleasures*, a Channel 4 documentary narrated by Daniella Nardini and directed by Anne Parisio, focuses on the sexual needs of individuals so disabled as to need help with every aspect of their lives. The film articulates these individuals' self-understandings as sexual beings and highlights the difficulties they face in satisfying their erotic needs. The point is to show that while their disabilities may represent obstacles to sexual fulfilment, the real problem lies with the various forms of institutionalised assistance they receive, all of which are predicated on assumptions about disabled persons as non-sexual beings. Programming comments connect von Trier's fiction film with a documentary that precisely aims to make public issues that have been so shrouded in the veils of privacy as to have been virtually non-existent, if existence is held to involve a certain public acknowledgment, a certain degree of mutual belief or shared awareness. The film, then, is construed, or at the very least appropriated, as a means of provoking a complacent society into rethinking its views on disability, into reconsidering certain institutional arrangements and the ideologies on which they are based.

Unlike *Forbidden Pleasures*, the second of the two relevant Channel 4 documentaries, entitled *Playing the Fool* (directed by Claire Lasko), is construed throughout as an explicit commentary on *The Idiots*. On the whole, the documentary seems to be trying to answer the following kinds of questions: To what extent is, or should, *The Idiots* be perceived as offensive? Can *The Idiots* function positively as a resource for undermining negative stereotypes about disability? The film begins by situating *The Idiots* within the larger context of von Trier's oeuvre, where disability is shown to be a guiding thematic concern. Reference is made to the central character's congenital and progressive blindness in *Dancer in the Dark*, which was awarded the Palme d'Or at Cannes, with the prize of best actress going to the Icelandic singer, Björk, in her role as the Czech immigrant, Selma. Mention is also made of the somewhat simple-minded Bess (Emily Watson) who, in *Breaking the Waves*, is shown to engage in increasingly self-destructive sexual behaviour in order to gratify various fantasies experienced by her bedridden husband, Jan (Stellan Skarsgård). Attention is rightly drawn to the 'Greek chorus' in the popular hospital series *Riget* (*The Kingdom*). This chorus comprises two dishwashers played by Morten Rotne Leffers and Vita Jensen, both of whom suffer from Down's syndrome. The main intent, however, behind *Playing the Fool* is to capture responses, on the part of both the able and the disabled, to von Trier's most systematic treatment of disability, *The Idiots*. The interviewer records a series of negative and positive reactions, with both kinds of responses being articulated by interviewees with disabilities and by those without. The journalist Penny Bould is shown to object to *The Idiots* on the grounds that it provides fuel for misconceptions about the disabled. In particular, the film suggests that there is a direct connection between disability and socially obnoxious behaviour. The film critic, Paul Darke, who is shown seated in a wheelchair, adopts a rather different position. The viewer hears some of Darke's introductory remarks about the film, which was screened at the Leamington Spa Film Festival in an attempt to generate public debate, not only about disability, but about cultural diversity and the pressure on outsiders or newcomers to conform to dominant norms. Judith Stevenson, a key figure in the Council of Disabled People, is equally supportive of von Trier's provocative work. The film, she points out, is very good in spite of the fact that it in many ways involves bad taste. In her view the film uses 'disability as a metaphor for an agent of rebellion against social control'. The seriously disabled actor, Jamie Beddard, objects vehemently to her interpretation. If disability is being used as a metaphor, then it is not an 'adequate' one, he insists, for there is something deeply offensive about using the lives of real people as metaphors. Beddard further registers his offence at the 'pot pourri' quality of von Trier's film, which in his mind showcases a grab-bag of disabilities mixed together in an incoherent manner.

It could be argued that von Trier's film targets the very same concept of disability 'as personal and accidental, before or without sociopolitical significance' (Wilson and Lewiecki-Wilson 2001: 2) with which the burgeoning field of disability studies is variously engaged. A case could also be made for seeing the film as an attempt to foreground the fact that whereas 'most disabled people spend their lives in the "majority world"' (Priestley 2001: 3), very few able-bodied people have even a dawning awareness of what it means to inhabit that world with a disability. In many ways the film mirrors on a more general level the transformative strategies that figure centrally in the identity politics of the disabled. Wilson and Lewiecki-Wilson point out that 'discourse ... aid[s] collective action' when, for example, 'the term cripple' is seized and turned 'against itself into the proactive label crip culture' (2001: 3). In von Trier's film a term traditionally loaded with negative connotations – 'spastic' – comes to designate a project of retrieval, a means of collective purification and a path towards inner authenticity. The point here, however, is not to decide whether *The Idiots* is ultimately objectionable or not, but to note that the film, abetted by the publicity that Dogma 95 affords, provokes discussions about disability. That this is no trivial contribution is clearly suggested by recent works, such as *The New Disability History: American Perspectives*, edited by Paul K. Longmore and Lauri Umansky (2001), and *Disability and the Life Course: Global Perspectives*, edited by Mark Priestley (2001). While Longmore and Umansky point out that disability finally 'won a place in the "national [i.e. American] conversation"' with the 'passage of the Americans with Disabilities Act (ADA) in 1990' (2001: 1), Priestley draws attention to the ways in which the global phenomenon of disability has been 'framed within a minority worldview' derived from first-world experiences. What is needed, he points out, is greater awareness of the way in which uneven economic and political development impinges on the experience of disability in various parts of the world. While *The Idiots* is clearly tied to the basic framework of the Danish welfare state, the film can hardly be construed as endorsing Danish first-world attitudes towards the disabled. By breaking radically with propriety, good taste and political correctness, the film necessarily invites debates about disability, not just in the Danish context on which it reflects, but in each and every public space around the globe in which the film is shown. In this sense the film brings into public focus the very realities for which the counter-public centred around disability is claiming greater attention.

The representation of disability made *The Idiots* controversial, but it was the emphasis on nudity and the inclusion of explicit sex that led to its being censored in different national contexts. In the US the film was released with 'ludicrous large black rectangles obscuring male and female genitalia floating ridiculously over the middles of every exposed performer' (Williams 2001: 20; cited by MacKenzie 2002). In Hong Kong the film is available, but without the offending penetration shots. And in the Canadian province of Ontario and the Republic of Ireland, censorship takes the form of an outright ban on von Trier's film. In Britain, on the other hand, the film was released uncut by the British Board of Film Classification, which deliberated as follows about the film:

This challenging art film ... concerns a group of young people who have formed a commune founded on 'anti-middle class ideology'. As part of that philosophy, they pretend to be 'idiots' (i.e. people with learning difficulties) and behave accordingly in public places. The BBFC considered the possible offensiveness of this behaviour to members of the public who are disabled, and to those who are concerned with them. The view of the film, taken as a whole, is however a positive and sensitive one – particularly when real disabled characters are involved. The 'idiot' behaviour is most specifically a means for the young people of taking refuge from society and a token of their abdication from it. The BBFC also considered the public acceptability of a very short but explicit shot of sexual behaviour. The BBFC's draft classification guidelines, published in July last year, permit images of real sex in '18' rated films or videos providing they are brief and justified by context. There are precedents for content of this kind (notably the widely shown Japanese film *Ai no corrida* (*In the Realm of the Senses*), but it requires the clearest justification. The particular scene in *The Idiots* represents the critical point at which the commune oversteps its own boundaries of behaviour and begins to fall apart. Given the brevity of the image, and its importance within the narrative structure of the film, the BBFC concluded that sufficient justification existed to satisfy the standard set by the guidelines (cited by MacKenzie 2002).

As MacKenzie points out, *The Idiots* became a focaliser for public debate, particularly in the tabloid press, because it could be framed as a clear and undesirable consequence of new permissive BBFC guidelines (adopted in July 1998) allowing 'real sex' to be shown on British screens. While von Trier could hardly have anticipated the specific role that his film would play in the British context, the overarching intent was clearly to push the limits of various forms of acceptability and, as a result, to prompt reflection on the very norms in question. Implicit in the film's mode of address is not only an invitation to enter into an imagined world of make-believe, but also, in almost Brechtian fashion, the demand that the viewer take a stand on those aspects that somehow provoke discomfort, a sense of threat, disgust or offence. Inherently and intentionally controversial, the film anticipates its own discursive elaboration in modes extending beyond mere interpretation.

The Idiots was also at the centre of public debate in Norway, where pietistic religious sentiments remain strong. In this case, what prompted discussion was not *The Idiots* as an instance of what censorship law allows, but rather the astonishing decision on the part of the Norwegian Censorship Board seriously to stretch the letter of the law and release *The Idiots* uncut. Although images of sexual organs have been consistently banned from Norwegian screens, the board determined that von Trier's treatment of nudity, explicit sex and especially group sex revealed an overarching artistic intent that justified a departure from established interpretations of the censorship guidelines. Interestingly, the claim has been made that a pan-Nordic sense of belonging, rather than artistic intent, in fact was the decisive factor:

I don't think that the ban on sex and naked sexual organs suddenly has been lifted. But it is no longer as definitive as it was in the past,' ... [Arild Frøyseth, director of the distribution company, Fidalgo] says. He explains that the fact that *The Idiots* is a Danish film was very significant: 'Had it been an American film, the answer would have been NO. But because the film is Danish and very artistic, it got through' (Høyer 1998).

Vincent Chui's *Leaving in Sorrow*: Reverend
Lai quarrels with his wife, Ivy, about her
desire to abandon Hong Kong and re-settle
in the US

Here, it would appear, the dynamics of international recognition form the basis, not for
reflected glory at the national, but rather at the pan-national level. Lars von Trier's status
as one of the great internationally recognised contemporary *Nordic* film-makers guarantees the release, in uncensored form, of his controversial film in Norway. At the same
time, the inherently controversial nature of the film inevitably generates collisions among
censorship guidelines, precedents and a religiously inflected public opinion, which in turn
creates a publicity effect equal to that of a typical Nordic marketing campaign: 'Overall
the intense debate … has provided the kind of publicity that would have cost a million
kroner' (Frøyseth, cited in Høyer 1998).

While the right kind of thematic content can make any film relevant to public discussions about matters of general concern, the Dogma label embraces a striking
number of films that have functioned as effective vehicles of public criticism.
Inasmuch as the Dogma project brings with it its own kind of counter-publicity, Dogma
films clearly provide a convenient means of articulating the concerns of diverse con-
stituencies. Yet, while Dogma's links to public criticism may be partially explained by
the appeal of a certain pre-constituted (and already critical) publicity, there seems to
be something about the particular nature of the rules themselves that genuinely supports the exploration of issues that are both current and broadly political. The rules, it
has been argued (Livingston, this volume, pages 102–5), target not only Hollywood's
globalising practices but also, very importantly, its insistence on fantasy. Not surprisingly, then, Dogma film-makers typically understand themselves to be somehow
reaffirming a commitment to what Vincent Chui unabashedly calls 'reality' and 'real
life', to what might also be described as the driving concerns of various publics. In the
case of *Leaving in Sorrow* this emphasis on the 'real' finds expression in a unique
soundtrack involving 'excerpts from protest rallies, denunciations of government offi-
cials, [and] democratic speeches', a kind of 'mediatized record of HK's history of
democratic resistance to 1997' (Kraicer 2001: 2–3). Inasmuch as Chui's film invites
debate about Hong Kong identities in the light of post-handover developments, it provides further evidence of an internal connection – even in contexts of informal
appropriation – between the brethren's metacultural project and the dynamics of
public criticism.

CONCLUSION

Dogma 95 is a complicated and multi-layered phenomenon that continues to evolve in spite of statements, at regular intervals, to the effect that the movement is dead. A crucial aspect of Dogma's impact clearly has to do with the way in which the movement allows limitations, not only of the self-imposed variety, but also of those derived from the accidents of larger socio-historical configurations, to be transformed into the very conditions that make genuinely significant contributions to art and public discourse possible. Yet, to count as a significant contribution, the relevant cultural expression has somehow to find an audience, and it is here – in its understanding of the workings of publicity – that an important part of the promise of Dogma lies. By ingeniously linking metaculture to public criticism, Dogma 95 effectively mobilises and forges links between a series of counter-publics that are committed in various ways to challenging dominant arrangements. Dogma 95, in short, is about stimulating creativity and finding a voice, but it is also about building audiences – a network of audiences with a genuinely global reach.

REFERENCES

Anon, 'PHILMSNYDT: ATS-service for biografgængere', *Politiken*, 26 May, 1998.

Appadurai, A., 'Grassroots Globalization and the Research Imagination', in A. Appadurai (ed.), *Globalization* (Durham: Duke University Press, 2001).

Bech, C. M., 'Dogmepolitik imod menneskelig ligegyldighed', *Politiken,* 7 May, 2001.

Beck, U., *What is Globalization?* (Cambridge: Polity Press, 2000).

Björkman, S., 'Trier on von Trier', *Film* no. 9, 2000, pp. 11–12.

Calhoun, C. (ed.), *Habermas and the Public Sphere* (Cambridge, MA: MIT Press, 1992).

Castells, M., *The Internet Galaxy: Reflections on the Internet, Business, and Society* (Oxford: Oxford University Press, 2001).

Caves, R., *Creative Industries: Contracts Between Art and Commerce* (Cambridge, MA: Harvard University Press, 2000).

Ditlev, N., 'København er miljø-dogme-by', *Morgenavisen Jyllands-Posten*, 25 May, 2001.

Dovne 98, 'Dovne 98 – et manifest', *Information*, 27 May, 1998.

Feldbech Rasmussen, N., 'Politiske dogmeregler', *Morgenavisen Jyllands-Posten,* 3 May, 2001.

Gigliotti, C., 'The Ethical Life of the Digital Aesthetic', in Peter Lunenfeld (ed.), *The Digital Dialectic: New Essays on New Media* (Cambridge, MA: MIT Press, 1999).

Grove, G., 'Teatre vil indføre dogme-begrebet', *Morgenavisen Jyllands-Posten*, 6 August, 1998.

Habermas, J., *The Structural Transformation of the Public Sphere: An Inquiry into a Category of Bourgeois Society*, trans. Thomas Bürger, with the assistance of Frederick Lawrence (Cambridge, MA: MIT Press, 1989).

Hansen, M., *Babel and Babylon: Spectatorship in American Silent Film* (Cambridge, MA: Harvard University Press, 1991).

Hjort, M., 'Lars von Trier', in Y. Tasker (ed.), *Fifty Contemporary Film-Makers* (London: Routledge, 2002).

Høyer, J., ' "Idioterne" bryder censurgrænser', *Morgenavisen Jyllands-Posten*, 5 August, 1998.

Kraicer, S., *'Leaving in Sorrow*: A Review', <www.chinesecinemas.org/reelasian.html> (2001).

Lee, B., *Talking Heads: Language, Metalanguage, and the Semiotics of Subjectivity* (Durham: Duke University Press, 1997).

Longmore, P. K., and L. Umansky, 'Introduction: Disability History: From the Margins to the Mainstream', in P. K. Longmore and L. Umansky (eds), *The New Disability History: American Perspectives* (New York: New York University Press, 2001).

MacKenzie, S., *'Baise-moi*, Feminist Cinemas and the Censorship Controversy', *Screen* vol. 43 no. 3, 2002, pp. 315–24.

Manovich, L., 'What is Digital Cinema?', in P. Lunenfeld (ed.), *The Digital Dialectic* (Boston: MIT Press, 1999).

Negt, O. and A. Kluge, *Public Sphere and Experience: Toward an Analysis of the Bourgeois and Proletarian Public Sphere*, trans. Peter Labanyi, Jamie Owen Daniel, Assenka Oksiloff (Minneapolis: University of Minnesota Press, 1993).

Ou Ning., 'In the Name of the Indies', *Ying Hua (Filmmakers)* vol. 1 no. 2, 1999 (Shenzhen, China).

Polizzotti, M., *Revolution of the Mind* (New York: Farrar, Straus and Giroux, 1995).

Priestley, M., *Disability and the Life Course: Global Perspectives* (Cambridge: Cambridge University Press, 2001).

Schmidt, J. (ed.), *What is Enlightenment? Eighteenth-Century Answers and Twentieth-Century Questions* (Berkeley and Los Angeles: University of California Press, 1996).

Shu Kei, 'Save Those Bad Movies – On Denmark's Dogma 95', *Ying Hua (Filmmakers)* vol. 1 no. 2, 1999 (Shenzhen, China).

Turkle, S., *Life on the Screen: Identity in the Age of the Internet* (London: Phoenix, 1997).

Urban, G., *Metaculture: How Culture Moves through the World* (Minneapolis: University of Minnesota Press, 2001).

von Trier, L., *Idioterne – manuskript, dagbog* (Copenhagen: Gyldendal, 1998).

Warner, M., 'Publics and Counterpublics', *Public Culture* vol. 14 no. 1, 2002, pp. 49–90.

Williams, L., 'Cinema and the Sex Act', *Cineaste* vol. XXVII no. 1, 2001, pp. 20–25.

Wilson, J. C. and C. Lewiecki-Wilson, 'Disability, Rhetoric, and the Body', in J. C. Wilson and C. Lewiecki-Wilson (eds), *Embodied Rhetorics: Disability in Language and Culture* (Carbondale and Edwardsville: Southern Illinois University Press, 2001).

Wilson, R. and W. Dissanayake (eds), *Global/Local: Cultural Production and the Transnational Imaginary* (Durham: Duke University Press, 1996).

woj, 'Kommentar fra kulisserne', *Politiken*, 24 March, 1995.

<www.dogma-dance.org>.

NOTES

1. Benjamin Lee's *Talking Heads: Language, Metalanguage, and the Semiotics of Subjectivity* (1997) provides an incisive discussion of various concepts of and approaches to performativity. I am using the term here primarily in the sense associated with the work of John Austin. That is, it is a matter of linguistic utterances somehow creating the events to which they refer.

2. I owe this idea to conversations with Ben Lee. Lee develops the point about circulation and transformation in 'The Problem of Circulation', the introduction to a forthcoming co-authored book provisionally entitled *Cultures of Circulation* (with Edward LiPuma).

3. Manovich (1999) provides an incisive account of how digitisation is affecting an established art form such as the cinema. The focus here, however, is not so much on the impact of the new media on existing arts, but rather on the 'elasticity', to use Manuel Castells' (2001) term, of the emerging digital arts themselves.

4. The view of Dogma as a cheap gimmick is articulated by the Duke in Baz Luhrmann's *Moulin Rouge*, where it is automatically discredited by the vile character of the speaker.

5. See her contribution to Calhoun (1992). For historical documents pertaining to relevant notions of publicity, see Schmidt (1996).

6. The connections between Dogma 95 and Surrealism are nowhere more evident than in *The Idiots*, which in many ways parallels André Breton's attempt in the second section of *The Immaculate Conception* 'to reconstruct the discourse of insanity from within' (Polizzotti 1995: 353).

10

Decoding *D-Day*: Multi-Channel Television at the Millennium

Martin Roberts

DESCRIPTION

D-Day [*D-Dag*], the code name for the project produced by the four Dogma directors for Danish television to commemorate the new millennium, is one of the least-known of their projects outside Denmark. Widely regarded as one of the least successful Dogma projects, it is also, as I hope to show here, one of the most conceptually interesting and certainly the most daring. Co-produced by the Danish Film Institute and Nimbus Film, the project consisted of four seventy-minute recordings shot on digital video, simultaneously and in real time, in central Copenhagen from 11:30 p.m. on New Year's Eve 1999 to 12:40 a.m. on New Year's Day 2000. Each film-maker remotely directed a DV camera operator and an actor (or actress, in one case) improvising a role according to predetermined rules, via a wireless link to a central control-room in Copenhagen's Tivoli Gardens (except for Lars von Trier, who for reasons which need not concern us here was based in *Filmbyen*). On the evening of New Year's Day 2000, the four video recordings were broadcast, simultaneously and unedited, on separate channels of Danish television. Additional channels showed a split-screen view of all four channels, as well as a behind-the-scenes view of the film-makers directing operations, chain-smoking and downing glasses of millennial champagne in the control-room. Viewers were invited to use their TV remote to surf between channels and thus obtain different views of the unfolding narrative, and thus to 'edit' their own film. As the introductory voice-over to each of the four channels observed, 'One thing is certain: no-one will see the same film.'

Collectively, *D-Day*'s four channels tell the story of an unsuccessful bank robbery, which takes place while the rest of the nation is out celebrating the new millennium. It eventually brings all four protagonists together in some of the most fascinating footage of the project, as camera operators dodge and weave around them at the bank, trying – not very successfully – to keep out of each other's frames. The New Year's Day broadcast was reportedly watched by an audience of some 1.4 million, approximately a quarter of the national population.[1]

'D-Day', as most people know, was the code name given to the date scheduled for the

Allied invasion of Normandy, 6 June 1944, generally regarded as one of the turning points in the Second World War. The term has since passed into common usage to denote any day of momentous significance, the turning of the millennium being an obvious case in point. Yet the 'D' of *D-Day* also stands, obviously, for Denmark, as well as for Dogma, and the superimposition of the three meanings encoded an ironic militarism which must have greatly amused Lars von Trier, celebrator of Baden-Powell and driver of a camouflaged golf-cart around the Zentropa studios. If *D-Day* marked the first day of the new millennium, it was also the day set for the Dogma brothers' symbolic invasion of Denmark, via that very organ of propaganda, national television.

As we shall see, the 'D' of *D-Day* also encodes other, less obvious meanings. In what follows, I attempt to decode both the obvious and less obvious meanings of *D-Day* from a variety of interdisciplinary perspectives, as a means of exploring the project's complex social, cultural and technological dimensions. The five sequences can be accessed in any order, and collectively aspire to reproduce the database structure of the *D-Day* project itself.

DENMARK

One of the most interesting dimensions of *D-Day* concerns its relation to Danish national cultural identity and the Danish public sphere. Like the British experience with the ill-fated Millennium Dome project, it raises interesting problems concerning the efforts of state governments to define an 'official' national public culture and the relative indifference, or even resistance, of national publics to this. As we will see, *D-Day*'s relative lack of popular success may have at least as much to do with this institutional dimension as with its particular qualities as a media text.

Within the Danish public sphere, *D-Day* could scarcely have occupied a more prominent position. The Dogma group has been criticised for its skills in self-promotion and *D-Day* was certainly no exception, receiving heavy advance publicity through press conferences, media gossip and the inevitable website (www.d-dag.dk) in the months preceding New Year's Eve. In institutional terms, *D-Day* was in many ways a specifically Danish project: the four Dogma directors themselves are widely regarded as a national treasure, and the project was financed by Denmark's national film institute. The fact that *D-Day* was broadcast not just on one national TV channel but on all of them – a privilege usually reserved for political broadcasts and the Queen's speech – and was scheduled immediately after the Danish Prime Minister's televised New Year's Day address to the nation make it clear that it was constructed as a media event of national significance. What made *D-Day* a national media event above all, however, was its interactive dimension: the invitation to its audience to 'edit' it at home using the TV remote, thus creating their own version of it. As Mette Hjort (2000a) observes:

> [V]iewers ... were highly attuned to the fact that they were engaging in a new communicative practice. They were, I assume, also focally aware of the likelihood of hundreds of thousands of fellow citizens being similarly involved in expanding their communicative repertoires ...

D-Day, Hjort suggests, 'fostered an intense experience of the social bond, in much the same way that popular events such as the world cup final do'. This meta-communicational aspect of *D-Day*, she argues, enables it to be seen as a contemporary version of a *Danmarksfilm*, a historical genre of Danish national cinema which purports to provide a portrait of Denmark and its people (Hjort 2000a; on the *Danmarksfilm* genre, see also Hjort 2000b: 114–15).

The temptation to read *D-Day* from the standpoint of Benedict Anderson's concept of imagined communities as the origin of the nineteenth-century nation-state is almost irresistible. Anderson argues (1991: 24), for example, that the nineteenth-century novel's structure of multiple, intersecting plot lines, or the collage structure of national news-papers, served to construct in their readers an idea of the nation as a large-scale social collectivity. The interwoven stories of the four protagonists of *D-Day* could clearly be read along similar lines, as providing a composite snapshot of the nation at the turn of the new millennium. Anderson's discussion of the social function of rituals of national synchronicity such as the singing of national anthems also illuminates *D-Day*'s function as a national media event:

> There is a special kind of contemporaneous community which language alone suggests –
> above all in the form of poetry and songs. Take national anthems, for example, sung on
> national holidays. No matter how banal the words and mediocre the tunes, there is in this
> singing an experience of simultaneity. At precisely such moments, people wholly unknown to
> each other utter the same verses to the same melody. The image: unisonance. Singing the
> Marseillaise, Waltzing Matilda, and Indonesia Raya provide occasions for unisonality, for the
> echoed physical realisation of the imagined community (1991: 145).[2]

D-Day clearly has much in common with such national rituals: the setting aside of an hour of national television creates the sacred time of ritual, during which the public is exhorted to engage in a form of collective play. 'Play' is the operative word here, indeed, since in contrast to public song or silence, *D-Day*'s public play, while synchronous, incorporates an element of indeterminacy: 'One thing is certain: no-one will see the same film.'

Much of the work inspired by Anderson's book *Imagined Communities* has been devoted to extending its arguments to twentieth-century mass media, which are now widely regarded as playing a key role in the emergence of national identities. According to a by now familiar narrative, the shift from national television networks – whether state-owned, public ones or commercial, as in the US – to today's deregulated, multi-channel televisual environment has resulted in the fragmentation of audiences, replaced broadcasting with narrowcasting, and facilitated the emergence of increasingly transna-tional identities. The example of *D-Day* seems to show, however, that the emergence of transnational media networks does not prevent television from continuing to play its older historical role as custodian of the national imaginary.

D-Day also exposes some of the limitations of Anderson's model, however. One of the problems of that model (Rajagopal 2000) is that it underestimates the role of the state in the production of national imagined communities, treating them as rather spontaneous, self-generating collectivities emerging from capitalist mass media. The fact that many twentieth-century national communications institutions such as radio, TV or film industries have been state-owned and controlled, thus enabling national governments to regulate what constitutes the national itself, clearly problematises a bottom-up, 'grassroots' model of the national imaginary. *D-Day*'s ties to the Danish state, via its dependence on the Danish Film Institute and national broadcast media, is a case in point, and these ties clearly set limits on the kinds of discourse on the national it could acceptably engage in (it is hard to imagine a project such as Lars von Trier's controversial film *Idioterne* [*The Idiots*] being deemed acceptable in such a context).

This state-sanctioned, 'official' nationalism of *D-Day* may in part account for the second way in which it poses a challenge to simplistic assumptions about media and imagined communities: the fact that only a quarter of the nation bothered to watch it anyway. The apparently large degree of public apathy about the project – leaving aside the dissatisfaction of those who did watch it – can be attributed precisely to its being a state-sponsored, top-down national initiative rather than a genuinely popular, collective one; for this reason it met with public resistance, or merely indifference, which such official national projects so often do. Across the channel, the Millennium Dome project has provided an even more striking lesson about the literal unpopularity among national publics of government efforts to define national cultural agendas and identities.

DOGMA

The fact that *D-Day* was an initiative of the four Dogma directors, not to mention its use of hand-held digital cameras, emphasis on improvisation and modest budget (approximately US$500,000), no doubt accounts for why it has been widely regarded as a Dogma project. However, the *D-Day* website makes a point of noting that the project does not adhere to the Vow of Chastity, while as Hjort points out, it contravenes it in a number of respects.[3] If *D-Day* does not follow the Dogma rules to the letter, however, it undeniably follows the spirit of the Vow of Chastity in that it remains based on a set of rules – not quite the same rules, to be sure, but rules nonetheless. While conceding that *D-Day* is 'not really a Dogma thing, … it just happens to be the four Dogma directors', von Trier adds, 'but it's very difficult – like Dogma in that way, because it's taking something very simple and then putting a lot of difficult rules on top and hoping something will come out of it' (cited in Kelly 2000: 136).

If one thing is clear about the Dogma movement, it is that it is obsessed with rules. Not since hair-splitting debates about seventeenth-century classical French drama, it seems, has there been so much attention to rules – adherence to or infringement thereof, merits or demerits thereof, or even what observing a rule actually means (Kelly 2000; Hjort 2000a). The rules themselves have been conceived in largely religious, and specifically Christian terms, from the tongue-in-cheek medievalism of the Vow of Chastity to the required public confession of one's 'sins' against it. This discussion of rules in religious terms has tended to distract attention from the more playful side of Dogma, however, and the fact that rules are also the defining principle of games. Rather than as a form of cinematic asceticism, Dogma is more productively viewed as an attempt to turn film-making into a kind of game, even a sport, in which, as in any game, rules provide a set of parameters within which serious play may take place. The analogy between film-making and sport is made explicit by Søren Kragh-Jacobsen in a discussion of the challenge of shooting *Mifunes sidste sang* (*Mifune*) on film rather than video:

> I did so much multi-camera work for television in the 1970s. But it was hard for me to think of shooting video in the countryside. And I said, 'This non-separation of image and sound – what's the problem if you have three cameras? It's too easy.' The challenge must be that you have one camera on your shoulder, you shoot film – I mean, that's sport, right? (cited in Kelly 2000: 158).

While not exactly played according to the Dogma rules-of-the-game, *D-Day* is clearly no less rules-based. As Thomas Vinterberg observed, 'This is a game that can be seen as an extension of the game we began with the first Dogma films' (cited in Hjort 2000a). Watching the elegantly attired directors in the control-room, one is struck by how similar their behaviour (smoking, drinking, laughing, etc.) and attitudes of intense concentration and enjoyment are to those of a group of gentlemen engaging in an after-dinner parlour game. But the game was not confined to the control-room, of course. The originality of *D-Day*, indeed, was that it took the 'Dogma game', as Vinterberg calls it, to another level, by being a game that we all – or at least we Danes – could play. Mette Hjort uses similar terms, noting that 'the rules of the game purport[ed] to convert mere consumers of TV fiction into co-producers or *co-authors*'. *D-Day*, she suggests, 'invite[d] viewers to engage in a game which somehow simulate[d] … the activities of film *editors*' [her italics] (2000a). On New Year's Day 2000, then, Danish citizens were invited to participate in a giant role-playing game, in which their assigned role was that of what might be called millennial national citizens. That the project was ultimately no more or less than that, and didn't 'really' turn its audience into authors, seems to miss the point: that it *was*, in the end, 'only a game', albeit one which almost a quarter of the population accepted the invitation to play.

From the Balinese cockfight to *Survivor*, 'deep play', in Clifford Geertz's useful term (1973), occupies a central position in the construction of social identities, whether of the village or the nation. Society itself is routinely conceptualised by social scientists as a kind of role-playing game: people are social actors; everyday life itself is a performance (Goffman 1959); you play by the rules or you take the consequences. Democracy itself is commonly seen as a kind of spectator sport in references to 'first past the post' or 'winner-takes-all' systems. With 'playing the game' come social identity, integration, often status. It is revealing, in this context, how the articulation of national identity so often involves vicarious or literal participation in game-playing, from the 'national game' of cricket or baseball to the national lottery. Getting people to play with you is a way of ensuring their participation, and national gaming thus can be seen as a necessary antidote to the apathy and inertia which, according to Jean Baudrillard (1973), are the natural state of the masses.

From this point of view, the ultimate significance of *D-Day* is not as a narrative, nor even as a fantasy of co-authorship, but as a collective video game whose players were also invited to participate, on a symbolic level, in the 'game' of the nation itself. While the project may have been generally felt to have been a failure, as anyone who plays games is always told, the point of a game is not in winning or losing, but in playing the game at all (as the Prince of Denmark himself might have put it, 'the play's the thing'). Ultimately, the success of *D-Day* should be evaluated not in terms of whether it 'worked', or did succeed in turning its audience into co-authors, but of how successful it was in persuading people to play its game at all. 1.4 million viewers, almost a quarter of the national population, might not seem like much of a success, yet even in 'little Denmark' – as the Danes affectionately like to call their country – it was clearly no small achievement.

DOCUMENTARY

Strictly speaking, *D-Day* is not a documentary: as is the case with other Dogma films, its narrative and characters are fictitious. Like those films, however, *D-Day* blurs the boundaries between fiction film and documentary in a number of ways, and in this respect is symptomatic of a larger shift in visual media in recent years, from reality-TV shows to fake *vérité* films such as *The Blair Witch Project* (1999).

To begin with, while its narrative is ostensibly fictional, *D-Day* was clearly intended to serve as a documentary record of events in the national capital at the turn of the new millennium. Going further than other Dogma films in its application of the seventh rule of the Vow of Chastity, *D-Day*'s fictional narrative takes place literally in the here and now, not only in the real public spaces of central Copenhagen but also the real time of its actual recording. *D-Day* was thus, in effect, a live public performance, recorded on video as it happened, in which the line between representation and reality in what we see on screen is often hard to draw: as the actors move through the city's public spaces, for example, they do so among 'real people', who often pause to stare quizzically at them and the camera operators.[4] As in other Dogma films, dialogue is largely unscripted and improvised within pre-arranged parameters, further enhancing the simulated spontaneity and authenticity of documentary.

Time is of central concern throughout *D-Day*, or more accurately, tim*ing*: the synchronisation of multiple temporal and spatial co-ordinates essential to successful criminal activity, immortalised in the familiar heist-movie injunction to synchronise watches. Pulling off a successful robbery, as any robber knows, is primarily a matter of ensuring that everything happens in the right place at the right time.[5] The *D-Day* bank-robbers are no exception in this regard, nervously consulting their watches at regular intervals prior to their rendezvous at the bank, and growing anxious when unforeseen obstacles come up which threaten to throw their timing off (most notably Boris' destitute former school friend, Jørgen, whom he vainly tries to shake off throughout the story).

Of course, the nervous glances at watches also serve a non-narrative purpose, since the real-time nature of the recording means that keeping an eye on the time is crucial to the project's success. The problems of space-time co-ordination facing the four producers of *D-Day* were in fact very similar to those of their characters, and the choice of a bank robbery as the project's narrative subject thus seems far from coincidental, a self-reflexive enactment of the project's own conditions of production. Flipping channels to the control-room, indeed, we observe a similar concern with timing: next to each director sits an assistant armed with a stopwatch who continually calls out the minutes remaining before key events are scheduled. It is, of course, the director's job to ensure that his actor/actress is in the right place at the right time. Much of the action of *D-Day* accordingly involves the actors scurrying anxiously from one location to another, although on occasion they also appear to be trying to kill time, with the accompanying risk of trying the audience's patience. If the characters seem tense, it is because the actors themselves are, albeit for different reasons.

The blurring of boundaries between reality and representation in *D-Day* also has much to do with the medium of production itself: as in other Dogma or fake *vérité* films, shooting on hand-held digital cameras gives *D-Day* the characteristically authentic look of a home movie. As if to underscore this, one of the four characters, Lise (Charlotte Sachs-Bostrup), herself carries a DV camera, on which, it emerges, she is shooting a video diary addressed to her husband. Although her footage was not shown as part of *D-Day*, it clearly could have been, and its narrative function seems to be to enhance the illusion of the authenticity of the footage we do see of her and the other protagonists. A further interesting aspect of *D-Day* in this context concerns the direction of the camera operators. Lars von Trier has noted that it is easy to imagine a film in which the audience would not have a problem with seeing the camera, and *D-Day* is certainly a case in point: although the directors often go to brilliant lengths to avoid having the camera operators shadowing their actors appearing in one another's shots, this becomes practically impossible once all four actors come together at the bank. Paradoxically, however, the glimpses we catch of cameras serve more to reinforce the illusion of authenticity than to undermine it: whereas classic realism in cinema pretends to provide an unmediated window on what it depicts and therefore attempts to conceal all traces of its technologies of production, documentary acknowledges – or even foregrounds – the camera's presence as a means of reinforcing its authenticity. This practice in turn, however, has now become codified as a stylistic device by which fiction films can simulate authenticity in what might be called hyperrealism.

In addition to the blurring of the fiction/documentary boundary within its narrative, *D-Day* also includes a non-fictional component in its video feed of the directors at work in their control-room in Tivoli Gardens. This was shot by Jesper Jargil, who has become something of an honorary fifth member of the Dogma men's club since producing documentaries of the making of von Trier's *The Idiots*, *De ydmygede* (*The Humiliated*), and his extraordinary 'Psychomobile' performance project, *De udstillede* (*The Exhibited*, 2000). Jargil's documentary footage of the control-room adds a further twist to the already vexed question of *D-Day*'s authorship (Hjort 2000a). Jargil's behind-the-scenes video further undermines the distinction in the project between fiction and documentary. As it makes clear, the audience of *D-Day* was invited to watch it on several levels at once, both as a fictional narrative and a non-fictional one about the former's production.

Much of the pleasure of watching *D-Day*, it can thus be argued, results from watching it at a meta-level, from the interplay within it between representation and reality, fiction and non-fiction, and the viewer's constant awareness of the collective ingenuity of directors, camera operators and actors in solving – or not quite being able to solve – the logistical dilemmas of the production process itself. A good example of this is the sequence towards the end of *D-Day*, when after leaving the bank, Carl and Niels-Henning break into the deserted (albeit well-lit, no doubt by prior arrangement) amusement park at Tivoli Gardens and go for a ride on the Ferris wheel. After seating themselves in the car, however, they are initially unable to get the ride to start: it becomes clear that this is unintended, and one senses the anguish of actors and directors at the likelihood that the carefully orchestrated ending of their story will fall flat. Luckily, they finally do manage to get the ride started (apparently with some off-camera assistance) and the pleasure of the scene comes as much from relief at its success as its narrative content. The final shot of the two men exultantly rising above the city, gulping from a champagne bottle, yelling New Year's greetings and framed by exploding fireworks, is one of *D-Day*'s finest moments.

DIGITAL

The Dogma directors have been at the forefront of the developing digital film-making movement, the shooting of feature films in digital video (DV) format on small, hand-held mini-DV cameras. Three of the four Dogma films made by the Dogma directors themselves – Thomas Vinterberg's *Festen* (*The Celebration*), Lars von Trier's *The Idiots* and Kristian Levring's *The King is Alive* – were shot on DV, while most of the twenty or so other Dogma-certified films have used the same format. Even films by the group which do not conform to the Dogma rules, such as von Trier's *Breaking the Waves* and *Dancer in the Dark,* were shot on DV. Such films are part of the much larger explosion of digital film-making that has been taking place in recent years.

The digital medium is in the process of transforming every aspect of film-making.[6] While some film critics today remain unimpressed by the resolution and saturation of the projected digital video image, film-makers are discovering the new possibilities, as well as some of the limitations, of shooting on DV. From the standpoint of production, perhaps the most important impact of the digital medium has been to shift the emphasis of production from production 'proper' to post-production (Manovich 2001: 303). As Lev Manovich explains, most of the work in classical film-making took place in the production phase: since film stock was expensive and had to be used sparingly, elaborate preparation of each shot was necessary (this is still true today of specialised film formats such as IMAX). Since film reels were of limited length and had to be spliced together, montage was developed as an aesthetic solution to the discontinuity of the medium (Manovich 2001: 144). Post-production offered relatively few options in terms of the visual effects that are standard today and, other than techniques such as optical printing, was confined largely to the craft of editing.

The advent of DV has been a mixed blessing for today's 'movie-makers': while on the one hand, the relative inexpensiveness of digital tape stock has vastly increased the volume of 'footage' that can be shot, the work of editing increases correspondingly as film-makers find themselves working with hours-more material than could have realistically been shot in the golden age of film-making. The much longer takes that DV makes possible also remove the necessity of montage, or at least reduce it to a purely aesthetic consideration. At the same time, computers have vastly expanded the range of options available in post-production, from digital compositing to the spatial montage of multiple frames on the cinema/TV/computer screen. While Hollywood films are increasingly produced by digital compositing, experimental film-makers such as Peter Greenaway (*Prospero's Books*, 1991, *The Pillow Book*, 1996) have begun exploring the possibilities of spatial montage.

D-Day itself is in many ways symptomatic of the impact of DV on the film production and post-production practices I have been describing. Each of its four seventy-minute tracks functions as a real-time, continuous video feed, deferring the process of editing and montage to the actual moment of reception, in the choices of the television viewer as he or she surfs between channels. It is interesting in this regard to compare *D-Day* with Mike Figgis' film *Timecode* (2000), which also involves four parallel, converging narratives. In Figgis' film, each of these narratives also unfolds unedited and in real time, as a continuous ninety-minute feed running in a different quadrant of the screen, similar to the multi-screen view of *D-Day* broadcast by the Danish channel TV3+. In contrast to *D-Day*, however, Figgis retains more editorial control over the film by modulating the volume of the respective soundtracks to direct the viewer's attention to one feed in preference to others at different points in the story. *D-Day*'s four channels, however, are spatially distributed across separate TV channels and selection of these is left entirely up to the viewer. The multi-screen soundtrack is simply an audio feed from the control-room, and in this sense complements the channels showing the control-room itself by simulating the directors' own viewpoint.

In addition to production, DV has in recent years also begun to transform the film, television and computer industries at the level of distribution and exhibition. Both in the US and Europe, digital broadcasting is in the process of superseding its analogue predecessor, not only expanding the multi-channel TV environment but bringing new interactive multimedia services which blur the boundaries between film, television and computing (Brandrud 1999; see also Jensen and Toscan 1999; Steemers 1998). Digital television has arrived in Denmark as in other European countries (Søndergaard 2000; *Development of Digital TV in Europe* 2000) and, although its market is still small, *D-Day* would undoubtedly have been watched as a digital broadcast by a small percentage of Danish viewers. While the broadcast version of *D-Day* did not offer any of the new services that digital television will provide, it did anticipate some of these, such as multiple camera angles of the same event. In this sense, as Mette Hjort observes, '*D-Day* provided a foretaste of the kinds of communicative competencies that might figure centrally in a future shaped by new technologies' (2000a). While set in the present, like other millennium projects *D-Day* thus had its eyes set firmly on the future and can thus be seen as a kind of digital time capsule, characterised by its peculiar sense of temporality: its orientation towards the historians of the future, its future-anterior sense of 'that which will have been'.

DATABASE

When I first began working on *D-Day* and set about obtaining a copy of it, I was not sure what to ask for. The problem was that it was far from clear exactly what *'D-Day' was*: was it, for example, the four seventy-minute DV recordings each directed by the four film-makers? Or a randomly chosen videotaped 'mix' of the original multi-channel broadcast, necessarily only one particular iteration among over a million others that could poten-tially have been made? Since the broadcast also included the additional split-screen and control-room channels which would presumably have been included in any viewing experience, should these channels also be treated as part of the text of *'D-Day'*? In the end, I obtained videotapes of each of the six channels, only to be faced with the problem of how to watch them: other than booking a session in a TV control-room to recreate the original viewing experience, the only option was to watch the tapes individually, either one after the other or laboriously switching back and forth between them.[7] What I had received, it became clear, was a video database, albeit without a suitable interface to nav-igate it. *D-Day*, indeed, can be seen as an exemplary instance of the emergence, in the age of new media, of the database as a cultural form.

In *The Language of New Media* (2001), Lev Manovich discusses a number of instances of the database form in cinema, from Dziga Vertov's *Man with a Movie Camera* (1929) to the films of Peter Greenaway. Vertov's film, for example, is described as resembling a database 'laid out flat' of film styles. *D-Day* has many fascinating parallels with *Man with a Movie Camera*, not least its search for a new kind of film language, and the self-reflexive appearance of camera operators in each other's frames. Whereas Vertov's data-base of the modern Soviet city is laid out sequentially and temporally, however, in the linear unfolding of the film itself, *D-Day*'s Copenhagen is laid out simultaneously and spatially across the multiple channels on which it was broadcast, as four simultaneously unfolding and intersecting narratives.

The database model of the media text is already an integral part of some areas of contemporary media production: as Manovich observes, in electronic and other pro-grammed musics the creative manipulation of musical samples is central to the art of the DJ. While on one level any film or TV broadcast can be seen as a 'mix' from a database of source materials, film and TV have been slower to exploit the possibilities of the database model, although the increasing frequency of director's-cut editions of well-known films is a step in that direction: Coppola's *Apocalypse Now Redux* (2001), for instance, is essentially a remix which expands his earlier film by interpolating new narrative segments drawn from the original database of footage. Mike Figgis goes a step further in *Timecode*, a film that exemplifies Manovich's database model via spatial montage within the frame: the cueing of individual channels through the modulation of sound makes the finished film itself a mix, and Figgis apparently planned to do live mixes of the film at special screenings after its release (Willis 2000: 35). Interesting as these examples are, neither goes as far as *D-Day* for several reasons: in the first place, neither relinquishes the control of the author/*auteur* over his film text, and neither involves the audience in the mixing process. In this respect, *D-Day* could be seen as a harbinger of the cinema or television of the future, in which, rather than being presented with a single, author-ised version, as is still largely the case today, the viewer is provided with a database from which to produce a personal mix. As is already the case with electronic music, one can thus imagine a proliferation of mixes of popular film and TV texts being exchanged – often illicitly – over broadband networks, no doubt accompanied by the legal struggles over 'intellectual property' associated with music, video and software piracy today.

Given the contingencies of *D-Day* as a media text, one can understand why the promised film version has yet to materialise: leaving aside the lukewarm reaction of both directors and critics to how the project had worked out in practice, such a film, in necessarily imposing a single, author-ised version of the text, would arguably contradict much of what made the project interesting in the first place: its nature as an open text. Rather than a film, indeed, *D-Day*'s interactive dimension makes it in many ways more appropriate for a video-game format, with the player/director being invited to mix her or his film from a multi-screen interface simulating that of the control-room from which the original project was directed. It is interesting, in this connection, that Nimbus Film (which had originally planned to produce the film version of *D-Day*) now plans to release a DVD edition of *D-Day*, a format that certainly offers the possibility of a more interactive version of the type outlined above. At the time of writing the DVD *D-Day* had not yet been released, but when it is it will be interesting to see what decisions have been made regarding the boundaries of the project itself, as well as how it attempts to simulate the interactive dimension of the original broadcast.

There is one aspect of *D-Day*, however, which even a DVD edition will be unable to reproduce: its collective dimension. Much of the appeal of *D-Day* for those who chose to participate in it was the awareness that many others elsewhere in the country were also doing so at the same time. As Hjort (2000a) observes, this collective dimension of *D-Day* had much to do with its meta-communicational force, and its role in fostering the sense of an imagined national community. Until recently, by contrast, playing video games was a predominantly individual activity: even when playing together in groups in arcades, players still had to take turns. This has changed over the past decade with the advent of networked role-playing and other games, in which hundreds of players may interact simultaneously in a shared textual or multimedia environment (Turkle 1995; Stone 1996). Interestingly, such groups have often come to imagine themselves as communities (see, for example, Dibbell 1998), with the line often blurring between playing and simply participating in a community. The phenomenon of the player-citizen in online communities paradoxically recalls how social participation in real-world societies can be seen as a kind of collective role-playing game, as well as the role of collective game-playing in the formation of imagined national and other communities. From such a perspective, one limitation of *D-Day* as a ritual of national identity was that it extended only to Danes residing in Denmark itself rather than the large number who live abroad. Beyond the DVD *D-Day*, then, one is left to speculate on how a *D-Day* webcast might have enabled Danes not just in Denmark but potentially anywhere in the world to connect to a worldwide imagined community.

ACKNOWLEDGMENTS

I would like to extend my sincere thanks to Dr Mette Hjort of the University of Hong Kong, Department of Comparative Literature, for initially providing me with tapes of *D-Day*, and for her help and dialogue throughout this project. Quite simply, I would have been unable to complete it without her. Thanks also for their assistance at various stages to Jeanette Nielsen in Copenhagen and Suzanne Quigley and Charlotte Ragert in New York.

REFERENCES

Anderson, B., *Imagined Communities: Reflections on the Origins and Spread of Nationalism* (New York: Verso, [1983] 1991).

Baudrillard, J., *In the Shadows of the Silent Majorities, or, The End of the Social, and Other Essays*, trans. Paul Foss, Paul Patton and John Johnston (New York: Semiotext(e), Inc, 1973).

Brandrud, R., 'Digital TV and Public Service in the Nordic Counties', in J. F. Jensen and C. Toscan (eds), *Interactive Television: TV of the Future or the Future of TV?* (Aalborg: Aalborg University Press, 1999).

Development of Digital TV in Europe: Denmark/1999, Institut de l'Audiovisuel et des Télécommunications en Europe (2000).

Dibbell, J., *My Tiny Life: Crime and Passion in a Virtual World* (New York: Henry Holt & Co, 1998).

Digital Denmark: Conversion to the Network Society, Copenhagen: Ministry of Research and Information Technology, Denmark, <www.detdigitaledanmark.dk> (1999).

Fiennes, S., 'Jesper Jargil. Dogma 2000? The Danish Director Co-Conspires', *Res* vol. 3 no. 1, 2000, p. 11.

Geertz, C., 'Deep Play: Notes on the Balinese Cockfight', in *Interpretation of Cultures: Selected Essays* (New York: Basic Books, 1973).

Goffman, E., 'Performance', in *The Presentation of Self in Everyday Life* (Garden City, NY: Doubleday, 1959).

Hjort, M., 'Reflections on Authorship: The Dogma Brethren's "D-Day"', paper delivered at University of East Anglia (2000a).

Hjort, M., 'Themes of Nation', in M. Hjort and S. MacKenzie (eds), *Cinema and Nation* (New York and London: Routledge, 2000b).

Hjort, M. and I. Bondebjerg (eds), *The Danish Directors: Dialogues on a Contemporary National Cinema* (Bristol: Intellect Books, 2001).

Kelly, R., *The Name of this Book is Dogme95* (London: Faber and Faber, 2000).

Manovich, L., *The Language of New Media* (Cambridge, MA: MIT Press, 2001).

Nichols, B., *Blurred Boundaries: Questions of Meaning in Contemporary Culture* (Bloomington: Indiana University Press, 1994).

Rajagopal, A., 'Mediating Modernity: Theorizing Reception in a Non-Western Society', in J. Curran and M. Park (eds), *Dewesternizing Media Studies* (New York and London: Routledge, 2000).

Søndergaard, H., 'Has Public Service Broadcasting a Role to Play in the Digital Age?', unpublished paper, University of Copenhagen, Department of Film and Media Studies (2000).

Steemers, J., *Changing Channels: The Prospects for Television in a Digital World* (Luton: University of Luton Press, 1998).

Stone, A. S., *The War of Desire and Technology at the Close of the Mechanical Age* (Cambridge, MA: MIT Press, 1996).

Turkle, S., *Life on the Screen: Identity in the Age of the Internet* (New York: Simon and Schuster, 1995).

Willis, H., 'Mike Figgis Redefines the Screen in *Timecode 2000*', *Res* vol. 3 no. 1, 2000, pp. 32–35.

NOTES

1. Since by its very nature as a national TV broadcast *D-Day* will not have been seen outside Denmark, Mette Hjort's (2000a) synopsis is invaluable and I therefore reproduce it in full below. As Hjort explains, these synopses are based on sequential viewings of video channels which were broadcast simultaneously and which viewers were intended to surf between, so that they represent a flattened-out version of the project. I return to the particularities of *D-Day* as media text and event in the 'Database' section.

Synopsis 1: Lise (Charlotte Sachs Bostrup) drops off her sister at her mother's place, parks her van, and then walks through downtown Copenhagen, addressing herself to her husband, Ulf, for whom she is making a home movie with her video recorder. Her remarks point to marital conflict. Lise informs her husband that she is on her way to his office. Lise retrieves a number of agendas from the vault that she and her fellow bank robbers break into in the Jyske Bank. She returns to her apartment where she confronts her husband with the agendas and an anonymous letter listing days on which he allegedly was unfaithful to her. They look up one of the dates and discover a D. Ulf invites her to check the other dates for Ds but informs her that such lack of trust would destroy their marriage. After some hesitation Lise returns the agendas to him unopened. She is joined by her sister with whom she drinks a New Year's toast.

Synopsis 2: Niels-Henning (Nicolaj Kopernikus) walks swiftly towards a hotel where, it turns out, he is to rendezvous with a contact who will provide him with a small bomb. En route, he receives a call from his mother on his mobile phone and responds emotionally when she informs him that he has forgotten to take the pills that prevent him from experiencing sight problems when nervous. Once in the bank, he manages to detonate the bomb after some hesitation about the wires. He subsequently meets up with Carl, who informs him that there was no money in the vault. Disappointed, they break into Tivoli, where they produce a chorus of exuberant 'Happy New Year's', having managed to start one of the rides.

Synopsis 3: Boris (Dejan Cukic) nervously records a message to his lover, Eva, in his yuppie apartment. He informs her that he is about to execute a risky scheme, which could entail a lengthy separation. On his way to the bank he encounters Jørgen, a former classmate and victim of bullying. Boris makes every effort to rid himself of Jørgen, who, as a result, finally pulls out a pistol, which turns out to be a toy. Boris' role in the robbery is to deactivate the alarms. He behaves with extreme nervousness throughout and at one point scares the others with the water pistol. Having faced the empty vault together with Carl and Lise, Boris and Jørgen leave the bank together. Boris invites Jørgen back to his slick apartment. Jørgen makes Boris a gift of a wad of bank notes and reveals that he found the money elsewhere in the bank.

Synopsis 4: Carl (Bjarne Henriksen) is on his way to a New Year's party together with his lover, Line (Helle Dolleris). He claims not to be able to join her and, having dropped her off, proceeds to the hotel where he meets up with Niels-Henning. He encounters a suicidal man on the hotel's roof and, having extracted the cause of his grief, promises that a woman will come to him before 00:15 when he intends to jump. He interrupts his criminal activities at the bank long enough to call a woman who is promised 10,000 kroner if she'll accommodate the man on the roof. On discovering the empty vault, Carl blames Lise and hand-cuffs her to a file cabinet. He meets up with Niels-Henning and takes the initiative to break into Tivoli. Together they produce an exuberant chorus of 'Happy New Year's' from one of the rides.

2.   One thinks also here of the minutes of public *silence* periodically observed to commemorate the national 'unknown soldier' or after football stadium disasters.

3.   'D-Day relies unashamedly on certain genre conventions and features a weapon – a water-pistol that is mistaken on two dramatic occasions for the genuine article – as well as what might be described as superficial action' (Hjort 2000a). Leaving aside the issue of genre, the assumption that the water-pistol is a 'prop' is open to question here, since while it is mistaken several times for a 'real' pistol it is still ultimately revealed as a 'real' water-pistol. One can imagine the fun the directors must have had debating such issues.

4.   For anyone caught on camera while *D-Day* was being recorded, of course, there was the additional pleasure of trying to spot themselves during the broadcast the following evening, like people who attend football matches and watch the TV coverage later.

5.   Correspondingly, much of the pleasure of watching such films derives from the suspense of waiting for the inevitable moment when something goes wrong, as for example in Jules Dassin's celebrated 1955 film *Du Rififi chez les hommes*.

6.   The transformation of film-making by the digital medium extends even as far as the concept of a 'film' itself: since a film owes its name to its medium, to call a digital video recording a 'film' seems at best anachronistic, which may be why it has become more common to use the less medium-specific terms 'movies' and 'movie-making'. The notion of 'footage' seems equally antiquated in this context.

7.   For example, watching, say, ten minutes of one tape before switching to another. Since the new tape would then be ten minues 'behind' the previous one, however, it had to be fast-forwarded so that its narrative would remain chronologically simultaneous with that of the previous tape – with the corresponding interruption of the actual viewing process this entailed. Needless to say, it quickly became clear that this method was unworkable. Another problem was that of language: since *D-Day* was a production of Danish television and was therefore, unsurprisingly, in Danish without English subtitles, I had to arrange to view them with Danish friends providing simultaneous translation.

11

Dogma Dance

Sally Banes and Noël Carroll

The Dogma Dance manifesto reads:

> YES to the development of dance technique for film – YES to a sharing of knowledge between dance and film – YES to the development of choreographic structure in film – YES to technology which aids rather than hinders – YES to human dancers – YES to the creation of a new genre – YES to safe dancers – YES to the encouragement of dance filmmakers – YES to a new hybrid form.
>
> NO to unsafe dancers – NO to the primacy of equipment and technology over human creativity – NO to the breakdown of choreographic structure – NO to purposeless hierarchies – NO to grossly unbalanced wages – NO to the dominance of film in Dance film.[1]

To those familiar with both contemporary dance and contemporary film, the manifesto and the twelve rules that accompany it (see pages 182–3) clearly call for a hybrid art of dance-film, since these documents allude directly to well-known earlier declarations in the worlds of both dance and film. On the one hand, the manifesto itself echoes the famous 1965 manifesto Yvonne Rainer (then a choreographer, and later a film-maker) wrote in regard to post-modern dance, in which she criticised the state of modern dance by declaring 'a very large NO to many facts in the theatre today', including 'spectacle … virtuosity … magic and make-believe', and, finally, 'no to moving or being moved' (Rainer 1965). While registering their own different (but not unrelated) set of protests against the state of dance-film in 2001, the members of Dogma Dance begin not with 'NO' but with 'YES', distancing themselves from Rainer's aesthetic of denial – even while overtly acknowledging their debt to her – and proposing an aesthetic of affirmation. The twelve rules, on the other hand, clearly recall, without precisely replicating, the famous Dogma 95 manifesto and Vow of Chastity issued by the collective of Danish film directors known as the 'Dogma brothers': Søren Kragh-Jacobsen, Kristian Levring, Lars von Trier and Thomas Vinterberg. Moreover, a third reverberation may be found in the world of screen dance itself, in Douglas Rosenberg's 1999 manifesto calling for more ideas and fewer technological tricks in screen dance. At the 1999 International Dance and Technology Conference, Rosenberg declared:

Dance and technology is a misnomer. It is really more often technology and dance … I call for the end of technological rhetoric, an end to the language of privilege, an end to obfuscation, an end to dogma, an end to the gendered, dogmatic, and hierarchical divisions of cyberspace that lurks beneath the veneer of egalitarianism and technological democracy … The dance and technology pendulum has swung dangerously away from the art of dance and toward technocracy. This is a call for balance … It is time for a recorporealization of dance and technology, time to reinscribe the body on the corpus of technology (Rosenberg 1999).[2]

But clearly the Dogma Dance group did not follow Rosenberg's call for an end to dogma, choosing, rather, to embrace it emphatically (though theirs is a dogma close to Rosenberg's fundamental principles).

Founded in October 2000 by Litza Bixler, Deveril and Katrina McPherson, three dance film-makers based in Great Britain who have training in both dance and film, Dogma Dance aspires to change both the process and the product of dance-films – the conditions of production as well as the look of the finished dance-films.[3] According to McPherson, the group's desire to set up a set of generative rules for creating dance-films emerged from a shared feeling 'that, perhaps in an attempt to be taken seriously in the world of television and film, dance films are losing the connection to dance. We see many dance films in which the focus is the design, the lighting or the telling of a story through the conventions of narrative film, with the dance content becoming an afterthought.' The Dogma Dance group wanted to 'get the dance back into dance films'.[4] And this interest led them to invite others to join them.

In late October 2000, various listservs, including the Dance-Tech list, carried an email from Deveril that read, in part:

> Please forward to anyone else you think may be interested.
> DOGMA DANCE – provocative, radical, dogmatic dance on screen.
> DOGMA DANCE is a newly established manifesto-based, artist-led organisation founded as a production forum for dance film makers to 'push the envelope' in terms of low budget, high concept dance on screen.
> DOGMA DANCE intends to offer a challenge to dance-film-makers to make their work within the frame-work of 'artistic and production rules', evolved to encourage the radical development of the medium and the individual's own approach to making work.
> DOGMA DANCE also plans to enable the making of new work through a network of resources, potential collaborators and eventually, it is hoped, access to funds for commissioning new work.
> A fundamental part of DOGMA DANCE will be its Web Site – a place where ideas can be shared, personal articles 'published', information passed on and, ultimately, work distributed. We want to share our ideas for what DOGMA DANCE could become and involve other interested parties from across the globe. In the first instance we invite those interested to UNDER YOUR SKIN, a free, informal introduction screening on Sunday 29th October, 6pm @ the Diamond Dance Studio, 6/8 Vestry St, London, N1 (nr. Old Street Underground).[5]

Frustrated by watching the results of various British dance-for-the-camera commissions that brought together choreographers and film-makers who did not necessarily know about each other's art forms, the Dogma Dance group felt that they could – and should – play a role in creating 'a new genre which draws from both disciplines' and that also asserts the importance of human bodies (rather than other, non-human sources of movement) in dance-films. The camera should be involved from the beginning, not brought in after the dance is made; it is 'part of the choreography'.[6] But not only aesthetic issues played into the Dogma Dance manifesto. The manifesto also addressed political and economic issues that arise during the making of dance-films, ranging from what the group perceived as the hierarchical, nearly militaristic disposition of workers in the commercial and professional film world to the differently gendered aspects of film production (dominated by men) and contemporary dance production (dominated by women). Even the physical safety of dancers, who, they charge, are often valued less than the equipment, became a sticking point.

If in many ways, Dogma 95 aims to restore authenticity to filmed narratives by presenting life-like action, Dogma Dance, acknowledging that choreography makes action artificial, seeks authenticity of a different type. While the Dogma Dance members set down some of the same rules as Dogma 95 (a hand-held camera and the use of natural or local light) and many rules in the spirit of Dogma 95 (the use of only one camera, no special effects, a meaningful relationship between soundtrack and visual content), some of their rules depart quite noticeably from Dogma 95 (the maximum length of ten minutes and the requirement that the work be recorded only on mini-DV). Thus Dogma Dances could never be certified as Dogma films, but, rather, will always be uniquely Dogma Dance films.

A number of the Dogma Dance rules lead the dance-film artist to ask fundamental theoretical questions regarding the nature of dance. Though influenced by post-modern choreographers like Simone Forti, Steve Paxton and Yvonne Rainer, the Dogma Dance group departed from some of the most radical views of post-modern dance as a frame for appreciating ordinary movement.[7] For McPherson, Bixler and Deveril, the dance in a dance-film should be discernible from purely pedestrian activity or pedestrian activity that has been transformed into choreography simply as a result of the film-maker's editing. Choreography and editing should work together, not substitute for each other.

Dogma Dance's concern with the nature and structure of dance as an artfully contrived, human activity, and therefore with dance-film as a unique category of film with its own particular effects, appearances and purposes quite distinct from narrative film, led the Dogma Dance group to establish several rules unrelated to those set down by Dogma 95. The first two Dogma Dance rules make the special disposition of dance-film absolutely explicit. They read: '1. The term "dance film" will be used to describe the finished piece. A dance film is defined by its emphasis on the human body (still or in motion). In this context "dance" refers to the actions of human beings only. 2. The movement content of the film should display clear choreographic intent. It should not be mime, nor should it be purely pedestrian movement.' While, in the spirit of post-modern dance, these rules allow for a very broad interpretation of dance, including ordinary movement and even the absence of movement, they very stringently disallow 'dance films' made 1) without human performers and 2) without designed movement. Thus, given rule 1, if a contemporary film-maker made a purely abstract animation in the manner of Hans Richter's *Rhythmus 21* (1921), Fernand Léger's *Ballet mécanique* (1924) or Oskar Fischinger's *Composition in Blue* (1935) it would not count as a Dogma Dance film. Nor, given rule 2, would a film such as Gene Friedman's *Public* (1964), in which the film-maker creates a rhythmic, dance-like composition from footage he shot of the public walking through the sculpture garden at the Museum of Modern Art in New York, count as a Dogma Dance film.

On the one hand, rules 1 and 2 restrict Dogma Dance films to following a broad definition of dance: human performers doing movement that has been designed in advance or that is improvised according to a set of rules intended to generate a dance. On the other hand, rule 9 ensures that a Dogma Dance film is an art film, not simply a recording of a live dance. It reads: 'The dance film must be structured in screen time and space, i.e. it should be edited according to rhythms dictated by the film rather than for continuity of the live choreography.' Taken together, these three rules safeguard the hybrid nature of Dogma Dance films – they should err neither on the side of being only film nor on the side of being only dance, but should partake of both.

If the commitment to recuperate recognisable dance movement for the screen is a leading motivation for Dogma Dance, it is also the theme of the first Dogma Dance film, *East South East* (2001). The film quite clearly sets up a contrast between ordinary movement and dance movement for the purpose of drawing our attention to the differences between them and finally of suggesting the way in which to see, and, by extension, to film dance.

East South East, the first certified Dogma Dance film (and the only one certified at the time this article was written), was made by Katrina McPherson in collaboration with dance/choreographer Jovair Longo. A colour film, seven-and-a-half minutes long, it features two dancers and a musician, in shots that alternate between two London locations: a dance studio (Chisenhale Dance Space) and an open-air city market (East Market). The dancing itself is a species of Contact Improvisation, more vertically oriented than the typically American form, at first set amid ordinary, everyday shopping and strolling.

The film begins with a brief shot in the studio, an inviting light-filled space with brick walls at two ends, large windows, a cream-coloured ceiling and a wooden floor. The opening shot introduces us to two male dancers and their accompanist, a female violinist. The dancers and the musician stride into the room in silence – we hear their footsteps. The dancers, two men of unequal height (Longo and Rick Nodine), wear casual clothing – loose shirts and pants, bare feet in the studio and sneakers on the street. They warm up, bending their knees and circling their arms. The musician (Irmela Wiemann), a violinist whose fitted white T-shirt and beige pants look both informal and elegant, moves her bow rhythmically like a conductor's baton.

Suddenly we are in the market, where the performers and the camera move among the shoppers and vendors who look on at their unusual antics. The onlookers show a variety of reactions to this unexpected performance in their midst; some point, smile, frown or stare expressionlessly, while others simply go on about their business – buying vegetables, selling toilet paper, wheeling a stroller, carting goods, talking on a cell phone, riding a bicycle and, most of all, walking. Movement steadily criss-crosses the screen, forming a tapestry of ongoing motion which alternately frames and absorbs the dance. We hear both the violinist's music and the ambient (but not synchronised) sounds of the marketplace: shouts, chatter, clatter. In long shots and close-ups we see the two men, in their bright shirts, doing moves that are familiar from Contact Improvisation.[8] Always touching – shoulders, hips, arms, torsos, backs, legs, armpits or elbows – they partner one another, in constant, swirling, turning motion. They take turns lifting one another, they dip, they duck, they climb or jump up on one another, or one catches the other in a fall or a slide. The camera is like a third dancer, moving in and out and around the dancers, sometimes honing in on a torso so that the entire screen is filled with a green shirt, or with a hand reaching to a shoulder, or with ankles and feet, and sometimes pulling back to reveal the entire street scene – dancers, musician, shoppers and all – in deep perspective. As the onlookers in the film discover the dance in their midst, we the dance-film spectators come to see this film as being as much about watching and finding the dance as about the dance itself.

Soon we notice that, despite what at first appears to be a continuous, propulsive, swirling movement of bodies, camera and music, certain chunks of activity repeat themselves. Not once, but several times an elderly woman in a light blue top, talking to a vendor in a yellow shirt, points up to an item and then reaches down into her black purse. A blonde woman wearing gold earrings and a purple blouse gestures backwards, pinches her nose and smiles as she talks to a friend. A young man steers his female companion in front of him. Time here moves simultaneously in different ways that are surprisingly difficult to comprehend, for both the dance movement and the pedestrian activity are not continuous, but broken up, replayed, while the music goes on, apparently tracing a seamless narrative even as we see the visual evidence of the action's discontinuity.

And, eventually, on repeated viewings, surprising details emerge. The film, which at first seems rather straightforward, even simple, reveals itself as richly structured in subtle layers. Once, for instance, it seems that for a split second there are three people configured into the dancers' lift – has the musician been momentarily incorporated into the dance? You start to notice, in the market scenes, when a particular scene repeats only once, or more than once. Juxtaposed to the dancers' action and patterned through film editing, the pedestrian movement itself becomes dancerly; a man who lunges only once in profile in the foreground to pick something up and another in the background, who steps down repeatedly from a cart with his back to us, both seem to be part of a larger dance, as do two people who turn their heads in sequence, and a woman pushing a baby carriage from left to right against the tide of other wheeled vehicles moving right to left.

The two dancers' movements, fluidly spiralling and similar in energy levels, are harder to differentiate. About one-third of the way through the film, shots of the two men dancing in the studio begin to alternate with shots in the market, and then, in the last minute and a half, the dancing all takes place in the studio. You realise that it is easier to track movement under action labels than when you see pure dance. In the studio, the scene becomes intimate and almost abstract: close-ups predominate, we hear the music and the dancers' breathing, and the film seems more about energy levels and movement flow than about individual figures and actions. Finally, the dancers and the musician simply drop what they are doing, and walk away, as the camera focuses on the window and the sounds of the market resume. The two spaces momentarily merge aurally, though not visually, as the dance ends.

The setup of *East South East* immediately draws the viewer's attention to the ways in which we are differentially affected by dance movement versus everyday movement. One would think that dance, because of its specially marked qualities, would be the most immediately identifiable action on screen, but oddly, the everyday movement is more legible, since we can track it anecdotally, or because we understand the functions of the behaviours that we are seeing. The dance movement, though in one sense more formally structured, slips away from us almost immediately after we see it. It does not embed itself in memory as the ordinary movement does. Indeed, we only come to realise that shots are being repeated (through editing) because we recognise shots of everyday actions (not dance actions) returning. Except for the professional choreographer or dancer, few ordinary viewers would recognise that these dance phrases are recurring. Though geometrically more legible than the ordinary movement of the passers-by, the dance movement is less intelligible because it cannot easily be woven into memory in terms of familiar stories or functions.

For roughly the first half of the film, McPherson explores the theme of pedestrian or ordinary movement versus dance movement by juxtaposing dance studio footage with location footage – location footage where the two forms of movement jostle in the same frame. The difference between the two types of movement is underlined subtly but unavoidably. Yvonne Rainer once wrote that 'dance is hard to see. It must either be made less fancy, or the fact of that intrinsic difficulty must be emphasized to the point that it becomes almost impossible to see' (Rainer 1968). *East South East* shows us, once again, that – although one might expect exactly the opposite, that dance would stand out from pedestrian movement and be easy to see – dance is hard to see, hard to remember and hard to re-identify. Understanding this, McPherson stubbornly puts the dance back into dance-film for us. But then, in the second half of the film, having brought our attention to dance movement, with an appreciation of its anomaly, she also suggests a way of seeing it.

It is important to note that in the first part of this dance-film, the camerawork deliberately and conspicuously sets up the contrast between pedestrian and dance movement. For instance, the second shot of the first scene in the market is framed so the dancers are in the mid-ground of the shot, surrounded by ordinary people doing everyday things like weighing vegetables and walking down the street. By being set back from the dancers, the camera draws a distinction between their actions and the behaviour of the other people in the scene. We can see that the dance movement is something extraordinary that takes place amidst, alongside, in front of, and behind ordinary activity, and the camera constantly invites us to note the contrast between types of action. Through this considered differentiation between dance movement and pedestrian activity, the camera's placement declares allegiance to the second Dogma Dance rule, underscoring the group's position that 'the movement content of the film should display clear choreographic intent' and 'should [not] be purely pedestrian movement'. And this contrast is crucial to the film's status as a hybrid (in the best sense), for the studied use of the camera implements a primary Dogma Dance commitment: that both dance and film must make a creative contribution in order to fulfill the aesthetic requirements of a genuine Dogma Dance film. The camera here does not simply record, but functions to engage both dance and film in the creation of a unified artwork.

In the second half of the film, transpiring in the studio, distracting pedestrian movement is banished, having served its purpose. The time for illuminating contrasts is past. Now we are to see dance. But in what way? The camera stays close to the dancers. It does not frame them in long shots. It moves into the close circle of the two dancers as they lift and flip one another with seeming effortlessness. By not backing off from the dance, the camera does not emphasise the figure of the dance or the floorplan of the choreography, but rather the fluidity of the movement, its rhythm and energy. Action, rather than shape, is the focus. The camera's position makes this virtually our only option in this context, but by so limiting our options, it is as if the film-maker were saying, 'This is how you ought to look at the dance, how you ought to experience it – as motion and velocity, rather than as pictorial design.'

Thus, *East South East* begins by setting ordinary behaviour and dance movement side by side in order to get us to note their differences. But once having done that, McPherson invites us to attend even more closely to this strange phenomenon – dance – in terms of what she values most about it: its energy and pulse. This reflexive obsession with the phenomenon of dance, moreover, realises the aims of Dogma Dance doubly, since it is not only obviously a *dance*-film (a film comprised of dance), but a film about (and not merely of) dance.

The rules and manifesto of Dogma Dance are a means of generating a certain ideal of what a dance-film should be. The rules, especially, carve out certain possibilities and foreclose others. The threat of pedestrian movement, as the rules indicate, poses a real challenge to the prospects for *dance* film-making, because pedestrian movement is what is featured in most non-dance films. *East South East* confronts that problem directly, juxtaposing dance movement and ordinary movement until the audience can appreciate some of the differences, thereby reflexively coming to grasp what is at stake in the Dogma Dance project.

While the Dogma Dance rules limit what is allowable, the movement's founders see those restrictions as empowering. 'We felt that sometimes you come up with the most interesting ideas when you're limited,' Bixler explains. 'As individuals, we've been happiest with projects we've made on a shoestring budget with lots of constraints. Often ingenuity comes out of poverty.' Within the rule-bound process, a diversity of styles is possible. Bixler's interest in human movement that she describes as looking 'inhuman or impossible' is quite different from McPherson's use of Contact Improvisation. Deveril wants to find alternative representations, especially in terms of gender, to those found in commercial music videos. 'We are hoping,' he states, 'that new vocabularies will be developed, so people aren't just transposing their particular technique from stage to film ... One of the beauties of Dogma Dance is that we're saying to any film-maker, "You can take any idea you want and use our rules in whatever way you want to explore all sorts of things." '9

For the Dogma Dancers, the intimacy or potential 'closeness' of film can improve dance, endowing it with qualities live performance can't always offer. Bixler, who works in commercial film as well as dance-film, says that the reason she stopped working on the live stage was that 'everything I did was too small. No one could see it.' And she continues, 'People talk about film as detracting from intimacy, because you're not in the presence of a live performer. But from my point of view, film is actually more intimate,' especially since it allows for close-ups and for what Deveril calls 'the in-there-ness of film – you can get right into the experience' (just as McPherson, in *East South East,* gets into the 'circle' of the performance).[10]

Letting go of dance as a purely live event can increase dance's accessibility. And that, Bixler asserts, is another Dogma Dance 'passion'. For a generation raised on television, the limited audiences live concerts deliver can be frustrating. Bixler compares her Levis ad, seen by millions, to a dance company touring England that might garner a few thousand spectators. 'Dance-film is a way of getting dance out there into the world as quickly as possible.' The rule that Dogma Dance films must be shot on mini-DV aims to increase accessibility from the artist/producer's point of view. 'We want to keep it as open to people as possible,' Bixler declares. 'Film is expensive. So we decided to go with DV, which is a challenge, but it embraces the idea of democracy, of many people having access to technology. We want Dogma Dance to be open to film-makers who might not have a lot of funds.'[11]

Other ways to make dance-films accessible, and Dogma Dance in particular, include open screenings, such as 'Under Your Skin', international film festivals (such as the IMZ [International Music Centre/Internationales Musikzentrum] Dance Screen Festival, where McPherson won a 'Best Screen Choreography' award in 2000), lectures, university courses (Bixler and Deveril now co-teach a course at Roehampton that McPherson and Bixler formerly co-taught), a workbook that McPherson is currently writing and designing for dance artists interested in making work for the screen and, importantly, the website. Located at www.dogma-dance.org, the website currently posts the manifesto and the rules, but will eventually include articles and clips of certified Dogma Dance films, including *East South East* and a new film (as yet unfinished at the time this article was written) by Bixler and Deveril.

As its rules and manifesto suggest, the Dogma Dance group is committed to the production of a specific type of dance-film, one in which the film component does not dominate the dance. Their films are intended to be *dance*-films, rather than dance-*films*. They wish to exorcise the ghost of Busby Berkeley from their cameras. But, as we've suggested, there is another ghost in the background here – one that hails from the dance world: the ghost of Judson Dance Theater. Rather than following in their footsteps, making dances indiscernible from pedestrian movement, Dogma Dancers want their gestures to appear dancerly, to affirm the value of movements that are out of the ordinary. In this way, Dogma Dance pits itself against two preceding avant-gardes – one cinematic, the other choreographic. The disavowed cinematic avant-garde is the tradition of the utterly synthetic film, where the dance exists only on the screen. The rejected choreographic avant-garde is the post-modern tradition of pedestrian movement. Both challenge the prospects of *dance*-films, films where recognisable dance figures and forms hold court. Pedestrian movement obviously could not implement just such an aim, since a film of pedestrian movement would look like almost any other type of film – including, perhaps, a Dogma film.

Thus, Dogma Dance departs from both post-modern dance and Dogma film. Importantly, it expands the Dogma concept in several directions, moving it beyond both national and artistic borders – not only from Denmark to Great Britain, but from narrative film to screen dance.

DOGMA DANCE

YES to the development of dance technique for film – YES to a sharing of knowledge between dance and film – YES to the development of choreographic structure in film – YES to technology which aids rather than hinders – YES to human dancers – YES to the creation of a new genre – YES to safe dancers – YES to the encouragement of dance filmmakers – YES to a new hybrid form. NO to unsafe dancers – NO to the primacy of equipment and technology over human creativity – NO to the breakdown of choreographic structure – NO to purposeless hierarchies – NO to grossly unbalanced wages – NO to the dominance of film in Dance film.

1. The term 'dance film' will be used to describe the finished piece. A dance film is defined by its emphasis on the human body (still or in motion). In this context, 'dance' refers to the actions of human beings only.
2. The movement content of the film should display clear choreographic intent. It should not be mime, nor should it be purely pedestrian movement.
3. Only one camera should be used.
4. A movement phrase (whatever the length) should be filmed in one type of shot only, i.e. not 'covered' by several different angles or sizes of shot.
5. Film only on mini-DV.
6. The camera must be hand-held. Any movement or immobility attainable in the hand is permitted. A moving camera is a dancing camera.
7. Only one lamp may be used. It can be any size. Other than that, use only natural light or artificial light that already exists in the location.
8. The camera, location or any other extraneous equipment should not impede the dancers' movement. In order for a film to be a certified Dogma-Dance film, the performing dancers should sign a written confirmation that they have felt this rule has been adhered to.
9. The dance film must be structured in screen time and space, i.e. it should be edited according to rhythms dictated by the film rather than for continuity of the live choreography.
10. There must be no digitally created special effects, such as dissolves, created in camera or in the edit. Changes of speed are allowed, but only if they have intent with the choreography and not used to cover up poor dance/film making.
11. The maximum length for a dance film should be 10 minutes, with at least 80% of this time being filled with bodies (or parts of bodies) in frame.
12. There must be a meaningful relationship between the soundtrack and the visual content of the dance film. It is not OK to cut to a musical track (i.e. a dance film is not a pop promo) or slap on music afterwards.

REFERENCES

Banes, S., *Terpsichore in Sneakers: Post-Modern Dance*, 2nd edn (Middletown, CT: Wesleyan University Press, 1987).

Carroll, N., 'Post-Modern Dance and Expression', in Gordon Fancher and Gerald Myers (eds), *Philosophical Essays on Dance* (New York: Dance Horizons, 1981).

Carroll, N., 'Toward a Definition of Moving-Picture Dance', *Dance Research Journal* vol. 33 no. 1, 2001, pp. 46–61.

Jordan, S., *Striding Out: Aspects of Contemporary and New Dance in Britain* (London: Dance Books, 1992).

Novack, C., *Sharing the Dance: Contact Improvisation and American Culture* (Madison: University of Wisconsin Press, 1990).

Rainer, Y., 'Some retrospective notes on a dance for 10 people and 12 mattresses called *Parts of Some Sextets*, performed at the Wadsworth Atheneum, Hartford, Connecticut, and Judson Memorial Church, New York, in March, 1965', *The Drama Review* vol. 10 no. 2 (T30; Winter 1965), reprinted in Rainer (1974): 51.

Rainer, Y., 'A Quasi Survey of Some "Minimalist" Tendencies in the Quantitatively Minimal Dance Activity Midst the Plethora, or an Analysis of *Trio A*', in Gregory Battcock (ed.), *Minimal Art: A Critical Anthology* (New York: Dutton, 1968), reprinted in Rainer (1974): 68.

Rainer, Y., *Work 1961–73* (Halifax, Nova Scotia: The Press of the Nova Scotia College of Art and Design; New York: New York University Press, 1974).

Rosenberg, D., 'Opening Remarks and Manifesto, Dance for the Camera Panel', International Dance and Technology Conference, Tempe, Arizona, 1999 (IDAT99).

NOTES

1. The Dogma Dance manifesto and rules may be found at < www.dogma-dance.org>.
2. In an email to Douglas Rosenberg, 23 October, 2000, Deveril acknowledged the impact of Rosenberg's manifesto on the Dogma Dance group.
3. Although the Dogma Dance rules call for the use of high-definition video, and although we would prefer the term 'moving-picture dance' over 'dance-film', we are using the terms 'film' and 'dance-film' here not to specify medium, but because those are the terms the Dogma Dance founders themselves use for their work. On our preference for the term 'moving-picture dance', see, for instance, Carroll (2001).
4. Katrina McPherson, email correspondence, 2 September, 2001.
5. <www.dancetechnology.com/dancetechnology/archive/2000/0416.html>.
6. Interview with Litza Bixler and Deveril (conducted by Noël Carroll), London, 5 September, 2001.
7. On American post-modern dance, see Banes (1987) and Carroll (1981): 95–104. On British New Dance, a closely related movement, see Jordan (1992).
8. On Contact Improvisation, see Banes (1987): 65–69; Novack (1990); and the journal *Contact Quarterly*.
9. Interview with Bixler and Deveril.
10. Interview with Bixler and Deveril.
11. Interview with Bixler and Deveril.

12

Documentary Gets the Dogma Treatment

Claus Christensen

Two penguins are walking down towards the sea. On the way they turn round and walk back again. The narrator says, 'Penguins are forgetful creatures. So in a moment they'll be going back to look for what they went to find!'

Many of us would see this as an innocent scene from a nature film, but to Lars von Trier it is an assault on God's work. Von Trier is infuriated by nature films in which penguins are forgetful and golden eagles flutter along in slow motion accompanied by the music of the spheres as rendered by a synthesizer. After all, nature never moves in slow motion, and certainly never to the sound of a synthesizer; and what is going on in a penguin brain as its owner wobbles along with that characteristic penguin gait is very hard to tell.

But that is only the tip of the iceberg. From hard-hitting television journalism to the art documentary that adorns itself with the seductive effects of the fiction film, Lars von Trier thinks the genre has lost its way in terms of its original mission: to describe real life as objectively and credibly as possible.

So he has drawn up a set of rules banning image and sound manipulation (e.g. lighting, optical effects, music and commentary), a ban on using library footage and concealed cameras, and a stipulation that every clip must be marked by six to twelve frames of black. Furthermore, the director must explain the aim and concept at the start of the film, while the end must consist of a minimum of two minutes in which the 'victim' of the film (if there is one) can put his or her case uninterruptedly.

WE CALLED THEM B MOVIES

The accompanying manifesto states that the aim of *Dogumentary* is to revive 'the pure, the objective and the credible' and restore 'the public's faith' in documentaries. So far four film-makers (two television programme devisors and two directors) have been chosen to make one film each in accordance with these rules. One of them is Klaus Birch, a journalist, and although his own oeuvre is open to Lars von Trier's criticism he agrees wholeheartedly with the film director.

'In the last five years, during which commercial channels have really got wind in their sails in Denmark, the original idea of television documentarism has been watered down. A good television documentary is like a loaded gun pointed at the authorities, but if the gun gets into the wrong hands or programme makers abuse their stock-in-trade, documentaries may also turn into a soggy mess,' he explains.

> When I began making programmes for public broadcaster TV 2/Danmark's documentary slot, *Fak2eren*, we were motivated by anger at social injustice. I wanted to use journalism as a means of revealing skeletons and pointing the finger at unreasonable social conditions. In order to make our revelations understandable we developed a particular narrative technique in which we were inspired by the BBC tradition to use fictional elements to tell a story. The programmes were made according to a pattern, with a clear division into heroes and villains and loads of artistic effects: dramatised scenes, luxurious lighting, music, and so on. We described them as B movies, and as time went by we pulled the stops out more and more.

COLD TURKEY

However, a couple of years ago the dangers of using artistic effects was brought home to Klaus Birch for real. In a programme about burglaries he showed authentic footage of an elderly lady who was in a state of shock after her home had been broken into. But many viewers thought the scene had been staged, using an actress.

'For the first time I thought: Is it our fault that we've come so far out on a limb? Have we diluted the documentary by using all those powerful effects?' His colleague Michael Klint had had the same reservations, and together they approached Lars von Trier's film company Zentropa in the spring of 2001. They wanted to raise ethical standards for television documentaries, and as von Trier was also considering ways of bringing television documentary back to its core, *Dogumentary* and the nine commandments were soon a reality.

'It'll be pure cold turkey!' Klaus Birch laughs. He is going to go on filmic rations with Michael Klint (winner of the 1996 Journalist of the Year Award for two programmes about the Danish hospital service) and directors Bente Milton (*Children of Gaia*, *The Fifth Gate*) and Sami Saif (*Family*, a deeply personal documentary released in 2001). A Swedish director and a Norwegian director will be attached to the group, and Zentropa Real is preparing an international version of *Dogumentary*; the idea is to get broadcasters from the US, the UK, France, Germany, Denmark and Belgium to choose a director from each country to make a film in accordance with von Trier's rules.

A BOOST FOR THE GENRE

The first six films, aimed at the Scandinavian television market, are being financed by DR TV, the DFI, Nordisk Film & TV Fund, and Scandinavian broadcasters. Each film will be an hour long, and is expected to cost 800,000 kroner.

'The novelty is that we're selling each film on the basis of Lars von Trier's idea instead of a particular story,' producer Carsten Holst says. 'By doing so we give our directors the freedom to tell stories they're really passionate about. This freedom may yield positive surprises, while the rules will force the directors to do things in unaccustomed ways. They'll be given new spectacles through which to view the world.'

One important aim of *Dogumentary* is to provoke debate, and after the initial half-dozen films a seminar on the documentary medium is going to be held. Media scientist Frands Mortensen welcomes the idea.

'Lars von Trier's backing should provide a boost to the whole documentary genre. It certainly needs it. A lot of "documentary Light" is being made for television, but thoroughly prepared television documentarism has practically vanished from Danish TV channels. Von Trier's move may help to ensure that public service broadcasters go on making these programmes even though they're expensive,' says Frands Mortensen. On the subject of Lars von Trier's disavowal of media manipulation he says 'It's a complicated issue. We – including von Trier – all know that you can't make films that are not manipulative. Nothing can reproduce real life "as is". You always tell a story. But the way I see it, these directors will now point out that they are doing just that. They will put their cards on the table and visibly mark each clip. It's a way of making audiences aware of what's going on.'

THE PURE STORY

The idea of reproducing real life objectively can be found in the work of directors like Richard Leacock and Don Pennebaker from the Direct Cinema school of the 60s. The school's spokesmen also worked according to more or less explicit rules such as 'thou shalt not use commentary, thou shalt not use film lights, thou shalt not stage events …'.

But it is obviously more relevant to draw parallels with von Trier's own Dogma 95, which presented ten aesthetic commandments by which Dogma directors swore to abide during the production process with a view to putting paid to the technological cosmetics of mainstream cinema and focusing on the character-born plot. This resulted in superb low-budget films, including *The Idiots*, *The Celebration* and *Italian for Beginners*, but the question is whether the Dogma success can be applied to the documentary, which is not burdened by technological equipment, big film crews or laborious work practices.

'I have no doubt that the pure story will emerge more clearly,' Klaus Birch replies. 'Stories that can only be told using all kinds of artistic effects will automatically be excluded. As a devisor you'll be less inclined to be seduced by the superficial drama of a story if you can't film reconstructions, for example. You'll be forced to find genuine living people with tales to tell.'

A VIEWER'S CHARTER

Klaus Birch emphasises that *Dogumentary* is an important signal to viewers: 'We're saying "these are programmes of a kind you haven't seen before. And we want you to know the rules by which they've been made." It's a kind of viewer's charter, and seeing as there's even a certificate guaranteeing the sterling nature of each programme, I think these documentaries will make more of an impact on viewers.'

He thinks that the second commandment in particular – 'The end of the film must consist of two minutes of free speaking time by the film's victim' – will affect his journalistic methods:

Content manifesto:

' DOGUMENTARY '

We are searching for something that is between fact and fiction. As fiction is limited by our imagination and facts by our insight, the part of the world that we portray cannot be contained by a "story", neither can it be perceived from a "point of view".

What we are looking for can be found in the real world, from where the creators of fiction draw their inspiration, the reality journalists attempt to describe but cannot. They cannot show us true reality as they are blinded by their technology. Neither do they want to, as technology has become a goal unto itself, content has become secondary.

From Lars von Trier's documentary manifesto, March 2000

Dogumentarism relives the pure, the objective and the credible. It brings us back to the core, back to the essence of our existence.

The documentary and television reality which has become more and more manipulated and filtered by camera people, editors and directors, must now be buried.

This takes place with the following documentarist content guarantee:
The goal and content of all Dogme documentary projects must be supported and recommended in writing by at least seven people, companies or organizations who are relevant and vital. It is content and context which plays the primary role in Dogumentarism, format and expression are secondary to this process.

Dogumentarism will restore the public's faith as a whole as well as the individual's. It will show the world raw, in focus and in "defocus".

Dogumentarism is a choice. You can choose to believe in what you see on film and television or you can choose **Dogumentarism**.

Zentropa Real © 2001

Content Manifesto: Documentary

The documentarist code for Dogumentarism:

1. All the locations in the film must be revealed. (This is to be done by text being inserted in the image. This constitutes an exception of rule number 5. All the text must be legible.)

2. The beginning of the film must outline the goals and ideas of the director. (This must be shown to the film's actors and technicians before filming begins.)

3. The end of the film must consist of two minutes of free speaking time by the film's "victim". This "victim" alone shall advise regarding the content and must approve this part of the finished film. If there is no opposition by any of the collaborators, there will be no "victim" or "victims". To explain this, there will be text inserted at the end of the film.

4. All clips must be marked with 6-12 frames black. (Unless they are a clip in real time, that is a direct clip in a multi-camera filming situation.)

5. Manipulation of the sound and/or images must not take place. Filtering, creative lighting and/or optical effects are strictly forbidden.

6. The sound must never be produced exclusive of the original filming or vice versa. That is, extra soundtracks like music or dialogue must not be mixed in later.

7. Reconstruction of the concept or the directing of the actors is not acceptable. Adding elements as with scenography are forbidden.

8. All use of hidden cameras is forbidden.

9. There must never be used archived images or footage that has been taken for other programs.

Lars von Trier,
Zentropa Real©October 2001

ZENTROPA REAL APS • FILMBYEN • POSTBOX 505 • DK-2650 HVIDOVRE
TEL: +45 3686 8788 • FAX: +45 3686 8789 • WWW.ZENTROPA-FILM.COM • E-MAIL: ZENTROPA.REAL@FILMBYEN.COM
CVR NR: 25281705 • BANK: FORSTÆDERNES BANK • REG NR: 5470 • KONTO: 1572966

The Documentarist Code

Allowing the victim to give his version of what happened is enormously police-like. You won't allow yourself to be too dogmatic in your approach to events, and the risk of succumbing to the usual manipulative traps will be much reduced if you have to show everything to the people appearing in the film. The rule may also mean we see more portrayals of the middle and upper classes. People from these classes are often highly critical and difficult to persuade to appear in documentaries, but with von Trier's rules we can tell them 'You will be able to influence the product. You'll have the chance to make objections, and you can make your own comments on the film at the end without being interrupted or edited.'

VON TRIER THE WIZARD

Unlike Klaus Birch, Sami Saif is less interested in the rules themselves than in the element of provocation and play that the concept also contains.

'The rules have a certain degree of cynicism. If you merely follow them blindfolded you'll end up with something very rough and immediate. Working within the form of *Dogumentary* I will try to make something affectionate, sensitive, and amusing. A little film with a start, a middle and an end – a film that opens the door to a universe,' Sami Saif says. He regards the fourth commandment as the greatest challenge: 'All clips must be marked with 6–12 frames black.'

'This is definitely the most difficult rule because black gaps between clips ruin the flow and disturb the audience. So I may try to make a film without any clips at all,' he reveals. Not that Sami Saif has any objections to taking on a job where the form to a certain extent is predetermined. 'I think it will give me the courage to take more chances. The commission is playful and challenging by nature and the *Dogumentary* group's vibes are good because we're all so different. So if any of us comes a cropper it won't be so painful. You're not all on your own.' Klaus Birch also emphasises the partnership with other film-makers from *Dogumentary*. He is looking forward to being able to consult Lars von Trier:

'It's no secret that there is friction between television journalists and documentary directors. Plenty of directors think that television documentaries are rubbish. They think the form is vulgar and that subjects like the fraudulent use of state subsidies by shipbuilders are boring. Conversely, lots of television journalists think that artistic documentaries about old monks on top of Portuguese mountains are completely irrelevant. But hopefully von Trier's rules will bring the two worlds together and contribute to the creation of something new. *Dogumentary* is like an experiment involving a bunch of people, with Lars von Trier poised above us like a wizard, waving his wand to see what happens. Will we fly at each other's throats or will we make a few interesting films?'

NOTE

This essay originally appeared in *Film* no. 19, 2001, pp. 28–30. Reprinted courtesy of the Danish Film Institute.

13

Dogma and Marketing: The State of Film Marketing in Europe and the Achievements of the First Dogma Films

Mads Egmont Christensen

Film marketing is commonly thought of as combining the dual functions of advertising and sales. A more sophisticated understanding of this simple idea requires a closer look at how the movie business actually works in different contexts. To that end, we may examine the marketing of Dogma 95, asking in particular how such films as *Festen* (*The Celebration*), *Idioterne* (*The Idiots*), *Mifunes sidste sang* (*Mifune*) and *The King is Alive* were handled. These cases contrast sharply with the marketing of mainstream American films, for even though quite a number of actions and expressions used in the process seem to be more or less identical, the advertising and sales campaign of a major American film is something quite different from that of a mainstream European film, even if it is one of those rare films that manages to break out of the festival circuit and into the marketplace. Secondly it will be helpful to discuss advertisers' ambitions in relation to the problem of understanding the psychology of twenty-first-century consumers, especially since this task seems to be far more challenging and complicated than most of us imagine.

THE STATE OF EUROPEAN CINEMA

Over the last decade, general box office sales for European films – still the most important window of exhibition – have been declining. Not all of the well over 700 films produced within the countries of the European Community are adequately distributed even in their own home territories. Few of the films get distributed in other European countries, and only a very small number are distributed outside Europe. At the same time all European countries are great importers of non-European films.

It is thought-provoking to realise that this serious loss of market share has happened in spite of an increased support to the film communities all across Europe from local governments, as well as larger scale efforts from the MEDIA-programme of the European Union. The results are an ever-increasing trade deficit – as it now stands, well over $US5 billion – and a number of socio-cultural challenges pertaining to audiences' abilities to identify with and understand their own societies, since the stories conveyed by most of the films viewed in Europe take place in other cultures.

The reasons for this agonising situation have been discussed at great length. One plausible explanation lies in the film community's own present understanding of how the production process should be undertaken. In Europe, the making of films has become a kind of cottage industry in which the considerable number of different players remain fundamentally estranged from each other. Most European creators, producers, distributors and exhibitors operate in small units which do not communicate. Each of these units struggles to succeed within the limits of its own expertise – the result being that there are no firm links between the cornerstones of the production process as this is actually defined on the international marketplace, namely, development, financing, pre-production, production, distribution, marketing and exhibition. As a result, the European film 'community' is fragmented, domestically orientated and suffers from a lack of financial muscle at a corporate level. On the other hand, the top American players – the majors – are all organised in vertically integrated companies that take control of all aspects of film, from development through to delivery. These are companies that constantly monitor the marketplace and are able to bring this know-how to bear on the development process. And they are companies of sufficient size and financial strength to be able to raise ongoing financing through traditional corporate sources. Unlike their European counterparts they do not have to rely on stitching together a tapestry of funding on a project-by-project basis. Instead they work with a global export strategy, their primary concern being to make commercially viable films.

To carry the discussion of the consequences of these differences one step further, one could claim that as a result of the heavily subsidised nature of the European film community, too few producers have the commercial ambition of achieving distribution throughout Europe; and what is even worse, they do not have the wherewithal to export their films beyond Europe. The problem is indeed of a paradoxical nature, because with very few exceptions, today's independent producers are in fact packagers whose lives are spent trying to match scripts and talent with the available subsidy money. Instead of matching budgets to audiences, they match budgets to funds. With very few honourable exceptions, European producers make their living off subsidies, and not off box-office revenues. As a result, very few European producers have the expertise or the opportunity to follow a project all the way into distribution and marketing. But the subsidy system does not only create problems for the producers. Media-financed distribution and exhibition support schemes are aimed at local (and often small) companies or cinemas, the result being that there are too few multi-territory distributors. Those that exist are not well established, which means that the possibility of partnering with producers, as well as with exhibitors, becomes very rare indeed.

It almost goes without saying that in an environment like this, the *selling* of film becomes a secondary activity – almost considered a lucky strike and not the result of professional business management and artistically orientated co-operation – or partnering – in the early phases of a given film's history. Dogma 95, as we shall see, was in many ways an exception to this rule.

NEW PERSPECTIVES ON ADVERTISING

One of the charismatic theorists of the Danish School of Advertising, Claus Lembourn (co-founder of the agency BUHL), has characterised recent trends in the field of commercial communication as follows. Once upon a time we asked ourselves how advertising influenced consumers. Ten to fifteen years ago we started asking how consumers influence advertising. Today we have to ask ourselves what form advertising should take if consumers are to interact with it in the desired way. The simple idea that it is enough just to send someone a message or sales pitch – as long as the message is strong enough – has been completely discredited. The freedoms granted by modern democracies, combined with high levels of education and increasing awareness of social responsibility have turned the consumer in the western world into something very personal and unique. So particular advertisers claim that marketing can no longer work with the assumption that general segmentation charts provide a solid manner of understanding the needs and preferences of the population, as was the case back in the 70s, 80s and early 90s. One of the most interesting initiatives to have been introduced to overcome this problem has been labelled *planning*. This new trend in advertising was first established in the UK. The leading idea was that a planner was invited to participate in the traditional triad of art director, copy-writer and project manager, normally responsible for defining both the strategy and philosophy behind a given communication.

Briefly put, the theory of planning claims that in order to reach the consumer properly – amid an ever-increasing media bombardment of information – people devising a marketing strategy must not only have a thorough understanding of the product, but also of the sorts of feelings and reactions to which that product might give rise in the consumer's mind. In this regard we must acknowledge that the American entertainment industry has been far better geared to finding adequate ways of implementing such an approach by drawing upon new knowledge about consumers' attitudes. The buzz that runs ahead of a given film is by no means a coincidence, regardless of whether the word-of-mouth is launched via websites, large-scale print campaigns utilising a variety of media, or smaller initiatives with more specific targets. Such campaigns have been created by exploring, analysing and coming to terms with a variety of socio-cultural trends involving political, sociological, psychological, philosophical and many other human factors.

Even though one could argue that the expansion of the entertainment industry is all too closely linked to a rather simplistic understanding of an archetypal society inhabited by one-dimensional heroes, apparently the stories told are fulfilling audiences' expectations all over the world. The result has been a source of both jobs and profits for developers, producers, distributors and marketing experts who have been *partnering* in the manufacture of the audiovisual product and in its launching through especially designed pipelines, video and DVD outlets and cinema chains.

Perhaps the most obvious and successful result of this recent merger between new perspectives on advertising and the principle of vertical integration is that the best of the creators and executives working in the American entertainment industry acknowledge the impact that the very fact of witnessing or being part of the inception of an idea has on a film's marketing campaign. It is quite obvious that without a clear conception of *what* it is you are trying to tell, *how* you are going to tell it, to *whom* you are telling it and, finally, *when* and *where* you are planning to tell it, you will not be able to sell or to advertise any film effectively on a regular basis. Again and again, those film-makers and marketing experts who are able to approach a general audience with pertinent and effective information about a film are those who have been deeply involved in articulating the basic *concept* of the work, that is, what some advertisers metaphorically call the very 'soul' of the film. This is not just a theory, as this approach has shown a striking level of practical success. When I first asked Gerry Lewis, founder of Dreamworks SKG, Europe, to come to the European Film College in Ebeltoft to talk about his work in marketing from the point of view of the vertically integrated principle, he remarked: 'What a wonderful idea. I think I'll talk about the marketing of *E. T.*, because I was there the night Steven got the idea of telling a story about the astonishing friendship between an extraterrestrial and a little boy.' The point is that in our present situation it is almost impossible to launch and implement an effectively integrated audience-directed marketing effort in connection with the production, distribution and exhibition of most European films. This has very little to do with economics. The investments necessary for large-scale marketing campaigns for European films would probably be available if more films with a solid and clearly integrated concept were developed. But they are not, primarily because of our film-makers' lack of skill and discipline in creating films with substantial *marketability*. The latter term refers to how well the idea of a film can be communicated and sold to an audience. It may be contrasted with *playability*, which refers to the quality of response among audiences once they have seen the film. In general, European films have a fairly high degree of playability, but with all the films waiting on the distributors' shelves, this is most often not sufficient to keep them in the cinemas for as long as it takes to get word-of-mouth working effectively – and it is the latter which in most cases is decisive for the overall success of a film.

There are, of course, some noteworthy exceptions to these generalisations. Yet this general situation will not change radically as long as our woefully fragmentary structure remains unchallenged, and as long as our subsidy policies uphold the present division between, on the one hand, the commercial activities of distribution and exhibition, and on the other, the creative practices involved in the processes of development and production. This could very well be the most crucial factor to be dealt with if Europe is to win back its audiences for its own films. In such a context we can see that Dogma 95 – by virtue of its intrinsic mix of artistic and formal rules – achieved something very special by creating an initial marketable *concept*. The latter serves the purpose of distinguishing a film or group of films from other films, just as slogans such as 'Just Do It' and 'Connecting People' signal a product's distinctive quality. In marketing terms this means that you have to turn your film into a 'brand'. As the Danish communications guru Jesper Kunde puts it in his Danish best-seller, *Unique Now – or Never*:

> In order to be successful producers must deliver something very special to the audience, and in
> that process the main objective must be to provide special values, which really means something

of particular interest for the people with whom one is communicating. In other words, you need to know what it is that makes your particular product unique, for failing that, chances are that you will vanish in the mechanisms of the new market economy (Kunde 2001: 17).

THE MARKETING ACHIEVEMENTS

It is probably the case that only *The Celebration* – out of the first Dogma 95 films – constitutes the sort of desirable exception discussed above. The other films have had very different fates in the marketplace, so it is an exaggeration to use the notion of branding in connection with Dogma 95 – even if both *The Idiots* and *Mifune* have as a matter of fact been successfully sold for worldwide distribution, thereby placing Danish film as a whole in a much improved position. Yet the launching of the manifesto and the production of the initial Dogma films have managed to establish an interesting platform which reveals some feasible ways of improving the problematic situation evoked above. A key factor is the actual integration of marketing exercises in the production process. In an effort to pinpoint some aspects of what Lars von Trier and the Dogma brethren have managed to accomplish, I shall now discuss some of the manifesto's implications and take a brief look at the films and their performance.

PLAYING THE SUBSIDISERS

Any film-maker or producer in Denmark, and perhaps in all other European countries as well, would agree that the most important element of all film marketing is the targeting of the funding bodies. There is nothing wrong with that – any US independent would claim the same with the studios in mind. In both cases creators must, if they are to win initial financing for their films, explain their concept and basic story idea. Not so with Dogma 95, for in that context, the question is answered more in technical terms than in terms of storytelling. What is most amazing about the introduction of the manifesto was that, from very early on, this device fared remarkably well with the subsidy systems, which is all the more remarkable given that at that early stage no-one really knew what the films were actually about. A partial explanation for this success is that Dogma 95 was a formal (and relatively simple and inexpensive) scheme that meshed well with most film institute bureaucrats' ideas of risk-minimised innovation. Another important factor was that the plan was the brainchild of Lars von Trier. Add to this the fact that the latter's company, Zentropa Productions, under the leadership of producers Peter Aalbæk Jensen, Vibeke Windeløv and von Trier himself, had been especially good at playing the media, constantly positioning Zentropa as a genuine artists' company. This meant that even though the Danish Film Institute had to pull out of the project for political reasons, other providers of subsidy financing were quick to support a project which in the mind of the public had carried the seal of artistic quality ever since its introduction in Paris in March 1995. Another important contributing factor was Cannes festival director Gilles Jacob's admiration for Lars von Trier's work, as his acknowledgment of von Trier as one of the true creative innovators of cinema meant that Dogma 95 films were brought to Cannes.

PLAYING CANNES

As I have already indicated, the artistic merits of the manifesto served as the primary marketing vehicle behind both the financing of the films and the decision to open the first two films at Cannes. Yet by this point in the story, Zentropa had already experienced the economic results of playing a festival correctly in terms of selling and advertising their films. Von Trier's previous film, *Breaking the Waves*, had enjoyed both critical acclaim and a subsequent worldwide sale after its opening in 1996. The Zentropa people knew that the reason that festivals are so important in generating interest in potential buyers is that they are the only way to get these key figures to see the film in a context where they can observe how the audience and press respond. This is the most persuasive way of demonstrating to a distributor that a film is commercially viable. If a film is made part of the main competition, as was the case first in Cannes with *The Idiots* and *The Celebration*, and later in Berlin with *Mifune*, followed by *Italian for Beginners*, and if it is received in the way all of these films were, then the sales agents handling the films are in a fantastic position. Yet this is also a tricky situation where having had the right sort of prior experience is an important asset. Zentropa and the agents of Nimbus Film, which had produced *The Celebration*, jointly contacted Swiss sales agent, Christa Saredi, who agreed to take charge of the foreign sales of *The Celebration*. (*The Idiots*, on the other hand, was handled by Zentropa alone.) Saredi was aware of the extraordinary possibilities of striking worthwhile deals with distributors, not only because of the marketing platform that had brought the film to Cannes, but quite simply because it was a very good film. Saredi saw that the ideas expressed in the manifesto had been executed in the aesthetics of the film under the brilliant direction of Thomas Vinterberg. In a way she utilised the vertically integrated principle of marketing (from concept to audience) in the worldwide sales efforts of *The Celebration*, and one could even claim that it was the impact of Zentropa's initial *soft* sales, directed towards the funders and the festivals, that actually made Saredi's *hard* deals possible when she took over, just as it was von Trier's imaginative and practical concept that paved the way for the critical acclaim of Vinterberg's utilisation of the principles.

The result, as we all know, was that appropriate distribution was secured for both films. *The Idiots*, as was to be expected, went primarily to the art-house circuit, whereas *The Celebration* was picked up by distributors equipped to handle a crossover product, i.e. low-budget films that can perform successfully at the box office.

FROM CONCEPT TO AUDIENCE

As was pointed out earlier, *branding* is not the most interesting and worthwhile element in the marketing achievements of the Dogma films. Branding is the naming of a certain genre or type of films, which share similarities and can be commonly referred to, examples being a *Disney-film* or a *James Bond-movie.* The notion of branding is closely linked to the *what's-in-it-for-me* type of advertising, which is also built on the gratification theories evoked above. Admittedly the introduction of Dogma 95 had an effect first on the press, then on the funding bodies and subsequently on the festivals, which are all constantly searching for new cinematic trends and artistic innovation. But to claim that the consumer was affected in any specific way is to make too great a claim. Oddly enough, the box-office failure of *The King is Alive* proves the point. Neither on the Danish nor the international market did it help much that this was a Dogma film, even though Kristian Levring did manage to receive considerable praise and critical acclaim for his film.

The really outstanding consequence of the rules set forth in the manifesto is that the creators of the living images on screen – the screenwriters, directors, cinematographers and especially the actors – were forced to rethink their entire approach to the themes, narrative structure and aesthetics that they had employed in their film-making over the past fifteen to twenty years. The Dogma rules made the Danish storytellers explore something they knew something about, namely, everyday social life and the responsibilities human beings have towards each other. What these film-makers wanted to explore in the best of the early Dogma 95 films were questions about what people do when existential trouble threatens. And it was this new realism which, combined with the audience's common understanding of human endeavour, gave rise to the word-of-mouth that secured the long runs of *The Celebration*, *Mifune* and later, *Italian for Beginners*.

Modern advertisers would most certainly claim that in this respect the film-makers involved in Dogma 95 have created a genuinely effective concept, one that may even have the potential to work in unison with practically and commercially viable ideas of marketing. In this sense Dogma 95 serves as a platform for creatively integrating audience response and preferences in future achievements, primarily for the benefit of artistic innovations in the early development of the stories film-makers want to tell. Such a platform also helps meet the challenges of building marketability into the films we develop and produce.

THE WAY AHEAD

If Europeans are to succeed at creating more films with crossover potential, that is, films that can move beyond the festival and domestic circuits and break into the international marketplace, we must improve the links between development, production, distribution and marketing, striving for a greater correspondence between artistic ambition and business competence. We need to train and support film-makers who have the ability to meet the artistic challenges involved in a given project, as well as the ability to approach the funding bodies and institutions in creative and persuasive ways. And they must be able to deliver such projects to an audience. We must avoid further fragmentation by commonly agreeing that what determines success in the marketplace is control, at both an artistic and managerial level, of every element in the vertically oriented production process, all the way from the initial development of the concept to final audience consumption. To meet this challenge it is vital that European film-makers, marketing agents, distributors and exhibitors develop a coherent, creative and co-operative strategy, where project development and design, involving thorough research on audience tastes, trends, preferences and demands, become key elements in winning back market shares for European productions. Admittedly a process such as the one evoked here would demand an alternative perspective on the world dominance of US corporate-major cinema. Again and again we have been told about the artistically destructive consequences of power politics and monopoly capital which are said to be the name of the Hollywood game. It is indeed the case that the majors have had many problems over the years and that the industry has churned out many mediocre, unsuccessful – yet professionally marketed – products. Nonetheless it is a question of the need to acknowledge that the best films from Hollywood manage to incorporate a strong marketability as an integral part of their very being. Our competitors wield a strategic approach that has been well tuned to the global requirements of the distribution and exhibition of popular culture, and it would be a mistake not to study and learn from this approach. With Dogma the first corner-stones for the implementation of such a strategy have been created by the pragmatic genius of Lars von Trier, by the hard and efficient work of his fellow brethren and their crews, and by the professionalism of a few distinguished distributors. It is now up to the rest of the emerging European industry to continue this work.

REFERENCE

Kunde, J., *Unik nu – eller aldrig* (Copenhagen: Børsens, 2001).

PART FOUR

Appendix I:
Dogma 95 Manifesto and its Progeny

DOGME 95

… is a collective of film directors founded in Copenhagen in spring 1995.

DOGME 95 has the expressed goal of countering 'certain tendencies' in the cinema today.

DOGME 95 is a rescue action!

In 1960 enough was enough! The movie was dead and called for resurrection. The goal was correct but the means were not! The new wave proved to be a ripple that washed ashore and turned to muck.

Slogans of individualism and freedom created works for a while, but no changes. The wave was up for grabs, like the directors themselves. The wave was never stronger than the men behind it. The anti-bourgeois cinema itself became bourgeois, because the foundations upon which its theories were based was the bourgeois perception of art. The auteur concept was bourgeois romanticism from the very start and thereby … false!

To DOGME 95 cinema is not individual!

Today a technological storm is raging, the result of which will be the ultimate democratisation of the cinema. For the first time, anyone can make movies. But the more accessible the medium becomes, the more important the avant-garde. It is no accident that the phrase 'avant-garde' has military connotations. Discipline is the answer … we must put our films into uniform, because the individual film will be decadent by definition!

DOGME 95 counters the individual film by the principle of presenting an indisputable set of rules known as THE VOW OF CHASTITY.

VOW OF CHASTITY

'I swear to submit to the following set of rules drawn up and confirmed by DOGME 95:

1. Shooting must be done on location. Props and sets must not be brought in. (If a particular prop is necessary for the story, a location must be chosen where this prop is to be found).
2. The sound must never be produced apart from the images or vice versa. (Music must not be used unless it occurs where the scene is being shot.)
3. The camera must be hand-held. Any movement or immobility attainable in the hand is permitted. (The film must not take place where the camera is standing; shooting must take place where the film takes place.)

4. The film must be in colour. Special lighting is not acceptable. (If there is too little light for exposure the scene must be cut or a single lamp be attached to the camera.)

5. Optical work and filters are forbidden.

6. The film must not contain superficial action. (Murders, weapons, etc. must not occur.)

7. Temporal and geographical alienation are forbidden. (That is to say that the film takes place here and now.)

8. Genre movies are not acceptable.

9. The film format must be Academy 35 mm.

10. The director must not be credited.

Furthermore I swear as a director to refrain from personal taste! I am no longer an artist. I swear to refrain from creating a "work", as I regard the instant as more important than the whole. My supreme goal is to force the truth out of my characters and settings. I swear to do so by all the means available and at the cost of any good taste and any aesthetic considerations.

Thus I make my VOW OF CHASTITY.'

Copenhagen, Monday 13 March 1995

On behalf of **DOGME 95**
Lars von Trier
Thomas Vinterberg

MINNESOTA DECLARATION: TRUTH AND FACT IN DOCUMENTARY CINEMA

'LESSONS OF DARKNESS'

1. By dint of declaration the so-called Cinéma Vérité is devoid of vérité. It reaches a merely superficial truth, the truth of accountants.

2. One well-known representative of Cinéma Vérité declared publicly that truth can be easily found by taking a camera and trying to be honest. He resembles the night watchman at the Supreme Court who resents the amount of written law and legal procedures. 'For me,' he says, 'there should be only one single law: the bad guys should go to jail.' Unfortunately, he is part right, for most of the many, much of the time.

3. Cinéma Vérité confounds fact and truth, and thus plows only stones. And yet, facts sometimes have a strange and bizarre power that makes their inherent truth seem unbelievable.

4. Fact creates norms, and truth illumination.

5. There are deeper strata of truth in cinema, and there is such a thing as poetic, ecstatic truth. It is mysterious and elusive, and can be reached only through fabrication and imagination and stylization.

6. Filmmakers of Cinéma Vérité resemble tourists who take pictures amid ancient ruins of facts.

7. Tourism is sin, and travel on foot virtue.

8. Each year at springtime scores of people on snowmobiles crash through the melting ice on the lakes of Minnesota and drown. Pressure is mounting on the new governor to pass a protective law. He, the former wrestler and bodyguard, has the only sage answer to this: 'You can't legislate stupidity.'

9. The gauntlet is hereby thrown down.

10. The moon is dull. Mother Nature doesn't call, doesn't speak to you, although a glacier eventually farts. And don't you listen to the Song of Life.

11. We ought to be grateful that the Universe out there knows no smile.

12. Life in the oceans must be sheer hell. A vast, merciless hell of permanent and immediate danger. So much of a hell that during evolution some species – including man – crawled, fled onto some small continents of solid land, where the Lessons of Darkness continue.

Walker Art Center, Minneapolis, Minnesota
April 30, 1999
Werner Herzog

VOGMA MANIFESTO

[Vertov with a Mac and a modem]

vogma
a manifesto [in no particular order]

1. a vog respects bandwidth
2. a vog is not streaming video (this is not the reinvention of television)
3. a vog uses performative video and/or audio
4. a vog is personal
5. a vog uses available technology
6. a vog experiments with writerly video and audio
7. a vog lies between writing and the televisual
8. a vog explores the proximate distance of words and moving media
9. a vog is dziga vertov with a mac and a modem

<www.hypertext.rmit.edu.au/vog/index.html>

WEBDOGME MANIFESTO

On this last day of the 2nd millennium we freely commit that should we survive, we will dedicate ourselves to the promotion of a new kind of film. For the first time in the history of film, we declare that now is the time and this time everybody can not only view films – everybody can make and distribute films themselves! We aspire that everyone will love the simplicity of the new language and will use it to create a new global, accessible and democratic medium. We decree that films:

1. Are cheap to make.
2. Are quick to produce.
3. Are cheap and easy to distribute.
4. Employ only basic and free equipment, light and cast.
5. Any subsequent video or audio editing should be done using only free tools.
6. Distribution should be done through the internet.
7. All genres are equal.

Naom Bamberger Noam Knoller Lev Kol
16:20 30/12/1999 XXc.
Tel-Aviv, Israel, World.
<www.go.to/webdogme>

THE NEW PURITANS MANIFESTO

1. Primarily storytellers, we are dedicated to the narrative form.
2. We are prose writers and recognise that prose is the dominant form of expression. For this reason we shun poetry and poetic licence in all its forms.
3. While acknowledging the value of genre fiction, whether classical or modern, we will always move towards new openings, rupturing existing genre expectations.
4. We believe in textual simplicity and vow to avoid all devices of voice: rhetoric, authorial asides.
5. In the name of clarity, we recognise the importance of temporal linearity and eschew flashbacks, dual temporal narratives and foreshadowing.
6. We believe in grammatical purity and avoid any elaborate punctuation.
7. We recognise that published works are also historical documents. As fragments of time, all our texts are dated and set in the present day. All products, places, artists and objects named are real.
8. As faithful representations of the present, our texts will avoid all improbable or unknowable speculation about the past or the future.
9. We are moralists, so all texts feature a recognisable ethical reality.
10. Nevertheless, our aim is integrity of expression, above and beyond any commitment to form.

Nicholas Blincoe and Matt Thorne (eds), *All Hail the New Puritans* (London: Fourth Estate, 2000).

THE LARP (LIVE ACTION ROLE PLAY) VOW OF CHASTITY

1. It is forbidden to create action by writing it into the past history of a character or the event.
From the point of view of an organiser, the LARP may appear to be good because every character has an exciting story in the written background. This is a typical pitfall. From the point of view of the player, only what happens in the LARP has reality. LARP is not literature, LARP is action. The use of retrospect in the character description forces the player to relate to incidents that are not real.

The Vow of Chastity forbids all action in the written character description's past; all action of the story must take place during the play.

Examples as to how this may be solved, is to use fates, to leave it to the players to agree (and role-play) upon conflicts between themselves, or to use *static* conflicts in the backgrounds. It is not in conflict with this rule for players to invent a more detailed background, if they find this necessary for their immersion into the character.

2. There shall be no 'main plot'.

(The story of the event must be made for each player, not the whole.)

With main plots we here mean conflicts that are meant to touch the entire LARP, but do not directly involve all characters. Main plots are another typical pitfall; the conflict is important for the organisers and those players directly involved in it, but reduces the roles of characters that do not play a part in this plot to the position of an audience. The use of main plots almost universally leads to a division between important and less important characters.

This convention probably comes from organisers seeking to replicate movies, literature and theatre. A story in the non-interactive media necessarily has a limited amount of active characters. In LARP, an interactive form of art, the amount of actors and stories is theoretically unlimited.

Examples of alternative ways to bind a LARP together:

- The LARP may contain many smaller intrigues, where the intrigues are thematically connected.
- The LARP scenario may be a slice of reality. In real life, there are no main plots.

3. No character shall only be a supporting part.

Not only must every character be directly involved in the conflicts that touch it; the character must also in its own way play the lead part of the conflict. It is therefore not permitted to write a character whose most important function in the LARP is to help or support another character.

4. All secrecy is forbidden.

(Any participant who so desires shall in advance be shown all documents that pertain to the event.)

In conventional LARP, organisers often attempt to create tension by preventing the player from knowing what the organiser has planned for the character. Actually, things are often kept secret so that players or organisers can feel important – *I know something you don't know* – or out of habit.

The reality of the LARP is what is acted out, **not** what is kept secret and becomes known only after the LARP is over or to a minority during the event. By removing secrecy, we also remove part of the competition aspect of LARP. Some players may wish to know everything before the event starts, whereas others will not. Dogma #4 implies that all plans must be made available to the players who wish to know them, not that these must be published to all players.

5. After the event has begun, the playwrights are not allowed to influence it.
(Any use of staging and ad hoc organiser roles is forbidden.)

Organisers of conventional LARP use a number of methods to influence the LARP after it has begun. They do this to entertain players and to steer the event in the 'correct' direction.

As organisers take control during a LARP, the players become passive. This leads to players learning to expect organiser control, even demanding it. Only a LARP entirely without organiser influence will place the real initiative in the hands of players, where it belongs. As we learn how to make LARP's work independent of organiser control and influence, it will become possible to develop more constructive and activating methods of organiser interaction.

6. Superficial action is forbidden.
(The playwrights may not in any way plan or encourage the use or threat of violence as part of the event.)

The LARP medium is quite fit to create tension through the simulation of violence. The medium can, however, be used for far more than this – something which is often overseen in favour of combat. At the time of writing, it is for many LARPers difficult to imagine a combat-free LARP. We are of the opinion that it is about time playwrights and players learn to create LARPs without using these simplest methods to achieve thrill and suspense.

7. LARP inspired by tabletop role-playing games are not accepted.
LARP and tabletop role-playing are different media that, despite some similarities, work on different terms. In the tabletop role-playing game, the action is played out as the roles (players) and the fictional world (storyteller) meet. In a LARP the focus is on the roles (players) and what happens between them.

Some of the pitfalls that come from the tabletop heritage:

- The idea of 'game balance' (all players must have the same opportunity to find the treasure).
- Focus on solving the riddle/completing the adventure.
- Organisers wish to control the game.
- Division between important and unimportant characters ('PC' and 'NPC').

Most conventional LARP is inspired by tabletop role-playing games both in form and content. It is no longer original to make a LARP of a new kind of tabletop RPG. We also register that a majority of the clichés in current LARP are inherited from tabletop RPGs.

The most important argument, however, for not being inspired by tabletop role-playing games is that only through these means are we able to find out what LARP as a separate medium may achieve.

8. No object shall be used to represent another object.
(All things shall be what they appear to be.)

In conventional and most mainstream LARP a number of signs and substitutes are used, swords are made from latex-covered styrofoam, cordial is supposed to be wine, the curtains are drawn because windows weren't invented in the middle ages, a rope is used as a city wall, tents instead of houses, make-up and masks are used to signify supernatural creatures etc.

Signs are most often an ingrown, but unfit, solution to the problems of transferring settings from other media to LARP. Exaggerated use of signs easily leads to absurdities in the play, as it is difficult for players to remember what the different signs represent. The focus of LARP disappears in the signs.

Human beings are, in this context, not to be considered 'objects'. A player may still be used to represent a character …

What we wish to end is the absurd certainty that for instance Styrofoam sticks are swords, and the assumption that this is the only way it can be done. The signs are not a part of the essence of LARP. Though they occasionally may come in handy, we wish to learn how to create LARP without their use.

9. Game mechanics are forbidden.

(Rules for the simulation of for instance the use of violence or supernatural abilities are not permitted.)

By 'game mechanics' we mean all rules used to simulate situations believed not to be possible to do for real in LARPs: violence, pain, intoxication, magic, poisoning et cetera.

LARP has developed from tabletop role-playing, which again has developed from strategy games. The use of game mechanics is merely a fossil remnant from the strategy games, and is unnecessary and generally impractical in both LARP and tabletop role-playing. Game mechanics may be easily replaced with trust in the players' ability to improvise.

Dogma #9 does not exclude rules for other purposes than simulation; such as security rules and fates.

10. The playwrights are to be held accountable for the whole of their work.

LARP has often been perceived as a hobby. In pact with this thought, players applaud their organisers no matter the product because the organisers anyway do a good job for their hobby. To the extent criticism has appeared after an event, it has often been for purely practical matters – food, fire security and such. We are not opposed to hobbyists in this way honouring the will to do something, but it helps little when one desires to develop the medium and art form. Which criteria LARP is to be criticised according to is another discussion.

Playwrights of a Dogma-event therefore refuse to wear the Emperor's New Clothes. We will be held accountable for our production, slaughtered for anything bad or imperfect, and merely receive positive criticism for what was original, well done and progressive.

The Future

We appeal to LARPers who share our goal of developing LARP as a diverse medium of expression to consider the following broad aims for the future:

The abandonment of conventional LARP – the current conventions of LARP are merely an infant stage and should be abandoned. In the future, it should be impossible to speak of 'conventional' LARP, as no conventions should exist. What we in the Dogma 99 manifesto term 'conventional' LARP might one day be called 'primitive', 'fallen' or 'corrupt' LARP.

To this end, training and handbooks must be made available for new scenes and troupes of playwrights, lest they fall into the pitfalls of convention.

Diversity – LARP playwrights and scenes must diversify the genres and methods of LARP events. We seek **the death of 'mainstream' LARP**, in that the diversity of LARP events should be so vast, no single genre or group of genres may be called 'mainstream'. We certainly do not want the current mainstream genres to disappear, but they should lose their dominant position.

We therefore appeal to the playwrights of the current mainstream to organise new and different LARPs, experiment with new methods, and explore or create other genres.

Publicity – LARP must become well-known in the eyes of the public as a new medium that takes diverse forms, not as a curiosity. To forward this end, LARPers should be conscious of the media attention they receive, and steer this away from 'feature' coverage towards in-depth journalism.

Fundamentalist and moral-panic critics must not be allowed to choose the battleground. Active and well-planned relations with the media are the best way to achieve a good, steady and objective coverage.

Recruitment – LARP must lose its profile as a young, slightly geeky, white middle-class activity. Recruitment should aim at all levels of society, and especially at groups from which recruitment has previously been scarce. We must abandon the misconception that conventional LARP is the best way of introduction to the medium; it is not.

Communication – The links between local, regional and national LARP communities must be strengthened. Forums (including magazines, the internet and conventions) must be opened for the exchange of ideas and know-how. LARPers must document their work, experiments and experiences, and make this documentation available to the international LARP community.

An exchange of knowledge with related media (drama, theatre, movie-making, storytelling, tabletop RPG) should take place, although the differences of the media should always be taken into consideration.

© 1999, 2000 Eirik Fatland & Lars Wingård

DOGMA 2001: A CHALLENGE TO GAME DESIGNERS

The Dogma 2001 Vow

(from <www.gamasutra.com/features/20010202/adams_01.htm>)

As a game designer I promise for the good of my game, my industry, and my own creative soul to design according to the following Dogma 2001 rules:

1. The design documents shall contain no reference to any object which is installed inside the outer case of the target machine. Input devices and the monitor screen itself may be mentioned in discussions of the game's user interface. Minimum acceptable machine specifications shall be determined by the programmers during development.

   Justification: Self-evident. Dogma 2001 game designs are about the game, period. As a Dogma designer, you renounce technology as part of your game's design.

2. The use of hardware 3D acceleration of any sort is forbidden. Software 3D engines are not forbidden, but the game must run at 20 frames per second or better in 640 x 480 16-bit SVGA mode or the nearest available equivalent.

   Justification: By adopting a simple, well-known display standard and sticking rigorously to it, both designers and programmers are freed to concentrate on tasks of real importance.

3. Only the following input devices are allowed: on a console machine, the controller which normally ships with it. On a computer, a 2-axis joystick with two buttons, or a D-pad with two buttons; a standard 101-key PC keyboard; a 2-button mouse.

   Justification: Most games that depend on gimmicky input devices are crummy games. You must not waste your time trying to design for them.

4. There shall be no knights, elves, dwarves or dragons. Nor shall there be any wizards, wenches, bards, bartenders, golems, giants, clerics, necromancers, thieves, gods, angels, demons, sorceresses, undead bodies or body parts (mummified or decaying), Nazis, Russians, spies, mercenaries, space marines, stormtroopers, star pilots, humanoid robots, evil geniuses, mad scientists, or carnivorous aliens. And no freakin' vampires

   Justification: Self-evident. If you find that doing without all of the foregoing makes it impossible to build your game, you are not creative enough to call yourself a game designer. As proof, note that it does not exclude any of the following: queens, leprechauns, Masai warriors, ghosts, succubi, Huns, mandarins, wisewomen, grizzly bears, hamsters, sea monsters, vegetarian aliens, terrorists, firefighters, generals, gangsters, detectives, magicians, spirit mediums, shamans, whores, and lacrosse players. One of the games that made it to the finals of the first Independent Games Festival was about birds called blue-footed boobies, so forget you ever heard of George Lucas and J.R.R. Tolkien and get to work.

5. The following types of games are prohibited: first-person shooters, side-scrollers, any action game with 'special attacks.' Also prohibited are: simulations of 20th-century or current military vehicles, simulations of sports which are routinely broadcast live on television, real-time strategy games focussing solely on warfare and weapons

production, lock-and-key adventure games, numbers-heavy role-playing games, and any card game found in Hoyle's Rules of Card Games.

    Justification: It is your duty as a Dogma designer to create new genres of games, not simply to make more technologically impressive games in old genres.

6. All cinematics, cut-scenes, and other non-interactive movies are forbidden. If a game requires any introductory or transitional material, it must be provided by scrolling text.

    Justification: The secret desire of game designers to be film directors is deleterious to their games and to the industry generally. This desire must be stamped out.

7. Violence is strictly limited to the disappearance or immobilization of destroyed units. Units which are damaged or destroyed shall be so indicated by symbolic, not representational, means. There shall be no blood, explosions, or injury or death animations.

    Justification: Although conflict is a central principle of most games, the current 'arms race' towards ever-more graphic violence is harmful and distracting. Explosions and death animations are, in fact, very short non-interactive movies. If you spend time on them, you are wasting energy that could be more profitably spent on gameplay or AI.

8. There may be victory and defeat, and my side and their side, but there may not be Good and Evil.

    Justification: Good versus Evil is the most hackneyed, overused excuse imaginable for having two sides in a fight. With the exception of a small number of homicidal maniacs, no human being regards him- or herself as evil. As a Dogma designer, you are required to create a real explanation for why two sides are opposed – or to do without one entirely, as in chess.

9. If a game is representational rather than abstract, it may contain no conceptual non sequiturs, e.g. medical kits may not be hidden inside oil tanks.

    Justification: The conceptual non sequitur is not merely sloppy; it is one of the things that actively discourages non-gamers from playing games. Gamers know that you're supposed to blow up everything in sight to see if anything might be hidden there, because they've played a hundred other games which have followed this pattern – games which were designed by adolescents for whom blowing things up is an end in itself. Ordinary people use their powers of reasoning to decide what should be blown up or not. Since it would not occur to a reasonable person that a medical kit could be found inside an oil tank, a reasonable person will not needlessly blow it up, and is therefore at a disadvantage when playing the game. A Dogma designer must do the design work necessary to reward reason rather than brute-force approaches.

10. If a game is representational rather than abstract, the color black may not be used to depict any manmade object except ink, nor any dangerous fictitious nonhuman creatures. Black may be used to depict rooms in which the lights are not switched on.

    Justification: Artists who make things cool by the simple expedient of making them black should be sent back to art college with a swift kick in the butt. This is also true of chrome and gunmetal grey, but black is the worst offender.

    'Finally, I acknowledge that innovative gameplay is not merely a desirable attribute but a moral imperative. All other considerations are secondary. Thus I make my solemn vow.'

Now I realize that, as with Hollywood and Dogme 95, nobody at EA or Sony or Blizzard is going to pay the slightest attention to Dogma 2001. This isn't a formula for commercial success, it's a challenge to think outside the box – in our case, the standardized boxes that are on the store shelves right now. But the rules are actually far less draconian than the Dogme 95 rules for filmmakers, and it wouldn't be that hard to follow them. I think it could do both us, and our customers, a lot of good.

If anybody takes the vow and builds a Dogma 2001 game, let me know!

JILL GODMILOW – DOCUMENTARY MANIFESTO 2000

DOCUMENTARY DOGMA 2000

have a real subject and a real analysis that is bigger than the subject –

don't produce the surface of things

don't produce 'real' time and space – your audience is in a movie theatre, in comfortable chairs

try not to exploit the experience of your social actors – just being seen in your film is not enough compensation for their bodies, voice and experience

avoid producing freak shows of the oppressed, the different, the criminal and please don't use your compassion as an excuse for pornography – leave the poor Beast Folk alone

neither produce awe for the rich, the famous, the talented, the highly successful – they are already everywhere – we feel bad enough about ourselves already and hating them doesn't help keep an eye on your own middle-class bias and your audience's

don't seek to conquer your material – to bend it to your will

watch that music – what's it doing? who is it conning?

avoid technical effects that mask or disguise construction techniques

don't weed out the interesting parts – the contradictions – remember that you are producing human consciousness even though you've got a focusing glass in front of your camera, know that scientific reductionism itself cannot fathom biological, social or historical complexity

don't address an audience of 'rational animals' – we have not yet evolved beyond the primitive urges of war, violence, killing, hatred, and social hierarchy

whatever you do, don't make 'history' – if you can't help yourself, try to remember that it's just a story and find a way to acknowledge your authorship

leave your parents out of this.

Appendix II: Dogma Filmography

Compiled by Emma Bell

Dogme #1: *Festen* (Denmark)
Released: 1998
Regional Titles: *The Celebration* (1998) (UK/USA); *Dogme #1 – Festen* (1998) (Denmark: series title); *Festen* (1998) (Denmark: short title)
Director: Thomas Vinterberg (uncredited)
Script: Thomas Vinterberg; Mogens Rukov
Production: Danish Film Institute (Mikael Olsen); DRTV Danish Broadcasting Corporation; Nimbus Film Productions; Nordic Film & Television Fund; SVT Drama (Sweden)
Producer: Birgitte Hald
Editor: Valdis Óskarsdóttir
Cinematography: Anthony Dod Mantle
Sound: Morten Holm
Music: Lars Bo Jensen
Appearances: Ulrich Thomsen; Henning Moritzen; Thomas Bo Larsen; Paprika Steen; Birthe Neumann; Trine Dyrholm; Helle Dolleris; Therese Glahn; Klaus Bondam; Bjarne Henriksen
Distribution: Scanbox Danmark A/S (Denmark)
Runtime: 106 minutes
Country: Denmark
Language: Danish/German/English
Colour: Colour
Sound Mix: Dolby Stereo
Certification: France: 12; Germany: 12; Netherlands: 12; UK: 15; USA: R
Technical Data: 35mm (1.37:1)
Link: <www.dogme95.dk>

Dogme #2: *Idioterne* (Denmark)
Released: 1998
Regional Titles: *The Idiots* (1998) (UK/USA); *Dogme #2 – Idioterne* (1998) (Denmark: series title); *Gli Idioti* (1999) (Italy); *Les Idiots* (1998) (France)
Director: Lars von Trier (uncredited)
Script: Lars von Trier; Mogens Rukov
Production: 3 Emme Cinematografica; Argus Film Produktie; Canal+; COBO Fund; DRTV (Denmark); Liberator Productions; Nordic Film & Television Fund; RAI Cinema Fiction; RO; La Sept Cinéma; VPRO; Zentropa Entertainments; ZDF/ARTE

Producers: Svend Abrahamsen (DRTV); Peter Aalbæk Jensen; Eric Shut; Marianne Slot; Peter van Vogelpoel; Vibeke Windeløv
Editor: Molly Malene Stensgaard
Cinematography: Casper Holm; Jesper Jargil; Kristoffer Nyholm; Lars von Trier
Sound: Per Streit
Appearances: Jens Albinus; Anne Louise Hassing; Anders Hove; Bodil Jørgensen; Knud Romer Jørgensen; Nikolaj Lie Kaas; Luis Mesonero; Trine Michelsen; Louise Mieritz; Troels Lyby; Henrik Prip; Anne-Grethe Bjarup Riis; Paprika Steen; Lars von Trier – *interviewer's voice* (uncredited)
Finance: COBO Fund; Danish Broadcasting Corporation; Nordic Film & Television Fund; October Films (US); Studio Canal+; Zentropa Entertainments (Denmark)
Distribution: Scanbox Danmark (Denmark)
Runtime: 117 minutes
Country: Denmark/France/Italy/Netherlands
Language: Danish
Colour: Colour
Sound Mix: Dolby Stereo
Certification: France: 16; Germany: 16; UK: 18; USA: R; Eire: Banned
Technical Data: 35mm (1.37:1)
Link: <www.dogme95.dk>

Dogme #3: *Mifunes sidste sang* (Denmark)
Released: 1999
Regional Titles: *Mifune* (1999) (UK/USA); *Dogme #3 – Mifunes sidste sang* (1999) (Denmark: series title)
Director: Søren Kragh-Jacobsen (uncredited)
Script: Søren Kragh-Jacobsen; Anders Thomas Jensen
Production: Nimbus Film Productions (Denmark)
Producers: Birgitte Hald; Morten Kaufmann
Editor: Valdis Óskarsdóttir
Cinematography: Anthony Dod Mantle
Sound: Morten Degnbol; Hans Møller
Original Music: Thor Backhausen; Karl Bille; Christian Sievert
Appearances: Jesper Asholt; Anders W. Berthelsen; Mette Bratlann; Sophie Gråbøl; Ellen Hillingsø; Iben Hjejle; Emil Tarding; Paprika Steen; Susanne Storm; Sidse Babett Knudsen
Finance: Nimbus Film APS (Denmark); DRTV Danish Broadcasting Corporation (Svend Abrahamsen); Danish Film Institute; Nordic Film & Television Fund; SVT Drama (Sweden); Zentropa Entertainments (Denmark)
Distribution: United International Pictures, UIP
International Sales: Trust Film Sales (Denmark)
Runtime: 98 minutes
Country: Denmark

Language: Danish
Colour: Colour
Sound Mix: Dolby Stereo
Certification: France: U; Germany: 12; UK: 15; USA: R
Technical Data: 35mm (1.37:1)
Link: <www.dogme95.dk>

Dogme #4: *The King is Alive* (Denmark/Sweden/USA)

Released: 2000
Regional Titles: *The King is Alive* (2000) (UK/USA); *Dogme #4 – The King is Alive* (2000) (Denmark: series title)
Director: Kristian Levring (uncredited)
Script: Anders Thomas Jensen; Kristian Levring; William Shakespeare (*The Tragedy of King Lear*)
Production: Ballistic Pictures; DRTV Danish Broadcasting Corporation; Danish Film Institute; Good Machine (USA); Newmarket Capital Group; Nordic Film & Television Fund; SVT Drama (Sweden); Zentropa Entertainments (Denmark)
Producers: Peter Aalbæk Jensen; Patricia Kruijer; Vibeke Windeløv
Editor: Nicholas Wayman-Harris
Cinematography: Jens Schlosser
Sound: Jan Juhler
Appearances: Miles Anderson; Romane Bohringer; David Bradley; David Calder; Bruce Davison; Brion James; Peter Khubeke; Vusi Kunene; Jennifer Jason Leigh; Janet McTeer; Chris Walker; Lia Williams
Finance: DRTV Danish Broadcasting Corporation; Danish Film Institute; Nordic Film & Television Fund; SVT Drama (Sweden); TV2 Norge (Norway); YLE 1; Zentropa Entertainments (Denmark)
Distribution: Asmik Ace Entertainment (Japan); Trust Film Sales, Good Machine International (non-USA); IFC Releasing (2001 USA); Newmarket Films RCV Film Distribution (Netherlands/Belgium/Luxembourg)
International Sales: Good Machine International (USA)
Runtime: 109 minutes
Country: Denmark/Sweden/USA
Language: English/French
Colour: Colour
Sound Mix: Dolby Stereo
Certification: Denmark: 11; UK: 15; USA: R
Technical Data: 35mm (1.37:1)
Link: <www.dogme95.dk>

Dogme #5: *Lovers* (France)

Released: 1999
Regional Titles: *Dogme #5 – Lovers* (1999) (Denmark/France: series title)

Director: Jean-Marc Barr (uncredited)
Script: Pascal Arnold; Jean-Marc Barr
Production: Bar Nothing; TF1 International (France); Tolodo
Producers: Pascal Arnold; Jean-Marc Barr; Emmanuelle Mougne
Editor: Brian Schmitt
Cinematography: Jean-Marc Barr
Sound: Pascal Armant
Appearances: Élodie Bouchez; Sergej Trifunovic; Jean-Christophe Bouvet; Irina Decermic;
    Philippe Duquesne; Thibault de Montalembert; Dragan Nikolic; Geneviève Page
Distribution: Camer-Ton-Film-Russ (Russia); ID Distribution (France); Nikkatsu
    Corporation (Japan); Prokino Filmverleih (Germany)
Runtime: 100 minutes
Country: France
Language: English/French/Serbo-Croatian
Colour: Colour
Sound Mix: Dolby Stereo
Certification: France: U; Switzerland: 12; Germany: 12
Technical Data: 35mm (1.37:1)
Link: <www.dogme95.dk>

Dogme #6: *Julien Donkey-Boy* **(USA)**
Released: 1999
Regional Titles: *Dogme #6 – Julien Donkey-Boy* (1999) (USA: series title)
Director: Harmony Korine (uncredited)
Script: Harmony Korine
Production: Independent Pictures Production in association with Forensic/391
Producers: Jim Czarnecki; Scott Macaulay; Robin O'Hara; Cary Woods
Editor: Valdis Óskarsdóttir
Cinematography: Anthony Dod Mantle
Sound: Brian Miksis
Appearances: Ewen Bremner; Werner Herzog; Joyce Korine; Evan Neuman; Chloë
    Sevigny; Victor Varnado
Distribution: An Independent Film Pictures Release (USA and non-USA); ED
    Distribution (France); Fine Line Features (USA)
International Sales: Independent Pictures (USA)
Runtime: 94 minutes
Country: USA
Language: English
Colour: Colour
Sound Mix: Dolby Stereo
Certification: UK: 15; France: U; USA: R
Technical Data: 35mm (1.37:1)
Link: <www.dogme95.dk>

Dogme #7: *Interview* **(Korea)**
Released: 2000
Regional Titles: *Dogme #7 – Interview* (2000) (South Korea: series title); *Intyebyu* (2001)
  (Korea)
Director: Daniel H. Byun (uncredited)
Assistant Director: Chang-ho Jo
Script: Daniel H. Byun; Jin-wan Joeng; Yong-kuk Kweon; Hyeon-ri Oh
Production: Cine 2000 (Korea).
Producers: Choon-Yeon Lee; Mi-yeong Lee; Seung-jae Lee
International Sales: Mirovision (Korea)
Editor: Sang-Boem Kim
Cinematography: Hyung-ku Kim
Sound: Kyu-shik Son
Original Music: Ho-Jun Park
Appearances: Jung-Jae Lee; Eun-ha Shim; Jae-hyeon Jo; Min-jung Kweon; Jeong-
  hyeon kim; Eun-yong Yang; Deok-jin Lee; Ho-il Jang; Charlotte Becquin
Runtime: 107 minutes
Country: Korea
Language: Korean
Colour: Colour
Sound Mix: Dolby Stereo
Certification: Hong-Kong: IIA

Dogme #8: *Fuckland* **(Argentina)**
Released: 2000
Regional Titles: *Dogme #8 – Fuckland* (2000) (Argentina: series title) F–kland (2000)
  (USA: Cable and TV title)
Director: José Luis Marquès (uncredited)
Script: José Luis Marquès
Production: Atomic Films S.A. (Argentina)
Producers: Diego Dubcovsky; Edi Flehner; Jonathan Perel; Jonathan Peret; Mariano Suez
Editor: Pipo Bonamino
Cinematography: Alejandro Hartman; José Luis Marquès; Guillermo Naistat; Fabián
  Stratas
Original Music: Sergio Figueroa
Appearances: Camilla Heaney; Fabián Stratas
Runtime: 87 minutes
Country: Argentina
Language: English/Spanish
Colour: Colour
Sound Mix: Dolby Stereo
Certification: Unrated
Link: <www.fuckland.com.ar>

Dogme #9: *Babylon* **(Sweden)**
Released: pending
Regional Titles: *Dogme #9 – Babylon* (Sweden: series title)
Director: Vladan Zdravkovic (uncredited)
Production: AF&P, MH Company (Sweden)
Country: Sweden

Dogme #10: *Chetzemoka's Curse* **(USA)**
Released: 2000
Regional Titles: *Dogme #10 – Chetzemoka's Curse* (2000) (USA: series title)
Director: Rick Schmidt (uncredited)
Script: Rick Schmidt
Production: FW Productions (USA)
Producers: Morgan Schmidt-Feng; Rick Schmidt
Editor: Chris Tow
Cinematography: Morgan Schmidt-Feng
Sound: Dave Nold
Appearances: Maya Berthoud; Adam Kelly-Karagas; Jessica Gillard; Stephen W. Gillard; Sue Gillard; Otis Roberts; John Sanders
Runtime: 81 minutes
Country: USA
Language: English
Colour: Colour
Sound Mix: Dolby Stereo
Certification: Unrated
Link: <www.dogme95.dk>; <www.lightvideo.com>

Dogme #11: *Diapason* **(Italy)**
Released: 2000
Regional Titles: *Dogme #11 – Diapason* (2000) (Italy: series title)
Director: Antonio Domenici (uncredited)
Script: Antonio Domenici; Georgio Formica
Production: Gruppo Minerva International; Flying Movies
Producers: Gianluca Curti; Paolo Luvisotti; Paolo Landolfi; Stefano Corti
Editors: Antonio Domenici; Roberto Mariani; Federico Stanisci
Cinematography: Frederic Fasano
Appearances: Alex van Damme; Melanie Gerren; Lea Karen Gramsdorff; Magdalena Grochowska; David d'Ingeo; Michel Leroy; Nicola Siri; Angelo Infanti
Distribution: Scanbox Danmark (Denmark)
International Sales: Gruppo Minerva International
Runtime: 90 minutes
Country: Italy
Language: Italian

Colour: Colour
Sound Mix: Dolby Stereo A
Certification: UK: 15; USA: R
Technical Data: 35mm (1.37:1)
Links: <www.dogme95.dk>; <www.minervapictures.com>; <www.rarovideo.com>

Dogme #12: *Italiensk for begyndere* (Denmark)

Released: 2000
Regional Titles: *Dogme #12 – Italiensk for begyndere* (2000) (Denmark: series title);
    Dogme 12 (2000) (Denmark); *Italian for Beginners* (2001) (International: English title)
Director: Lone Scherfig (uncredited)
Assistant Director: Niels Reiermann
Script: Lone Scherfig
Production: Danish Film Institute; DRTV Danish Broadcasting Corporation; Zentropa
    Entertainments (Denmark)
Producers: Karen Bentzon; Ib Tardini
Editor: Gerd Tjur
Cinematography: Jørgen Johansson
Sound: Rune Palving
Appearances: Anders W. Berthelsen; Peter Gantzler; Sara Indrio Jensen; Ann Eleonora
    Jørgensen; Lars Kaalund; Bent Mejding; Karen-Lise Mynster; Elsebeth Steentoft;
    Anette Støvelbæk
Distribution: Les Films Losange (France); Miramax Films (USA, 2001: subtitled);
    Sandrew Metronome
Runtime: 112 minutes
Country: Denmark
Language: Danish/Italian
Colour: Colour
Sound Mix: Dolby Digital/Dolby Stereo
Certification: Denmark: 7; France: U; USA: R
Technical Data: 35mm (1.37:1)
Link: <www.dogme95.dk>; <www.italienskforbegyndere.dk>

Dogme #13: *Amerikana* (USA)

Released: 2001
Regional Titles: *Dogme #13 – Amerikana* (2001) (USA: series title)
Director: James Merendino (uncredited)
Production: Apollo Media, Cologne Gemini Filmproduktion (Germany); Zentropa
    Productions (Denmark)
Producers: Frank Hübner; Bob Jason; Sabine Müller; Gerhard Schmidt; Sisse Graum Olsen
Appearances: Morgan Vukovic; James Duval
Country: USA/Germany
Link: <www.dogme95.dk>

Dogme #14: *Joy Ride* (Switzerland)
Released: 2000
Regional Titles: Dogme #14 – *Joy Ride* (2000) (Switzerland: series title)
Director: Martin Rengel (uncredited)
Script: Lukas B. Suter; Martin Rengel
Production: Abrakadabra Films AG (Switzerland)
Producer: Claudia Wick
Editor: Bernhard Lehner
Cinematography: Marco Barberi
Sound: Jürg von Allmen; Laurent Barbey; Philippe Combes
Appearances: Jaap Achterberg; Yangzom Brauen; Markus Cajöri; Agnes Dünneisen; Adrian Herzig; Sebastian Hölz; Tiziana Jelmini; André Jung; Claudia Knabenhans; Stephan Krauer; Mike Müller; Adrian Meili; Elisabeth Niederer; Edward Piccin; Gwendolyn Rich; Julia Roth; Klaus-Henner Russius; Monique Schwitter; Andri Zehnder
Finance: Abrakadabra Films (Switzerland); Annazarah Films (Switzerland); SRG/Schweizer Fernsehen (Germany); Teleclub (Switzerland)
Distributor: Frenetic Films (Switzerland)
International Sales: Abrakadabra Films (Switzerland)
Runtime: 90 minutes
Country: Switzerland
Language: Swiss-German
Colour: Colour
Sound Mix: Dolby Stereo Digital
Certification: Switzerland: 14
Technical Data: 35mm (Digi-cam transfer) (1:1.85)
Link: <www.joy-ride.ch>

Dogme # 15: *Camera* (USA)
Released: 2000
Regional Titles: *Dogme #15 – Camera* (2000) (USA: series title)
Director: Richard Martini (uncredited)
Script: Richard Martini
Production: Martini Productions (USA)
Producer: Richard Martini
Editor: Drew Friedmen
Cinematography: Richard Martini
Sound: Glen Matisoff
Original Music: Peter Rafelson
Appearances: Carol Alt; Rebecca Broussard; Angie Everhart
Distribution: Les Films Losange (France); Miramax Films; Sandrew Metronome
Runtime: 80 minutes
Country: USA

Language: English
Colour: Colour
Link: <www.dogme95.dk>

Dogme #16: *Bad Actors* (USA)

Released: 2000
Regional Titles: *Dogme #16 – Bad Actors* (2000) (USA: series title)
Director: Shaun Monson (uncredited)
Script: Shaun Monson
Production: Immortal Pictures (USA)
Producer: Nicole Visram
Editor: Shannon Sumo
Cinematography: Roger Olkowski
Sound: Lee Alexander
Appearances: Anjeanette Carter; Nikki Crosby; Amy Dowd; David Ivers; Nawzat
    Kattan; Chester Mayple; Jonas Mayabb; Shaun Monson; Cissy Wellman; Paul Witten
Runtime: 90 minutes
Country: USA
Language: English
Colour: Colour
Sound Mix: Dolby Stereo
Link: <www.badactors.net>

Dogme #17: *Reunion* (USA)

Released: 2001
Regional Titles: *Dogme #17 – Reunion* (2001) (USA: series title)
Director: Leif Tilden (uncredited)
Script: Kimberley Shane O'Hara
Production: O'Hara/Klein (USA); Reunion Films (USA)
Producers: Eric M. Klein; Kimberley Shane O'Hara
Editor: Gábor Szitanyi
Cinematography: Patricia Van Over
Sound: Rune Palving
Appearances: Dwier Brown; Andres Faucher; Marlene Forte; Steven Gilborn; Corey
    Glover; Rainer Judd; Jennifer Rubin; Billy Wirth
Runtime: 112 minutes
Country: USA
Language: English
Colour: Colour
Sound Mix: Dolby Digital/Dolby Stereo
Link: <www.reunion81.com>

Dogme #18: *Et rigtigt menneske* (Denmark)

Released: 2001

Regional Titles: *Dogme #12 – Et rigtigt menneske* (2001) (Denmark: series title); *En usynlig mand* (Denmark: working title); *Truly Human* (2001) (International: English title)

Director: Åke Sandgren (uncredited)

Assistant Director: Iben Snebang

Script: Åke Sandgren

Production: Sandrew Entertainments; Zentropa Entertainments (Denmark)

Producers: Peter Aalbæk Jensen; Ib Tardini

Editor: Kasper Leick

Cinematography: Dirk Brüel

Sound: Mikkel Groos

Appearances: Jesper Asholt; Klaus Bondam; Peter Belli; Søren Haunch-Fausbøl; Line Kruse; Nikolaj Lie Kaas; Peter Mygind; Troels Munk; Charlotte Munksgaard; Clara Nepper Winther; Susan Olsen; Anna Oppenhagen Pagh; Oliver Zahle

Distribution: Nordisk Films

Runtime: 95 minutes

Country: Denmark

Language: Danish

Colour: Colour

Sound Mix: Dolby Stereo/Mono

Certification: Denmark: 7; France: U; USA: R

Technical Data: 35mm (1.37:1)

Link: <www.dogme95.dk>

Dogme #19: *Når nettene blir lange* (Norway)

Released: 2000

Regional Titles: *Dogme #19 – Når nettene blir lange* (2000) (Norway: series title); *Cabin Fever* (2001) (International: English title)

Director: Mona J. Hoel (uncredited)

Script: Mona J. Hoel

Production: DIS Film (Norway)

Producer: Malte Forsell

Editor: Hélène Berlin

Sound: Ad Stoop

Appearances: Gørild Mauseth; Sven Scharfenberg; Karj Simonsen; Zbigniew Zamachowski

Distribution: Europafilm AS (Norway)

Runtime: 102 minutes

Country: Denmark/Norway/Sweden

Language: Norwegian

Colour: Colour

Sound Mix: Dolby Digital/Dolby Stereo

Link: <www.dogme95.dk>

Dogme #20: *Strass* (Belgium)
Released: 2001
Director: Vincent Lannoo (uncredited)
Script: Vincent Lannoo
Production: Radowsky Film (Belgium)
Producers: Pierre Lekeux; Gilles Bissot; Vincent Lannoo
Editor: Frédérique Broos
Cinematography: Gilles Bissot
Sound: Julie Brenta
Appearances: Lionel Bourguet; Carlo Ferrante; Pierre Lekeux; Hélène Ramet
Runtime: 70 minutes
Country: Belgium
Language: French
Colour: Colour
Sound Mix: Stereo
Link: <www.dogme95.dk>; <www.strasslefilm.be>

Dogme #21: *En kærlighedshistorie* (Denmark)
Released: 2001
Regional Titles: *Dogme #21 – En kærlighedshistorie* (2001) (Denmark: series title); *Kira's Reason – a Love Story* (2001) (International: English title)
Director: Ole Christian Madsen (uncredited)
Script: Ole Christian Madsen; Mogens Rukov
Production: Nimbus Film; DRTV Danish Broadcasting Corporation; Nordic Film & Television Fund; The Danish Film Institite; Zentropa Entertainments (Denmark)
Producers: Bo Ehrhardt; Morten Kaufmann
Editor: Søren B. Ebbe
Cinematography: Jørgen Johansson
Sound: Pétur Einarsson; Sigurdur Sigirdsson
Original Music: César Berti; Øyvind Ougaard
Appearances: Camilla Bendix; Lars Mikkelsen; Stine Stengade; Sven Wollter
Distribution: Trust Film Sales (Denmark)
Runtime: 92 minutes
Country: Denmark
Language: Danish
Colour: Colour
Sound Mix: Dolby Mono
Certification: Unrated
Technical Data: 35mm (1.37:1)
Link: <www.dogme95.dk>; <www.enkærlighedshistorie.dk>

Dogme #22: *Era Outra Vez* **(Spain)**
Released: 2000
Regional Titles: *Dogme #22 – Era Outra Vez* (2000); (Spain: series title, Galician title); *Érase Otra Vez* (Spanish title); *Once Upon Another Time* (2000) (International: English title)
Director: Juan Pinzás (uncredited)
Script: Juan Pinzás
Production: Atlantico Films, TVG (Spain)
Producer: Pilar Sueiro
Editor: Maria Lara
Cinematography: Gerado Moschioni; Tote Trenas
Sound: Johnny Bleep
Original Music: Juan Manuel Sueiro
Appearances: Monti Castiñeiras; Víctor L. Mosqueira; Jacinto Molina; Marcos Orsi; Pilar Saavedra; Vincente de Souza; Isabel Vallejo
Distribution: Cinema Indie Group (Spain)
Runtime: 93 minutes
Country: Spain
Language: Galician/Spanish
Colour: Colour
Sound Mix: Dolby Stereo
Link: <www.dogme95.dk>

Dogme #23: *Resin* **(USA)**
Released: 2001
Regional Titles: *Dogme #23 – Resin* (2001) (USA: series title)
Director: Vladimir Gyorski (uncredited)
Script: Steve Sobel
Production: Organic Film (USA)
Producer: Steve Sobel
Editor: Jessica Kehrhahn
Cinematography: Brent Meeske; Brett Crowe
Sound: Brandon Beckner
Original Music: Dogme
Appearances: Michael Glazer; Mia Kelly
Distribution: Organic Film (USA)
Runtime: 87 minutes
Country: USA
Language: English
Colour: Colour
Sound Mix: Dolby Stereo
Certification: USA: R
Technical Data: 35mm (1.37:1)
Link: <www.dogme95.dk>; <www.resin-themovie.com>

Dogme #24: *Security, Colorado* (USA)

Released: Pending

Director: Andrew Gillis (uncredited)

Script: Andrew Gillis

Production: Grammar Rodeo Ltd; Parts and Labor Films

Producers: Andrew Gillis; Erin Aldridge

Editor: Andrew Gillis

Cinematography: Steven Pedulla

Sound: Christof Gebert

Appearances: Karen Felber; Paul Schneider; Tiffany Eddy; Chuck Snow; Jeanette Hohman

Finance: Incomplete as of 11/9/01 – raising funds for transfer to 35mm film – Grammar Rodeo LTD and Parts and Labor Films (USA)

International Sales: Christa Saredi; Grammar Rodeo (USA)

Runtime: 94 minutes

Country: USA

Language: English

Colour: Colour

Sound Mix: Stereo

Technical Data: (1.33:1) Academy. Source medium–mini DV

Link: <www.dogme95.dk>

Dogme #25: *Converging with Angels* (USA)

Released: 2002

Regional Titles: *Converging with Angels* (2002) (International: English title); *Dogme #25 – Converging with Angels* (2002) (USA: series title); *Dogme 25* (2002)

Director: Michael Sorenson (uncredited)

Script: Alija Sighvatsson; Michael Sorenson

Production: Keynote Films/Artistry & Rhythm Filmworks

Producers: Thomas Jamroz; Degas Vertov

Editors: Antonia Tighe; Degas Vertov

Cinematography: Kimberly Kyle

Sound: Bryan Clavey; Lou Mallozzi

Appearances: Abu Ansari; David Wesley Cooper; Lisa Hunter; Ed Johnson; Anne Mayer; Ronald Bruce Meyer; Melissa Muniz; Richard Richards; Valerie Shull; Patrick Sheard; Joan Perniconi; Robert Tobin; Philip Wasik

Finance: Artistry & Rhythm Filmworks (USA); Electric Dream Releasing (USA)

Distributor: Electric Dream Releasing (USA)

International Sales: David Sikitch; Iltis/Sikitch Associates Inc.

Runtime: 162 minutes

Country: USA

Language: English

Colour: Colour

Sound Mix: Dolby Stereo
Certification: France: 16; Germany: 18; Netherlands: 12; Spain: 18; UK: Unrated; USA:
    Unrated as of 18/02/02
Technical Data: 35mm (1.37:1)
Links: <www.dogme95.dk>; <www.arflix.com/converge>

Dogme #28: *Elsker dig for evigt* (Denmark)

Released: 2002
Regional titles: *Open Hearts* (2002) (UK/USA); *Dogme #28 – Elsker dig for evigt* (2002)
    (Denmark: series title)
Director: Susanne Bier (uncredited)
Script: Susanne Bier; Anders Thomas Jensen
Production: Zentropa Entertainments4; Danish Film Institute (Vinca Wiedemann, film
    consultant); DRTV Danish Broadcasting Corporation (Ditte Christiansen and
    Marianne Moritzen)
Producer: Vibeke Windeløv
Associated Producers: Sisse Graum Olsen; Jonas Frederiksen
Editors: Pernille Bech Christensen; Thomas Krag
Cinematography: Morten Søborg
Sound: Per Streit
Original Music: Jesper Winge Leisner
Appearances: Paprika Steen; Sonja Richter; Mads Mikkelsen; Nikolaj Lie Kaas; Niels
    Olsen; Birthe Neumann; Stine Bjerregaard; Ulf Pilgaard
Distribution: Egmont Entertainments A/S; Nordisk Film Cinemadistribution A/S
Runtime: 105 minutes
Country: Denmark
Language: Danish/English
Colour: Colour
Sound Mix: Dolby Mono
Certification: France: 12; Germany: 12; Netherlands: 12; UK: 15; USA: R
Technical Data: 35mm (1.37:1)
Link: <www.dogme95.dk>; <www.elskerdigforevigt.dk>

Dogme #30: *Días de Voda* (Spain)

Released: 2002
Regional titles: *Días de Boda* (Spanish title)
Director: Juan Pinzás (uncredited)
Script: Juan Pinzás
Production: Atlantico Films, TVG (Spain), Cinema Indiegroup
Producer: Pilar Sueiro
Editor: Corte Digital
Cinematography: Gerardo Moschioni, Tote Trenas
Sound: Johnny Bleep

Original Music: Juan Sueiro
Appearances: Monti Castiñeiras; Comba Campoy; Ernesto Chao; Miquel Insua; Rosa
    Álvarez; Pilar Saavedra; Belén Constenla; Alfonso Agra; Javier Gurruchaga; Asunción
    Blaguer; Juan Manuel de Prada
Distribution: Cinema Indiegroup
Runtime: 104 minutes
Country: Spain
Language: Galician
Colour: Colour
Sound Mix: Dolby Stereo
Certification: Unrated
Link: <www.dogme95.dk>

Dogme #32: *Se til venstre der er en svensker* (Denmark)
Released: 2003
UK Title: *Old, New, Borrowed and Blue*
Director: Natasha Arthy (uncredited)
Script: Kim Fupz Aakeson
Production: Danish Film Institute 60/40; DRTV Danish Broadcasting
    Corporation; Nimbus Film Productions; Zentropa; Egmont Entertainments
Producers: Birgitte Hald; Birgitte Skov
Editor: Kasper Leick
Cinematography: Rasmus Videbæk, Dff
Sound: Hans Møller
Appearances: Sidse Babett Knudsen; Björn Kjellman; Søren Byder; Lotte
Andersen; Mette Horn; Lene Maria Christensen; Louise Mieritz; Vigga Bro;
Martin Buch; Lars Ranthe; Ibrahim Aygün; Jimmy Jørgensen
Distribution: Nordisk Film Biografdistribution (Denmark)
Runtime: 90 minutes
Country: Denmark
Language: Danish/Swedish (English and Swahili)
Colour: Colour
Sound Mix: Dolby SR
Technical Data: 35mm (1:1.66)
Link: <www.dogme95.dk>

Appendix III: Dogma-Related Films

Compiled by Mette Hjort and Scott MacKenzie

Title: *Confessions of Julien Donkey-Boy*
Released: 2001
Genre: Documentary
Director: Harmony Korine
Runtime: 15 minutes
Appearances: Ewen Bremner; Werner Herzog; Joyce Korine; Evan Neuman; Chloë Sevigny; Harmony Korine
Colour: Colour
Country: USA
Language: English

Title: *D-Dag*
Released: 2000
Genre: Drama
Directors: Søren Kragh-Jacobsen; Kristian Levring; Lars von Trier; Thomas Vinterberg
Runtime: 70 minutes
Appearances: Nicolaj Kopernikus; Charlotte Sachs Bostrup; Dejan Cukic; Bjarne Henriksen; Jesper Asholt; Helle Dolleris; Louise Mieritz; Klaus Bondam; Therese Glahn; Thomas Bo Larsen; Lasse Lunderskov; Stellan Skarsgård; Alexander Skarsgård
Colour: Colour
Country: Denmark
Language: Danish

Title: *D-Dag: Boris*
Released: 2000
Genre: Drama
Director: Søren Kragh-Jacobsen
Runtime: 70 minutes
Appearances: Dejan Cukic; Jesper Asholt; Helle Dolleris
Colour: Colour
Country: Denmark
Language: Danish

Title: *D-Dag: Carl*
Released: 2000
Genre: Drama
Director: Kristian Levring
Runtime: 70 minutes
Appearances: Bjarne Henriksen; Helle Dolleris; Klaus Bondam
Colour: Colour
Country: Denmark
Language: Danish

Title: *D-Dag: Lise*
Released: 2000
Genre: Drama
Director: Lars von Trier
Runtime: 70 minutes
Appearances: Charlotte Sachs Bostrup; Louise Mieritz; Stellan Skarsgård; Alexander
    Skarsgård
Colour: Colour
Country: Denmark
Language: Danish

Title: *D-Dag: Niels-Henning*
Released: 2000
Genre: Drama
Director: Thomas Vinterberg
Runtime: 70 minutes
Appearances: Nicolaj Kopernikus; Klaus Bondam; Therese Glahn; Thomas Bo Larsen
Colour: Colour
Country: Denmark
Language: Danish

Title: *D-Dag: Instruktørerne*
Released: 2000
Genre: Documentary
Directors: Søren Kragh-Jacobsen; Kristian Levring; Lars von Trier; Thomas Vinterberg
Runtime: 70 minutes
Appearances: Søren Kragh-Jacobsen; Kristian Levring; Lars von Trier; Thomas Vinterberg
Colour: Colour
Country: Denmark
Language: Danish

Title: *D-Dag: Den færdige film*
Released: 2001
Regional Titles: *D-Dag: The Editor's Cut*
Genre: Drama
Directors: Søren Kragh-Jacobsen; Kristian Levring; Lars von Trier; Thomas Vinterberg
Runtime: 65 minutes
Appearances: Nicolaj Kopernikus; Charlotte Sachs Bostrup; Dejan Cukic; Bjarne
     Henriksen; Jesper Asholt; Helle Dolleris; Louise Mieritz; Klaus Bondam; Therese
     Glahn; Thomas Bo Larsen; Lasse Lunderskov; Stellan Skarsgård; Alexander Skarsgård
Colour: Colour
Country: Denmark
Language: Danish

Title: *De ydmygede*
Released: 1998
Regional Titles: *The Humiliated*
Genre: Documentary
Director: Jesper Jargil
Runtime: 79 minutes
Appearances: Jens Albinus; Iris Albøge; Lars Bjarke; Louise B. Clausen; Palle Lorentz
     Emiliussen; Christian Friis; Anne Louise Hassing; Jesper Jargil; Bodil Jørgensen;
     Ewald Larsen; Nikolaj Lie Kaas; Troels Lyby; Luis Mesonero; Paprika Steen; Lars von
     Trier
Colour: Colour
Country: Denmark
Language: Danish

Title: *De udstillede*
Released: 2000
Regional Titles: *The Exhibited*
Genre: Documentary/Drama
Director: Jesper Jargil
Runtime: 81 minutes
Appearances: Carsten Bjørnlund; Regitze Estrup; Lotte Aske Fredskov; Betina Henriette
     Grove; Niels Peter Johansen; Karoline Lieberkind; Claus Løwert; Luis Mesonero; Bo
     Overgaard; Lars von Trier
Colour: Colour
Country: Denmark
Language: Danish

Title: *De lutrede*
Released: 2002
Regional Titles: *The Purified*
Genre: Documentary
Director: Jesper Jargil
Runtime: 74 minutes
Appearances: Søren Kragh-Jacobsen; Kristian Levring; Lars von Trier; Thomas
    Vinterberg; Mogens Rukov
Colour: Colour
Country: Denmark
Language: Danish/English

Title: *Lars from 1–10*
Released: 1998
Genre: Documentary
Directors: Sophie Fiennes; Shari Roman
Runtime: 10 minutes
Appearances: Lars von Trier
Colour: Colour
Country: USA
Language: English

Title: *The Name of this Film is Dogme95*
Released: 2000
Genre: Documentary
Director: Saul Metzstein
Script: Richard Kelly
Runtime: 50 minutes
Appearances: Jean-Marc Barr; Ewen Bremner; Richard Kelly; Harmony Korine; Søren
    Kragh-Jacobsen; Kristian Levring; Paprika Steen; Thomas Vinterberg; Lars von Trier
Colour: B&W/Colour
Country: UK
Language: English

Title: *Tranceformer: A Portrait of Lars von Trier*
Released: 1997
Genre: Documentary
Director: Stig Björkman
Runtime: 54 minutes
Appearances: Morten Arnfred; Jean-Marc Barr; Katrin Cartlidge; Tom Elling; Tómas
  Gislason; Peter Aalbæk Jensen; Ernst-Hugo Järegård; Stellan Skarsgård; Lars von
  Trier; Emily Watson
Colour: B&W/Colour
Country: Denmark/Sweden
Language: English

Title: *Von Triers 100 øjne*
Released: 2000
Regional Titles: *Von Trier's 100 Eyes*
Genre: Documentary
Director: Katia Forbert Petersen
Runtime: 60 minutes
Appearances: Björk; Catherine Deneuve; Udo Kier; Vladica Kostic; David Morse; Lars
  von Trier; Vibeke Windeløv
Colour: Colour
Country: Denmark

Index

Note: Page references in italics indicate the text of manifestos, entries in the Dogma Filmography and list of Dogma-related films in the Appendices.